# • THE ROOTS OF SOLIDARITY •

# THE ROOTS OF SOLIDARITY

## A POLITICAL SOCIOLOGY OF POLAND'S WORKING-CLASS DEMOCRATIZATION

## • ROMAN LABA •

PRINCETON UNIVERSITY PRESS, PRINCETON NEW JERSEY

Copyright © 1991 by Princeton University Press
Published by Princeton University Press, 41 William Street,
Princeton, New Jersey 08540
In the United Kingdom: Princeton University Press, Oxford

All Rights Reserved

*Library of Congress Cataloging-in-Publication Data*
ISBN 0-691-07862-9

This book has been composed in Adobe Laser Sabon and Gill Sans

Princeton University Press books are printed on acid-free paper
and meet the guidelines for permanence and durability of the
Committee on Production Guidelines for Book Longevity of
the Council on Library Resources

Printed in the United States of America by
Princeton University Press, Princeton, New Jersey
1  2  3  4  5  6  7  8  9  10

*To the memory of* **Andrzej Mróz**

# • C O N T E N T S •

# I L L U S T R A T I O N S

# ACKNOWLEDGMENTS

ALTHOUGH the writing of this book was very much a solitary enterprise, it could not have been accomplished without a great deal of help. In the first instance, I would like to thank Professor Melvin Croan, who suggested this topic. In addition to Professor Croan, I am much indebted to my other professors, Seweryn Bialer, Murray Edelman, Edward Friedman, James Scott, and Elizabeth Valkenier, whose teaching will always be with me. Field research in Poland was sponsored by the International Research and Exchange Board and the Fulbright Doctoral Dissertation Abroad. I am particularly thankful to Dr. Allen Kassof of IREX.

In Poland, I was sponsored by the Academy of Science and Professor Władysław Adamski. My major debts are to the members of the Gdańsk Solidarity region, Joanna Wojciechowicz, Antoni Wręga, Bogdan Borusewicz, Lech Kaczyński, Lech Wałęsa, and the 1970 historical research team, Ewa Dering, Aleksander Klemp, Janusz Krupski, Wiesława Kwiatkowska, Jan Andrzej Stępek, and Krzysztof Żórawski. I am also indebted to Andrzej Paczkowski, Krzysztof Wójcicki, Halina Bortnowska Andrzej Celiński, Jan Kielanowski, Jan Józef Lipski, Maciej and Anna Kozłowski, Jan Jerschina, Jan Malanowski, Romauld Smieck, Krzysztof Wyszkowski, Piotr and Krystyna Wojciechowski, Piotr and Gaja Malinowski, Andrzej and Wanda Paszewski, Mary and Walker Connor, Andrzej and Astrid Mentuch, Jean-Yves Potel, Jean-Louis Panné, Patrick Michel, Lawrence Weschler, Jane Kramer, and Vincent Crapanzano.

The Rockefeller Foundation, and particularly its three officers, Lawrence Steifel, John Stremlau, and Marcin Sar, made it possible to write. A start was made at the Blue Mountain Foundation. The Russian Research Center at Harvard University was the main academic sponsor of this work and provided constant support and a most congenial environment. I am grateful to Adam Ulam, Marshall Goldman, Mary Towle, Rose DiBenedetto, Lubomir Hayda, Hugh Olmstead, Z. A. Pelczynski, Tadeusz Szafar, Aleksander Leyfell, Norman Naimark, and especially Priscilla McMillan, Janet Vaillant, and Henry Norr.

Other Harvard sponsors were the Center for European Studies, personified for me by Stanley Hoffmann, Abbie Collins, and Charles Maier, and the Program on Non-Violent Sanctions of the Center for International Affairs, headed by Gene Sharp. Last revisions were carried out at the University of California at Santa Cruz and the Hoover Institution.

I am also much indebted to my mother, Olha Laba, my uncle, Teodor Kokorudz, and to Barbara Correll, Abraham Brumberg, Anne Porter,

Graham Blaine, Douglas Powell, Mary Hyde, Don Morrison, Susan Pharr, Ellen Seidensticker, Julieta Almaida Rodrigues, Dot Sapp, Lidia Pasamanick, Susan Woodward, John and Patricia Thackray, Burt Angrist, Nell Goodwyn, Barbara Mitchell, Irena Grudzińska-Gross, and Hania LaBorn.

The advice of the two reviewers for the Princeton University Press, Teresa Rakowska-Harmstone and Michael Kennedy, was unfailingly helpful in the final revision, as was the editorial work of Sherry Wert, Cindy Hirschfeld, and Gail Ullman.

The support of Lawrence Goodwyn and Edward Friedman was crucial in the completion of this book. It surpassed all possible requirements of scholarly solidarity or friendship.

# • THE ROOTS OF SOLIDARITY •

# Introduction

WHEN IT emerged out of the strikes of August 1980, the Solidarity movement seemed to be a severe judgment of history on the Soviet workers' state. With its constituent base in the industrial working class, its organizational strength in interfactory strike committees, its elaborate system of worker delegates and worker spokesmen, and its programmatic dedication to local democracy, Solidarity appeared to be an ultimate negation of the Leninist model of the state. It also seemed to be a refutation of the operative justification of the Leninist system—namely, the belief that the working class, acting alone, was capable only of limited trade union or materialistic consciousness. Solidarity demonstrated that ordinary people such as workers were, indeed, capable of coherent political activity without consciousness-raising or leadership by elites.

Specialists have come to a different conclusion. The opinion among the political class of Poland and the specialists is that Solidarity occurred because of the leadership, the actions, and the theories of the intellectual opposition, and that consequently it is the intellectual opposition who are the main agents of the Solidarity revolution.

## The Elite Thesis

The consensus that intellectual elites fashioned the Solidarity movement is broad. For the philosopher Leszek Kołakowski, the energizing intellectuals may be found in the democratic opposition group KOR (Committee for the Defense of Workers).[1] Says Kołakowski, "Although the intellectuals grouped in KOR did not cause the strikes out of which Solidarity emerged in the summer of 1980, KOR's influence on the way the workers voiced their grievances and articulated their demands was certainly essential."[2] The Polish Communist party has agreed with Kołakowski. Very early in its political struggle with Solidarity, the Polish party claimed that the 10-million-member union was brought into being and manipulated by vanguard extremists of KOR. Former premier and first secretary M. Rakowski, a prominent Polish Communist, stated "It is impossible not to notice that KOR activists, among them Jacek Kuroń, prepared the future leaders of Solidarity long before the July-August strikes. They nurtured them in a spirit of struggle with really existing socialism. They openly boasted of this in 1981 as did Wałęsa and many other union activists."[3]

The opinion that intellectuals created and led Solidarity extends beyond politically engaged Poles into academic scholarship. The French and Polish team led by sociologist Alain Touraine is incisive on what Solidarity was, but when it turns to the reasons for Solidarity's rise, it flatly states that the intellectuals created workers' newspapers and organized free trade unions. "Here the KOR (Worker's Defence Committee) played a major role and workers were able to progress beyond riots."[4] A Polish sociologist explains why this is so:

> Only after the 1976 insurrection, when the Polish intelligentsia entered into a close collaboration with the leader of the workers, did they affect the 1980 change in the Polish society. No force other than the working class can challenge the powerful political elite in the People's Democracies, but this class must be provided with the leadership of more enlightened people.[5]

For one American political scientist, KOR "acted as a disseminator of information and an agent for 'consciousness raising' among both workers and intellectuals. And it helped to provide the workers with an integrated ideology, both socialist and democratic, that was crucial later on in the development of the workers' own representative organizations."[6]

Sometimes individuals within the intellectual opposition are identified as having created Solidarity through their superior vision. Jonathan Schell, a writer for *New Yorker*, finds the cause of Solidarity in "a prophetic essay" entitled "A New Evolutionism," written by Adam Michnik. Adam Przeworski, an American political scientist, discovers the "key to the success of Solidarity" in workers "staying in factories rather than going into the streets," which he says is "to a great extent a fruit of the strategic genius of Jacek Kuroń as expressed in his slogan, 'Let us not destroy [party] committees. Let us form our own.' " This slogan, explains Przeworski, "guided workers through the summer of 1980."[7]

Occasionally intellectuals other than those grouped in KOR are given precedence. Adam Bromke, a Canadian political scientist, asserts that "the workers' demands were drawn largely from a report on the Polish economic crisis issued by some prominent Polish intellectuals including both Catholics and communists who are known as the Experience and Future group."[8] The French writer Jean-Yves Potel agrees with Bromke that the work of the Experience and the Future group had "tremendous repercussions." In fact, says Potel, their findings "provided the underpinning for many of the demands."[9] In short, intellectuals close to the party were essential to Solidarity.

There are some divergences within this consensus that Solidarity was inspired by other than its worker members. In one alternative, workers became genuinely politicized and democratic, thanks to the conscious-ness-raising of the intellectuals. While conceding the presence of a political learning process among workers, English journalist Timothy Garton Ash concludes, "KOR worked very much as Lenin recommended (in "What Is To Be Done?") that the conspiratorial communist party should work, raising the political consciousness of the proletariat in key industrial centres." Though KOR members were by no means party-oriented Marxists, Garton Ash finds that their "Leninist" organizational approach "played a major role in helping discontented workers to generalize their grievances, formulate remedies, and coordinate their activities." In discussing the workers' twenty-one demands, Garton Ash writes, "The drafting hand of the opposition activists is very evident here: in the top priority given to independent trade unions; in the breadth of interests represented—workers, students, prisoners of conscience, believers of *all* denominations."[10]

In his history of KOR, Warsaw literary historian and KOR activist Jan Józef Lipski also states the thesis of elite leadership forthrightly. "KOR was involved in the preparation of the worker's consciousness for the strikes . . . it familiarized workers with the idea of the strike . . . it indicated the possibility of strike demands that would go beyond economic issues."[11]

In these interpretations, intellectuals played the necessary role, in Garton Ash's phrase, of "raising the political consciousness of the proletariat." For Garton Ash and Lipski, without the help of the intellectuals, workers would not have given priority to free unions or considered a range of social interests; they would not have been capable of being conscious human actors. Other observers will not grant the workers even that. Instead, these analysts assert that workers remained a brutish and primitive but explosive force. They remained politically incompetent and unstable in their commitment to democratic values. The leading role was played by intellectuals with their superior language skills, wider political horizons, and coherent political ideologies. For Polish sociologist Jadwiga Staniszkis, for example, the working class is "profoundly authoritarian" and afflicted with a "semantic shame and incompetence" when faced with semantically competent party or opposition intellectuals. Their "aggression . . . reveals the self-hatred of workers rooted in a depth of frustration connected with their own limited semantic competence."[12] These sweeping generalizations are not supported by any empirical investigation into workers' symbolic or semantic abilities.

In a similar vein, Aleksander Smolar, a KOR spokesman in Paris, sees workers as trapped between passive, limited economism and outbursts of unreflected violence. KOR's crucial contribution, he feels, was to bring a "geopolitical wisdom" to temper the "crude and brutal language" of workers.[13] Agreeing on these basic dynamics, Soviet observers disagree only on the usefulness of the result. A correspondent for *Izvestiia*, writing in 1985, draws these inferences:

> Tens of thousands of young men, most often from the countryside, first-generation proletarians lacking in class consciousness, poorly developed in a political sense, . . . unburdened with the revolutionary and labor traditions of Silesian workers or even by family ties, . . . had come from all over Poland to such major facilities as, for example, the Katowice Metallurgical Combine, the automotive plant in Tychy, and the new mines in Jastrzębie. It is hardly surprising that it was this large mass of people that proved most susceptible to the demagoguery of the extremist leaders of the notorious Solidarity![14]

Some writers, marginally more optimistic about working people, are not sure that KOR has yet succeeded in raising the workers' consciousness, but they hold out hope. To J. M. Montias, an American scholar, the workers' mental incapacities are not necessarily permanent: "KOR may gradually supply the workers with the elements of an ideology—a set of symbols to which they can relate their experience. This ideology is essentially patriotic, legalistic, socialist, and democratic. With its emphasis on legalism, KOR may enable workers to formulate more abstract system-related demands."[15]

Like Kołakowski, Lipski, Rakowski and Garton Ash, Adam Michnik, a Polish activist and member of KOR, sees KOR's teaching role as central. In a comprehensive treatment of this specific issue in 1985, Michnik strongly states the thesis of worker incompetence and elite competence. Employing the word "mass" as a descriptive term for Solidarity's members, he presents the union's significant internal politics solely in terms of conflicts among competing groups of intellectuals. He explains Solidarity's rise as the result of a conscious agent—KOR—acting on a "disorganized" and "disoriented" society. According to Michnik, "The Gdańsk agreement was possible thanks to the functioning of a political strategy perfected in the KOR epoch. . . . At the moment the Gdańsk agreement was signed, KOR's historical role was fulfilled."[16]

There are, of course, views that diverge from the consensus about the central role of elites in Solidarity. There are generally found in the form of brief, unelaborated assertions. English sociologist George Kolankiewicz, for example, offers this explanation for Polish workers' radicalism: "This qualitative change [in workers] can only be explained in terms of the specific heritage of 1970–71 which had remained rooted in the consciousness of the populations on the northern seaboard, in Gdańsk, Szczecin, and Elbląg."[17] More elaborately, Jan B. De Weydenthal, in his article on workers in Polish politics written in 1977, steps outside the elite consensus in pointing out the gradual emergence since 1970 of "workers as a distinct albeit unorganized political force." The 1970 change was important because workers stepped beyond "narrowly defined economic interests" and the "confines of individual factories." It was "an active attempt to self-organize."[18]

When the question "Why Solidarity?" is discussed by the most distinguished activists and students of Polish affairs, the results are paradoxical and surprising. Many hold that Solidarity was the result of consciousness-raising by the political intellectuals. If they are correct, with Solidarity, Lenin has triumphed at the moment of his defeat. His teachings about the low democratic and political possibilities of those he called "the masses" and the consequent need for elites are confirmed by the lesson of Solidarity.

## The Problem of Gatekeepers

The elite thesis can be examined in terms of the evidence supporting it. Polish workers were held under very tight political controls until 1980. It was very difficult for independent journalists or academics to enter Polish factories, to conduct research, or to publish any significant findings. As a result, discussion of workers was almost always limited to how they were seen by, appealed to, or affected by intellectuals. In published accounts, workers are treated as passive recipients of the actions and attitudes of intellectuals. This problem is well known to social historians and students of social movements. It is simply much easier to study an organization within a social movement that produces documents and has articulate members than it is to study the social movement itself.[19] George L. Mosse is sardonic: "The intellectual occupies the foreground, for he systematizes thought, making it understandable to historians."[20]

This introduces a problem that is particularly severe for the student of foreign systems. Especially in repressive situations, intellectuals act as gatekeepers who interpret their own societies for foreigners. But intellectuals occupy a particular niche in their societies and have categories of thought and deep ideologies shaping their presentations. That the origin of Solidarity has been passed over as entirely self-evident and has been taken for granted by persons at such diverse ends of the political spectrum commands attention.

## A Question of Evidence

A related problem is almost never mentioned. In postwar Poland, there is no social history of Polish workers, no sociology of the working class. Polish political activists were not obliged to deal with this problem of documentation, but it is surely different for the many historians and social scientists who have been ready to express sweeping judgments on shaky evidence.[21] A rare exception is Jan Malanowski, a senior Polish sociologist and member of Solidarity and the party's Central Committee in 1981. In his book on Polish workers, Malanowski lamented that ideological pressure had pushed social investigations into designated areas known as "safe problems," and that "problems which the workers' explosion of 1980 showed as central to the lives of workers were clearly neglected." Summing up the work of postwar Polish social scientists, he wrote that there was not one study on the state of health of the working class; the same was true of its material situation and its political consciousness. Even the Polish statistical yearbooks avoided elementary data. "We did not have and we still do not have information on such fundamental problems as aspirations, needs, structure of wages, and character of work." Malanowski concluded with a sweeping judgment: "We did not create and we are not creating any body of knowledge on the working class."[22] The lack of evidence made it possible to assert undocumented and unexamined opinions.

This study aims to shed more light on the activities and attitudes of a key sector of the Polish working class in the period 1970–1980. As part of Solidarity's post-August effort to recover its own history, documents were preserved that illuminate these matters in extensive detail.

As Baltic Coast workplaces went on strike in August 1980, they sent their demands to the Gdańsk Lenin Shipyard, the headquarters of the regional strike committee. After the successful strike, these demands, together with other relevant documents relating to the August strike, were deposited in the archives of the Gdańsk Solidarity Region.

In the fall of 1980, Gdańsk and Szczecin Solidarities started gathering evidence of their histories; their work took on added momentum as the seacoast union chapters prepared for the tenth anniversary of the December 1970 strike, which was to fulfill one of the frequently voiced 1970–71 demands that a monument be erected in honor of the fallen shipyard workers. Early in 1981, the Gdańsk region created a six-person historical team to investigate the 1970 strikes.[23] The team worked continually for eleven months and produced a second body of evidence. It gathered many documents and conducted dozens of interviews, including discussions with local party and factory officials. It also unearthed a number of demands written during strike meetings in December 1970 and January 1971 and subsequently preserved by worker committees and by individual workers. Among them was the one-page protocol of the agreement between the strike committee of the city of Gdynia and the city's president, Jan Mariański. Also preserved was the folder containing all demands written by factory work teams in the general strike of the city of Szczecin. After that particular three-day strike, led by the Warski Shipyard, this folder and three others, constituting the basic archive of the strike committee, were locked in the safe of the Warski Shipyard director, where they remained until they were turned over to the Solidarity union in 1980.

The Baltic workers' demands and interviews reviewed in the following study are unique in that they are self-produced. In 1970 and 1980, the workers created their own meaning and salience, at a time when the state's authority had weakened. Beyond this, the great number of interviews generated and preserved concerning "the coastal massacre" permits a detailed reconstruction of the social dynamics that formed the Baltic uprising. When arranged in sequential order and subjected to sustained analysis, this material illuminates with unusual clarity and specificity the policies of the party, the army, and the police, but most particularly the development of the working class. Thus the data from 1970, 1971, and 1980 provide a rare basis for informed general analysis, now making possible an understanding of what changed and what remained the same in the political and social consciousnesses of the workers of the coast.[24]

A political sociology of Poland's working-class democratization diverges from informed opinion in Poland and academic research at several points. Interest in workers as a significant factor in social change has progressively dwindled away in the twentieth century. C. Wright Mills in 1960 pointed to the "really impressive historical evidence that now stands against this expectation, a legacy from Victorian Marxism that is now quite unrealistic." He proposed instead "that attention be directed to the cultural apparatus—the intellectuals as a possible immediate radical agency of change."[25] Not only in Poland has research into social change followed Mills's prescription.

The growing scholarly interest in the prospects for democracy in authoritarian regimes has been directed correspondingly toward elite-negotiated political processes, leaving out wide-scale social movements. Narrowly political and short-term in its focus, the literature so far has not devoted much attention to underlying structural factors,[26] and was based on the proposition that there were no prospects for democratization in Leninist regimes in the foreseeable future.

## A Structural Argument

The argument in this study addresses two areas: structure and political action. In Western Europe and the United States, the turn to a service economy has reduced the political importance of workers. The political and technological structure of the Soviet Union and the countries of the Soviet Bloc causes one to pause before dismissing workers entirely in those very different economies. The Soviet system has three essential features. First, it is a police state that denies its citizens civil and political rights; second, the state dominates the economy and the society through the device of "nomenklatura," or the power of nomination to key bureaucratic posts; and third, it is a big steel economy—a product of state-managed industrialization where the working class is huge (half or more of the working population as compared to under 20 percent in the U.S.). Workers in this system remain poorly compensated—at the technological level of the first and second industrial revolutions. This system depends on steel and chemicals. Its growth is extensive rather than intensive, and it stands like a dinosaur before the necessity to carry out what some call the third industrial revolution—the transition into postindustrial technology.

Yet the same technological rigidity of the Soviet system that causes it to lose out in the world market forces some attempt at transition. This objective appears to be the main motive for Gorbachev's reform campaign. Still, Gorbachev's Soviet Union and all the other countries under the Soviet system have to face not only an outmoded economic structure but also a class of insecure party functionaries and even a class of workers threatened by the reform.

Marx's general point about the relation of class struggle to changes in technological levels has been fundamentally modified by Barrington Moore's observation that it is not rising classes that generate revolutionary upheavals, but rather dying classes.[27] If we combine the insights of Marx and Moore with the 1980 upheaval in Poland, it is tempting to identify the industrial proletariat in Soviet systems as a dying class on the point of becoming revolutionary, just as small artisans and peasants became revolutionary in the nineteenth and twentieth centuries.

Several characteristics of the working class in the Soviet system increase this temptation. Industrial workers constitute a very large proportion of the working population, 67 percent in the U.S.S.R., far above that in the West today. This class occupies a strategic ideological position, since the Leninist party rules in its name. The working class has engaged in an implicit social contract—minimal social security in exchange for minimal work. It also occupies a strategic geographical position. In the U.S.S.R., restive ethnic groups on the Soviet peripheries are less dangerous than would be restive industrial workers in the Russian Federated Republic.

Seen this way, what is present in China, the Soviet Union, Poland, and Eastern Europe is a crisis of systems that have legitimated themselves by building nineteenth-century economies and proletariats. While these twentieth-century states have treated their proletariats materially better (universal education, health care, and job security) than English elites did when they created the English working class in the early nineteenth century, both economics in the shape of the world market and war in the shape of security confrontation among states force them to face technological change while saddled with antiquarian tools. They are rigidified Leninist states entangled with oversized and outdated working classes.

## A Political Action Argument

Thus the structural argument presented here shows the socialist proletariat as a dying class. The other half of the argument concerns political action, as structural conflict is resolved in particular places by particular groups and individuals. "Structure determines the ways in which human agents act; but those agents are responsible for recreating the structure and they do this task in subtly different ways. As a result they frequently change the structure in some manner . . . so to identify the specifics is theoretically important because without understanding specifics we cannot fully understand the creation of new structures."[28]

Out of the structural crisis emerge the political action arguments. The first is that the main characteristics of Solidarity, its master frames, were created autonomously by Polish workers six years before the creation of KOR and ten years before the rise of Solidarity. The sit-down strike and the interfactory strike committee are the organizational breakthroughs. The programmatic frame or breakthrough is the demand for free trade unions, independent of the party. These findings push the direct origins of Solidarity in its programmatic and organizational dimensions back six years earlier than is generally thought. They also change the dynamic agent from the intellectuals to the workers.

Another political action argument is that the origin of Solidarity was regional, among the shipyard workers of the Baltic Coast. Considerable attention is devoted to showing how the conflict with the Polish party, army, and police shaped the perceptions of and possibilities for workers. This allows a presentation of the state's behavior and performance at the central, provincial, and factory levels.

This study will show that the workers' movement was an attempt to build a democratic project as an answer to the contradictions, crises, and pathologies inherent in Leninist states. The available interview data and primary source materials illustrate quite clearly a process in which Polish industrial workers substituted assertion for subordination, in effect transforming themselves from the objects to the subjects of politics.

The account begins with a detailed analysis of the 1970 crisis on the Baltic Coast. Chapters Two and Three place the workers of the coast in the structural crisis. These chapters are meant to show a developmental sequence of new forms of ideology, association, and tradition. Succeeding

thematic chapters develop analytic categories that are present in the narrative account. The analysis tries not only to deal with certain issues in
greater depth but also to demonstrate the links between the events of
1970 and Solidarity in 1980 and 1981. Chapter Four is a brief discussion
of the decade between the workers' strikes of 1970 and the rise of Solidarity in 1980. Chapter Five explores the Polish workers' search for adequate organizational formulas of resistance against the state. Chapter Six
examines underlying factors in the sociology of the Baltic Coast and the
shipyards that may have influenced workers' radicalism. Chapter Seven is
concerned with the creation of a specific countertradition on the coast
and a popular consciousness manifested in Solidarity's rituals and symbols. Chapter Eight compares the political content of demands written by
workers on the coast in 1970, 1971, and 1980. Chapter Nine examines
the conceptual categories by which this workers' movement has been understood in Poland and the West, summarizes the general findings, and
discusses some of their implications.

# The Demystification of the Party-State

# Massacre and Memory: Gdańsk and Gdynia, 1970

AFTER World War II, the small group of Polish Communists consolidated power with the help of the Soviet army. To create a base of social support in a hostile country, the communists carried out a revolution from above that changed the social and economic face of Poland. The capitalist and large landholder classes disappeared while the technical and cultural intellectual classes grew manyfold. The index of urbanization increased from 33 percent in 1946 to 52 percent in 1970. Millions of underemployed peasants were given work in new industries, and by 1970 the population not deriving a living from agriculture stood at 70 percent, of whom 50 percent were workers. The Communists had created their own proletariat.

The Stalinist model of industrialization started with high rates of growth in the 1950s but began to slow down in the succeeding decade even as the state maintained high levels of investment at the cost of consumption and wages. In the 1960s, the Gomułka regime tried to introduce a corrective in the agricultural sphere by greatly increasing investment, but because of its ideological commitment to wear down and eventually drive out the private farmers, who held 85 percent of arable land, it funnelled this capital almost exclusively to the quite unproductive state and *kolkhoz* farms. A failed harvest in 1969 and a 1970 decision by Gomułka to cease all imports of grain for feed stock had catastrophic effects on food supplies in the fateful year 1970.[1]

In the industrial sphere, the drop in the growth rate from 18 percent in 1950–55 to about 8 percent—much of it useless stocks—in 1961–68 convinced the leadership that there should be a shift from quantity to quality in Polish industry. At the Fifth Congress in 1968, party leaders resolved to try to break out of the Stalinist model of extensive industrialization to intensive utilization of labor materials and capital. But how could this be achieved?

In the first instance, Gomułka and his associates looked abroad for help. At that particular juncture, before *Ostpolitik* and the glut of petrodollars that marked the 1970s, Gomułka did not want to borrow from the West. He therefore looked to the Soviet-led Comecon for help. The

Poles proposed that, in place of the autarkic duplication of industry, aggravated by the lack of a convertible currency, the socialist countries of Comecon create a socialist division of labor. They hoped that the consequent rationalization of industrial effort would assure markets and capital loans for Poland, and permit them to catch up to world technological levels. For Gomułka, Poland was "menaced by falling far behind in the scientific-technical revolution in which all countries are engaged." Gomułka spoke of this danger in dramatic terms:

> History has given terrifying lessons to Poles because they neglected Poland's development, as Poland fell behind, and she became weaker and weaker in relation to her neighbors. Comrades, do you think that today weakness and backwardness have a different meaning than they did in the past? Do you believe that being in the Socialist camp means that we belong to a charitable association for aid to the destitute and helpless? In life, the weak everywhere and always, were, and will be, beaten.[2]

When it became evident in 1969 that the Comecon countries were unable to agree on such a socialist division of labor, Gomułka decided to solve the economic problem by domestic means. In the short time available before the start of the new five-year plan for 1970 to 1975, the Gomułka regime applied three drastic internal strategies.

As inflation of the cost of consumption goods continued at 8 percent per year, state spending on housing, health, and other services was drastically reduced. In order to free capital for primary investment, the regime decided, in addition to reducing social consumption, to pursue a strategy of triage of Polish industry. Certain industries were targeted for "selective development," while others were to be wound down or even closed. Shipbuilding and aviation, in particular, were singled out to be shut down.[3] Exceptionally for a socialist leader, Gomułka anticipated creating a pool of 500,000 unemployed out of a total working population of 10 million in order to force the workers to work harder.[4]

Gomułka's attempt to rationalize Polish industry threatened vested interests within the party, state, and industrial bureaucracies. While Gomułka struggled with these bureaucratic interests, the Fourth Plenum, which took place on November 29, 1969, extended the ferment to all industrial workers by starting a campaign under the slogan "Efficient Use of Production Reserves." Employing its unions and other administrative and managerial means, the party now tried to squeeze more labor out of its workers. According to its own analyses, 50 percent of machinery and 80 percent of work time was not being utilized. The workers viewed their situation differently. They saw themselves as overworked and underpaid.

On May 19–20, 1970, the Fifth Plenum of the Central Committee discussed a new wage scheme for Polish workers under the slogan "Material

Incentives." Though the term might seem to imply an industrial wage policy based on rewards according to work accomplished, the ensuing campaign in fact limited overtime, thus lowering wages, and excluded wage increases, premiums, and bonuses for at least the first two years of the new five-year plan. The party's policy of "broadest possible consultations" translated into a seemingly unending series of exhortative meetings in which workers were criticized for their laziness and general resistance to guidance. Determined as it was to reduce absenteeism and sick leave, the party pressed ahead in the face of worker resistance. But sharpened work discipline, reduced pay due to reduction in overtime, and a rise in work norms aroused workers' anger and, more ominously, led to exchanges of opinions among work forces at factory meetings. Pay schedules were changed at least a dozen times in the course of one year and, by the party's own admission, grew so complicated that even its own economic experts did not understand them. Gomułka's economic initiatives, implemented through the tactic of "consultation," had the effect of mobilizing workers throughout the country.[5] The party, which as a rule did not permit any discussion, had inadvertently carried out "consensus mobilization," which preceded the coming "action mobilization."[6]

The crisis in the Polish work force was most severe in the shipbuilding industry because it, like the aircraft industry, had been selected for elimination after twenty-five years of expansion of capital and work force. All the great shipyards—Warski in Szczecin, the Paris Commune in Gdynia, and the Lenin Shipyard in Gdańsk—were threatened, but the crisis was most immediate in the Lenin Shipyard. From the start of the 1966–70 plan, there was a sharp drop in capital investment in the Lenin Shipyard. Then, after the Second Plenum in 1969, the shipyard's management and workers realized that shipbuilding was not on the list of industries chosen for selective development. Gomułka's closest associate, Zenon Kliszko, fed the fears within the shipbuilding industry when he stated flatly that the Lenin Shipyard was so unprofitable that it should be "plowed into the ground."[7]

The policies of the party had awakened the Polish workers. The party's perceived need to improve Poland's place in the world market translated into intensified exploitation of workers—implemented through a political doctrine that compelled the assent of the work force through managed union party and council meetings. The situation was most severe in the shipbuilding factories of the Baltic Coast with their relatively young, better-paid, better-educated work forces. Now the shipyard workers were on a collision course with the Gomułka regime. As Henryk Lenarciak, a metalworker and strike leader in the Lenin Shipyard, described the mood as Christmas 1970 approached, "When you over-drive a screw, the screw or the screwdriver breaks."[8]

For the party elite, after 25 years of rule, the Polish working class that it had largely created was truly a "mass" to be molded, directed, out-smarted, and manipulated at will. The contempt of the elite was almost boundless. It controlled this "mass" through party organizations in the factories that were reinforced by various other bureaucracies, such as unions.

The crisis opened by the party on December 11, 1970 was to reveal a different political reality in People's Poland. It was to show that the prole-tarian "masses" believed they were the real representatives not only of the nation but of socialism. It was to show that the proletarians generally assumed that in a political struggle, the army would be with them, as would students and intellectuals. They thought that the ruling party was made up of traitors who stole from the people to pay their Soviet masters. In the conflict, the people found the simple courage to say what everyone knew and felt but did not say: that the people were one against an alien state of unproductive and incompetent exploiters who served foreign masters. The crisis revealed a far different Poland beneath the facade pro-jected through a combination of expediency and compulsion. But the cri-sis also pushed the people of the coast into a desperate search for new forms of resistance and new ideas. This new Poland, which embodied the fundamental ideas of the Solidarity that swept the coast ten years later, was to be the product of one chaotic and bloody week of struggle.

## "Comrade, It Will Be Hard But We Will Manage"

The coastal rising had its immediate origins in two facts of Polish life: in 1970 almost half of a worker's income was allotted for food; and at a meeting of the Politburo on December 11, the Gomułka regime com-pleted plans for large, immediate, and broadly applicable food price in-creases.[9] Although the price changes had been in preparation for some time, their proportions were a surprise even for most members of the Politburo. One account of that meeting originated with Stefan Jędry-chowski, Minister of Foreign Affairs, who less than a week before had presided over the greatest foreign policy success of People's Poland—the signing of a peace treaty with the Federal Republic of Germany. Jędry-chowski reported that he alone opposed the price changes:

> I pointed out the lack of real knowledge of the social effects of the price rises; for example, how much the cost of living would rise for different groups of workers and employees and how far the lowering of prices on certain industrial items would compensate. I also argued that the new incentive system was due to go into effect January 1, and this price change might well meet with opposi-tion from the working class and society. To this Comrade Gomułka replied: "Whatever the position of the party, that will also be the position of the work-

ing class and society." He then turned to Edward Gierek, member of the Polit-buro and first secretary of the PZPR in Katowice, and asked his opinion. "Comrade," replied Gierek, "it will be hard, but we will manage." Other members of the Politburo accepted the proposal without comment.[10]

The Politburo then sent a letter to all primary party organizations explaining the need for the price rises. The Politburo's letter began by listing reductions in prices on consumer durables—many too expensive for ordinary workers or simply unavailable. It opened the subject of price rises with the claim that "the price adjustment may temporarily lower the real income of an average family by 1.5 percent," and then finally listed the increases: meat prices rose by an average of 17.5 percent; lard, 33.4 percent; fish, 11.7 percent; jams and marmalade, 36.8 percent.[11]

Manual workers saw the price rises as a physical threat to themselves and their families. A "spectre of hunger" suddenly rose before them. They realized that when the price rises went into effect, their children faced the prospect of going hungry.[12] Coming after months of party-directed discussion of the new wage scheme and the open attack on the shipbuilding industry, the Christmas price increase seemed to verify the gratuitous meanness of a miserly government determined to squeeze every possible złoty out of its people. By lowering prices on luxury items that workers had little hope of acquiring in the first place, Gomułka's announcement merely heightened the workers' anger and despair. In his forced retirement, former Politburo member Roman Zambrowski puzzled over the decision. "One thing was sure," he said,

> This entire price operation shows to what extent Gomułka isolated himself, lost his sensitivity to poverty and cares of working peoples. . . . It is even harder to explain the fact, smacking of a provocation of the entire country, of decreeing the rise 10 days before Christmas. Such an insult to the deepest national traditions ignores elementary social psychology. German historians have a word for such behavior: *Caesarwahnsinn* ('leader madness').[13]

On Saturday, December 12, a working day in Poland, primary party organizations all over the country met to hear the Politburo's letter. In the Gdańsk Lenin Shipyard, Stanisław Kociołek, vice premier and Politburo member, returned to his primary party organization, Shop W-3. Three thousand party members—workers of the shipyard—gathered to meet him. It was already 4 P.M., only eight hours before the prices were to go into effect, when the "consultation" with party members took place. The unseemly haste contributed to the popular revulsion toward the regime's action.[14]

The briefings of the party members, as they later reported, "were stormy and difficult to control. Cleaning ladies cried, lamented their children and their empty cooking pots. One of the party secretaries read the regime's statement and then, thoroughly fed up, declared that he was broken."[15] At the main meeting in the Lenin Shipyard's Shop W-3, a confidential internal party report reported that "Kociołek couldn't establish common ground with the crowd. He was listened to out of politeness. His civil courage in coming alone was appreciated, but when he returned he said that the situation was bad."[16] The crowd's immediate reaction seemed an ominous portent. Adam Sarad, a party member and strike leader in Shop P-1, said, "When I returned home that night, I was convinced that the serious conflict we had expected for months was going to begin."[17] In the workplaces that Saturday, party activists tried to defuse hostility. In some factories, workers were asked on the spot to sign the Politburo's letter as a sign of assent. A party member in the ZNTK rail repair shops refused, telling a party functionary that "we had now lived twenty-some years since the war to vegetate no more."[18]

As disastrous as the party meetings were, some accounts by nonparty members showed a different view—of outsiders looking on an alien and hostile proceeding. According to Bronisław Duda, chairman of the metalworkers union in the engine shop, there were no meetings or discussions in the unions or among the union leadership, and since he was not a party member he wasn't invited to the party meetings.[19]

Outside the ponderous machine of political control within the shipyard, a counterleadership was forming during the day. As one worker put it, "We already knew about the price rises on Saturday because of the briefings of the party activists. Among our trusted colleagues we agreed that on Monday we were not going to work."[20]

The Politburo letter was read in all factories in Poland on Saturday afternoon and had the effect of a detonator. In Szczecin, "People's reactions varied from silence to tears to salvos of laughter."[21] At 8:00 P.M. Saturday, Gomułka announced the prices rises on television and radio. Now the entire country knew. Its people had one day to reflect. On Sunday, a shipyard worker stated, "all stores were open (with the new prices already put up) . . . a graveyard quiet hung over everything . . . that's how I remember that Sunday."[22]

Stanisław Michel, an employee of a planning bureau neighboring the Lenin Shipyard, tried to explain Saturday's events to himself. In his notes he wrote,

> The coming holidays were to be the last feast before January, tightening of our belts. This sudden unexpected price rise in December is impossible to explain. Why before the holidays? What do they care about these few days? Why are they unnecessarily irritating people who are already anxious and worried? Over a glass of red wine, I played the prophet. I imagined how a furious people would seize all the food it needs for the holidays without paying anything. It wasn't so much prophecy as logic. No reasonable person would raise the prices

just before Christmas. That Saturday I said what I felt and what I wanted every worker in Poland to feel.

In his notes for Sunday, Michel doubted his prophecy: "Nothing is happening. Have we capitulated?"[23]

## December 14—The Party Refuses to Talk

That Monday, Michel's question was answered. When the workers of the Lenin Shipyard arrived by bus and trolley on the morning of December 14, it was still dark. Saturday's stormy meetings with party members and activists had mobilized shipyard directors to frenetic preventive efforts. Henryk Jagielski, a leader of the strike in one of the most determined shops, W-4, said, "We noticed right away how the Saturday operation was pretty effective—the managers and foremen were hyperactive—pushing everyone to get to work and not loiter in the lockers. Part of the workers went, part stayed. Those who went didn't go to work anyway. We hung around the cabins or any other shelter and we talked about what we were going to do next."[24]

On Monday, the decisive first step was taken by the tool-and-die engine workers, the most skilled and well-paid workers in the shipyard. "In S-4, at 6 A.M., the engine workers struck from the very moment work was to begin. They stood in small groups at their workplaces. It looked harmless, but they kept talking until 6:30 and on, which convinced me that this was really a strike. The news that the S-4 workers were on strike spread rapidly across the shipyard. It was passed on by workers whose jobs require going from shop to shop and by persons starting work at 7 A.M."[25]

In a neighboring engine shop, one of the white-collar employees whose work started at 6:45 A.M. described how it looked as he walked through the shipyard on the way to his post:

> When I entered the Gdańsk Shipyard, I could feel the tension. As usual, everyone was going to their workplace, but on each face you could see something serious was going on. When I reached the hangar of S-5, above which was my office, I noticed that all the machines were shut off even though the workers started their shift at 6:00 while we started at 6:45. The workers stood in one place talking. Someone was trying to explain to them but he was immediately drowned out with whistles and yells.[26]

At 7:45, the union council and the director of the shipyard were informed that S-5 demanded the cancellation of the December 13 price changes. The demands began to escalate immediately. The second was to cease the constant lowering of pay for piecework. By 7:30, other engine shops had joined. The secretary of the party's primary organization now directly ordered party members subject to party discipline to return to work. Some party loyalists worked—as loudly as possible: they beat steel plates with their hammers to create the impression that everything was going on as normal.

In an attempt to squelch the spreading strike, shipyard director Żaczek demanded that S-4 work until the breakfast break at 9 A.M. The workers' representative, Bronisław Duda, replied, "The work team will not begin work. You, the director yourself, cannot settle this affair without the provincial authorities."[27]

In a meeting of the entire S-4 work force that began at 9:15, the director tried to buy off the strikers, promising them a pay premium of 10 percent and changes in the work norms. But the events begun in S-4 had already escalated. In the midst of the meeting with the various engine shops, the director received the news by telephone that 1,000 workers had assembled in front of his offices. He abandoned the meeting and the engine workers followed after him.

Meanwhile, in another part of the shipyard, the work team of P-1 had marched into its meeting hall. After short speeches, P-1 elected a strike committee of seven people, secured their work stations, and rooted out "provocateurs" and "stoolpigeons." The strike leader noted the flight of the entire management of P-1 along with the party secretary and the chairman of the trade unions.[28] Both the party apparatus and the plant management began melting away. The same had already happened in the engine divisions. Around 7:30 A.M., hundreds of workers in their work clothes and helmets began chanting "Join us! Come with us!" What one witness described as "two enormous rivers of workers, one of the hull welders of K-3 and another from the islands," converged on the square.[29]

Seen from a distance, the events take on an appearance of purpose and logic that masks the actual confusion and tentative groping for a coherent course of action. For many, the initial motivation to strike was pure curiosity. Mirosław Marciniak, for example, was on his breakfast break when he heard the shipfitters of W-3 chanting, "Come with us. Come to the director's." As he put it, "So, partly out of curiosity I went. I didn't have the faintest idea there was going to be a strike. In fact, I didn't know what a strike was."[30]

The gathering in front of the shipyard director's building lasted from about 9 to 11 A.M. As more work teams and workers drifted in, Director Żaczek attempted to speak to the crowd. In reply, workers proposed that the shipyard public-address system be turned on, and, this accomplished, a kind of public conversation began. Żaczek told the workers to return to work because their action "wouldn't have any effect anyway."[31] He offered a 5 percent work premium. The shipyard party secretary also spoke to the crowd, but conceded that he couldn't explain the government decision or offer any concession.[32]

Some workers then entered the director's building and began to speak over the PA system to the crowd. Their demands immediately soared beyond simple repeal of the price rises to include reform of the pay and premium system and the "resignation" of the ruling regime. Departures were specifically suggested for First Secretary Gomułka, Premier Cyrankiewicz, General Moczar, and Vice Premier Kociołek.[33]

Bronisław Duda, the engine workers' leader from S-4, entered the union offices on the first floor of the director's building and found that "utter consternation reigned."[34] From the union offices, he saw workers sitting on their helmets, waiting. They had already demanded that party authorities from the provincial committee come to speak to them.

After nearly an hour's wait, someone in the crowd proposed that they march to the party committee "to let the town know that we've stopped work, that we're striking."[35] It was now 11 A.M. About a thousand workers marched out through Gate 2, intermittently singing the "Internationale" and the Polish national anthem. The downtown area of Gdańsk was only a few hundred yards away. In case they were attacked by the militia, some marchers had clubs and others their tools.

Picking up more participants on the way, the marchers continued past the main railroad station to party headquarters. They found all its windows closed and the blinds drawn. The marchers occasionally glimpsed party employees peering out from behind the curtains. During the long wait that ensued, the crowd chanted, "We want bread! Down with Gomułka!"[36] In front of the shuttered building, two nervous policemen studiously ignored workers who wrote slogans in red shipworking crayons—"Paid lackeys! Lackeys of Moscow!"[37]—on the wall of the headquarters. The crowd expected Alojzy Karkoszka, the Provincial First Secretary, but he was away at the Central Committee Plenum in Warsaw and it was his assistant, Provincial Secretary Jundziłł, accompanied by the Shipbuilding Association Director Stanisław Skrobot, who finally came out to speak. Jundziłł first proposed that the crowd choose delegates to represent itself during talks inside the building. Speaking for the workers, Henryk Jagielski replied, "We won't go and talk it over and we won't be electing anyone just yet because if we do you'll arrest them all."[38] His answer summarized the distrust and suspicion the party had earned among Polish workers.

Jundziłł then ordered a sound truck to be driven up in front of the provincial committee. But Jundziłł, like the shipyard officers, had no more to offer them than the advice to get back to work as soon as possible. He was hooted and whistled down as the crowd seized the sound truck and began to discuss what to do next. With their provincial leaders in Warsaw, the party bosses left behind were too fearful and too powerless to negotiate. A rumor spread that a workers' delegation that had entered the building was under arrest. Fights broke out as some workers tried to enter the building to free them. Another rumor spread: "The Cegielski Works in Poznań and the Ursus Tractor Factory in Warsaw have stopped work. So have the Lenin steelworks in Kraków. So we're not alone."[39]

Some eyewitness accounts assert that a workers' delegation did enter the party headquarters and was arrested. In response, the crowd is said to have left the committee and the arrested workers in order first to gather reinforcements from the other shipyards and then to force their release at 4:00 P.M.[40] Internal evidence from the accounts suggests that this was a rumor that passed into legend. It recurs in explanations of what happened the next day. It is also unlikely—from a psychological standpoint—that a crowd of several thousand would abandon its emissaries to the police. Moreover, at this time party authorities were not making any decisions. The repression was to begin four hours later.

The marchers had been ignored by the shipyard management, the party, and even the police. It occurred to some workers that perhaps larger numbers would force the party to speak to them. In an open meeting around the sound truck, the crowd arrived at a plan to march through the town, first to the shipyard area and then to the Gdańsk Polytechnic, to seek the support of students and intellectuals. At 4:00 P.M., as the city center filled with people returning from work, the marchers would reassemble at party headquarters. As for the next day, there was to be a general strike throughout the city.[41]

Trying to gather more forces, the crowd, pushing the sound truck, returned to the Lenin Shipyard, then toured the Repair Shipyard, and finally reached the Northern Shipyard just as the guards were trying to shut the gates. They pushed through and agitated for a strike.[42]

Sometime after 2 P.M., the crowd, still pushing the sound truck, reached the Polytechnic, only to find the university gates closed and the students locked up in their classrooms. The workers broke open the gates and entered the large square in front of the main building. Students could be seen peering out windows, so several shipyard workers spoke over the megaphone to them: "We shipyard workers have begun a strike and we appeal to you to join us out of solidarity."[43]

Some students finally came out. Two school officials appeared and, in an interesting display of prerogatives, moved to the workers' sound truck and promptly used it to direct the students not to join the protest. The speaker, the rector, was unceremoniously thrown out of the sound truck. But the great majority of students remained inside their classrooms.[44]

No student-worker alliance ensued. In succeeding days, the regime easily spiked student protest by cancelling classes and granting early Christmas holidays. In the midst of strikes, demonstrations, and shootings, delighted students cleared out of Gdańsk to return to their families. Worker hopes for a common worker and intellectual front went unanswered.

The crowd of workers now divided. Some went to nearby student dormitories and the rest to a radio station several hundred meters away. The aim was to announce the Gdańsk strike to the nation and to call on "the rest of Poland to begin a national strike."[45] A worker delegation entered the radio station but was told by management that the station's power had been disconnected. Some demonstrators proposed that they attack and seize the station, but this did not strike the crowd's fancy.

It was now after 3 P.M. The workers, aimless and uncertain, set out along wide Grunwald Avenue back toward the party committee building, where they had agreed to reconvene at 4 P.M. At intervals the procession would stop so that "everyone who had something to say could say it over the loudspeaker."[46] One worker took advantage of the offer and promptly "declared a democracy."[47] As the day wore on, the messages over the loudspeaker became markedly more political and the crowd more boisterous, alternately chanting and singing revolutionary songs such as the "Internationale."[48] The ringleaders near the sound truck continued with some difficulty to retain a loose control over those permitted to speak. The crowd meanwhile grew steadily, augmented by workers leaving the shift at 3 P.M. One of the oracles on the loudspeakers started a provocative refrain: "We want butter just like the comrades! We don't want know-nothings ruling the country! We don't want party committees running factory councils and unions! Down with the red bourgeoisie!"[49]

The crowd's actions to this point had been disoriented, its members indecisive. The crowd could not find an interlocutor. When faced with a transparent but firm excuse that the power had been cut off at the radio station, the workers wandered on. Though the small group of shipyard workers who controlled the sound truck allowed anyone to speak, speeches they judged to be overly demogogic were suppressed. As a welder from the Gdańsk heating station later recounted, "When I said Gomułka's name and criticized him too fiercely, they took the microphone away from me right away."[50]

The party, too, was uncertain—or perhaps simply routinely complacent. While local functionaries in Gdańsk waited for instructions, the Sixth Plenum of the Central Committee of the Polish United Workers Party met in the morning. Officially, no announcement of the strikes and street demonstration in Gdańsk was made at the meeting, although the news spread in the anterooms and corridors. The meeting took place as planned around the theme of "Key Tasks of the Economic Situation in 1971." The main address was given by Politburo member Bolesław Jaszczuk, who was followed by no less than fourteen speakers. In the late afternoon, Gomułka concluded the session with the observation that raising prices was always unpopular, and lowering them was always popular.

> I would like to be well understood. We are not discussing a sharp turn or deep change in the direction of our economy. Sharp turns can occur in the political realm only after other elements have come to maturity which together cause the change of a specific political course.

In clear Marxist language, Gomułka delivered an authoritative political assessment: important political changes are preceded by changes in the socioeconomic structure. It was a good one-sentence summary of his coming predicament.[51]

At 9:10 A.M., the Gdańsk authorities made their first report to the party secretariat: the shipyard had ceased work. At noon, Politburo member Kociołek and Gdańsk Party Secretary Karkoszka left the Central Committee meeting for the coast. They were soon joined by a militia general. Only after they arrived in Gdańsk was the belated decision made to mobilize security forces and disperse the demonstration.

About 4:00 P.M., a unit of motorized militia—ZOMO—ordered the crowd of 3,000 still pushing the sound truck to disperse at the rail station at the entrance to the Gdańsk city center. The ZOMO intervention set the stage for the December events.[52]

Antoni Tomaszewski, an older Lenin Shipyard worker with two grown sons who also took part in the demonstration, happened to be at home on sick leave that day. He took for granted on hearing of the march that he would take part.

> I used to discuss politics with my neighbor Nowicki.... And I told him a half-year before the December events that the Polish working class was going to turn in the bills for its work. I was at home that Monday when I heard that the shipyard workers were demonstratively parading through the streets of Gdańsk. It was 3:30. I met the march near Victory Avenue and I joined it. At the head of the procession, they were pushing a sound car. Near the main railroad station stood a cordon of militia, equipped with helmets, batons, arms, and shields. The first clashes broke out there. I myself yelled "Gestapo! Gestapo!" and "SS!" Most of the crowd with the sound car broke through. I with other groups also broke through and joined them again.[53]

At 4 P.M., as the crowd surged forward to party headquarters, the police received orders to use night sticks "and other defensive means" because the demonstrators were "acting aggressively."[54]

The party's decision to suppress the march generated direct combat between police and workers. As an irate worker later described the dynamics, "Some of us decided on street fighting with stones and other instruments. We tried to smash those militiamen who interfered with us instead of upholding law and order."[55] Calls of "Thieves from the Polish working class! Thieves! Thieves!" were replaced by the chant, "We want bread! We want truth!" Over the truck's megaphone someone proposed, "Let's go to the Press House—the press lies!" The workers began to move out to the Press House as night began to fall.[56]

The crowd started to wander off, but it was attacked at 5:45 P.M. by large groups of militia, who attempted to seize the sound truck and arrest those around it.[57] Some were dragged away as stones were thrown to drive the police back, and the confrontation grew more violent. A flurry of stones also beat out windows in the National Bank and the Press House as part of the crowd moved off to party headquarters.[58]

The militia, continually reinforced by new units, intensified its attacks on the crowd with gas grenades and clubs. But workers from the railroad brought stones from the tracks. "People were so angry," said one worker, "they didn't react to the militia's gas—on the contrary, they would catch the grenades and throw them back on the militia. In the end they pushed the militia back beyond the party committee. That's when we tried to burn the committee."[59] They started in the cellar where "someone" threw a bottle of benzene and a few rags.[60] A second attempt to start a fire was made on the other side of the building. Eventually the printing shop of the party committee building was burned out.

While this was happening, a new crowd of about 1,000 workers and sailors set out from the New Port to join demonstrators in Gdańsk. The protest now extended across factories in a worker's solidarity. Along the way, the crowd demolished cars and furrier shops. In addition to symbols of state power, they were attacking symbols of luxury and privilege.[61] A dockworker described the march in language that illustrated the mood that developed after the first street clashes:

> We called all the workers to support the shipyard by marching to the town. We moved through the New Port to Region II. They joined us and we continued towards Gdańsk past the Wrzeszcz Hospital and under the railroad bridge. Our march had a couple thousand—it's hard to say exactly. The slogans were "Work!" "Bread!" and "Poland still lives!" At the Błędnik Bridge, we met the first police, but in spite of their flares and gas grenades, we made them retreat. Around the railroad station two kiosks were burning. A fire engine appeared but had to retreat amid a rain of stones—the workers wouldn't allow them to extinguish the fire. There were many wounded and bloodied demonstrators, but the shipyard workers now knew that they didn't stand alone, that we, the longshoremen of Gdańsk, were with them.[62]

Destruction and pillaging of stores and kiosks now began with an almost systematic thoroughness. Fragments of conversation in the crowd have been preserved in the copious documentation of the December events: "Burn the committee, but how? Get alcohol and bottles in the stores!"[63] As a party member observed, "The cars standing on the parking lot in front of the Hotel Monopol started to burn. If you take into account that one person rides in an automobile and the other doesn't have bread to eat, it's not so strange that cars irritated people."[64] In the socialist reality, luxury stores and cars were political targets.

A worker from the Gdańsk Shipyard remembered, "I saw militiamen run up to a kiosk with flares and other flammable materials and set the kiosk on fire."[65] Numerous accounts also agree, however, that petty criminals taking advantage of the fighting in the square formed by the committee building, the Monopol Hotel, and the railroad station, looted the numerous small stores in the back of the Hotel Monopol and the party committee.[66]

As police and army reinforcements continued to arrive, fighting took the form of successive rushes and retreats between the party building and the Błędnik Bridge. Fighting spread onto the smaller side streets of the old town, the police keeping to the lighted areas, the rioters to the dark. Because the militia attacked people passing through the railroad station, its methods effectively provoked new recruits for the demonstration. Police invaded the trams and rail cars and "clubbed any young person they could find."[67] Police drove up on the rail platforms and threw captured demonstrators into the paddy wagons.

Within the apparently unorganized crowd, some people were trying to establish a purpose and a plan for the next day. A joint meeting of workers and students had been called for 7 P.M. at the Polytechnic. Its purpose "was to elect a city-wide strike committee and decide what to do next."[68] Anna Walentynowicz was one of about 200 workers who arrived for this meeting at exactly 7:00 P.M. She later recalled, "The square was empty, dark, light extinguished—not a student to be seen."[69] Henryk Jagielski also came with an organized group from the shipyard. "Unfortunately, we didn't encounter a single student. . . . All the dormitories were locked up. The students told us, 'Listen, we can't help you because we've been quarantined. The rector will expel us from school if we take part in this.' "[70]

Having failed to find students at the agreed meeting place, Jagielski returned to the shipyard director's office, where he found a group of around thirty self-appointed members of a "strike committee" discussing what to do next. There was no chairman. As Jagielski remembered, "The watchword was that we had to free those who had been arrested out of the sound car. There were six of them taken away, and the next day we had to free them. So around midnight I went home and slept soundly all night."[71] A plan of sorts had materialized.

As for the party, planning for the next day was the special preserve of central authorities sent from Warsaw. As street fighting and arson attempts continued around party headquarters, Vice Premier Kociołek summoned 160 soldiers of Internal Security Troops (WOW) to the party building. Over radio and television, the president of the People's Council appealed to the workers "who had rebuilt Gdańsk out of ruins not to tear it down on their own heads." During the night, all telephone and telegraph lines connecting Gdańsk with the rest of Poland were cut.[72]

Two members of the Politburo—Zenon Kliszko, Gomułka's closest associate, and Ignacy Loga-Sowiński, chairman of the national trade unions—arrived by air in Gdańsk at 11 P.M. They were accompanied by General Grzegorz Korczyński, vice minister of national defense and commander of Internal Security Forces, and Poland's foremost specialist on quelling internal disorder. The newcomers labored through the night to prepare for the next morning.[73] Let us note what in other social systems would appear to be a colossal overreaction. By now the party had dispatched three Politburo members, including Gomułka's righthand man—Kliszko—and the leading Polish policeman. The next day, they were joined by the army chief of staff, Bolesław Chocha, and other generals. Still, the almost pathetic wandering of workers around Gdańsk on December 14, 1970, which culminated in the police attack in the city center at rush hour, generated a sense of taboos being tested and finally broken. Not since the uprising in Poznań in 1956 had government buildings been attacked on such a scale. It was a barrier that, once broken, was easier to violate again. On contemplating the party headquarters that night, with its windows beaten out, drapes and curtains blowing in the night, and half-extinguished fires at the front and back, a Lenin Shipyard worker wrote in his diary that just two days previously, "no one would have thought it possible that this could happen in our system."[74]

Many workers clearly assumed on December 14 that their efforts were part of a national movement, an assumption reflected in the rumors of strikes in other towns and in the march to the radio station. The shipyard marchers took for granted a class and national solidarity and assumed that if others learned of their action they would join them. The workers also assumed that they possessed natural allies in the students of Gdańsk Polytechnic. Their failed efforts to rouse the students revealed, however, that the universities remained politically broken by the witch hunts of 1968.

Intellectual and student opposition circles had been severely manhandled in 1968. Many of the most determined and courageous leaders had been forced into exile. Many others who were to play a major role in Solidarity were still in prison—for example, Jacek Kuroń, Adam Michnik, and Karol Modzelewski. This, however, does not explain the extraordinary detail of gleeful students delighted with their unexpected holidays. December 1970 was a working class rising without support from students, creative or technical intelligentsia, or the local or national church.

There is also the party's reaction to consider. The fact that some of the highest political authorities in the country descended upon Gdańsk to face a wandering procession of several thousand persons reflected the fundamental insecurity of the party elite. Their reaction betrayed a gnawing fear that, as impressive as the party's instruments of control looked on paper, they could all disappear suddenly. Everything the central leaders discovered upon arrival on the coast served to increase their anxiety. In the factory shops, the *aktyw* (the party activists) had scattered as soon as the disturbances started. Party leaders desperately tried to mount a counterdemonstration to disperse the march at the Polytechnic that afternoon, but the trusted party members they recruited either went home or joined the march.[75] The party leaders were still the generals, but after the unprecedented events of December 14, they must have begun to wonder if they had an army to command.

## December 15

### The Party Headquarters Burns

The relationship between workers and the state had now changed. As the day's first shift started in the Gdańsk port at midnight, longshoremen refused to begin work. The word was, "General strike at 7:00 A.M."[76] By 4 A.M. on December 15, the entire port was on strike. As the second shift started at 6 A.M., workers at the Lenin, Northern, and Repair Shipyards arrived but took for granted that this would not be a normal work day. They traded news of the previous day's events, determined who had been wounded or arrested, and discovered that during the night the police had made home arrests of workers who had spoken publicly at the assemblies the day before.[77] As in Poznań in 1956, much of the workers' radicalism can be explained by their fundamental insecurity as police entered homes by night and arrested those who had spoken up by day. Mutual self-defense and solidarity were the defensive reactions that drove the protests.

The arrests of their workmates changed the course of the events of December 15. "We dressed in our shipyard workers' clothing with helmets and gloves for the march on the town." The goal now was, "We're marching on the city to free those who are locked up."[78] Workers from other factories around Gdańsk debated what to do. The events of December 14 had clearly activated a number of workers besides those at the shipyard. At 6:45 A.M., a 1,000-man contingent from the Railroad Repair Yards (ZNTK) moved out to the city center.[79]

At the same time, two hullworking shops, K-3 and K-2, were the first to arrive at the Lenin Shipyard's administration office to demand that prisoners be freed. Shipyard authorities had attempted to prevent further strikes that morning by transferring certain individuals and brigades to other sectors of the shipyard. Now, First Secretary Pieńkowski attempted to speak to the crowd, but, as he saw it, "The conditions for serious discussion were not present and the brief assembly ended in whistles and offensive remarks."[80]

At party headquarters in downtown Gdańsk, Politburo member Kliszko suddenly discovered that he was besieged. The police detachment of 150–200 officers that Kliszko had posted outside the shipyard was swept aside by the workers.[81] Dressed in work clothes and helmets, they walked "swiftly with clenched fists and occasional shouts." Some carried work tools, iron bars, and steel cables. In the semi-darkness, an approving middle-class bystander, a lawyer, said to a friend, "We've waited for this moment for twenty-five years."[82] Like a Polish Sancho Panza, the lawyer then went off to work as he had for twenty-five years. Barely pausing at party headquarters, the marchers continued past to the city police station on Świerczewski Street. They scattered the militia who were blocking the way to the station and, using crowbars, stormed the entrance, entered the ground floor, and smashed in the metal doors leading to the station courtyard and jail. In the initial assault, the crowd almost captured the police station's armory. At the last moment, police rescued "several score machine pistols with magazines."[83]

The first casualties occurred at the police station. As a participant recalled,

> We swept everything before us. I only got as far as the entrance to the police precinct, but my workmates did go inside. They burned the equipment. They threw out the furniture. . . . A group of 25–30 militia came from the direction of Okopowa Street where they were guarding the city hall. We settled accounts with them, too. We surrounded them, crushed them against the walls—7 or 8 lay there. At that moment, it was around 8:30, I heard the first shot. Next to me a young worker from the carpentry shop fell, shot in the leg. The mates picked them up and carried them away. Red and white flags immediately appeared. Fearing a third shot, we ran for cover to the station walls. There were no more shots, but the first one killed the 21-year-old shipyard carpenter.[84]

By 8:45 A.M., the crowd besieging the police station was pushed back to an adjacent crossroad. Police cars burned while demonstrators gathered stones from street excavations and threw them at the lines of police.

Others now commandeered trucks, secured the steering wheels, and sent them racing full speed into the lines of police. It is instructive to note that, symbolically, the street fighting was seen by the workers as a national uprising, a patriotic act. Marches were preceded by national flags, and some strikers donned red and white armbands. The behavior of the crowds was quite ritualized—in a sense, lawful. At the Polytechnic on Monday, the crowd had scrupulously refrained from trampling rosebeds, another example of the selectivity in the rhythms of worker protest. Destroying the party headquarters was an authentic expression of worker grievance—a "lawful act"—unlike the harming of state representatives such as police, military, or government workers. Militia who fell prisoner were frequently protected by the crowd against those who wanted to beat them.[85] Abstractly, the workers made a distinction between social property that was to be protected and the physical symbols of state power and privilege that were fair game for destruction.

Only a small percentage of the crowd, which was estimated at as many as 15,000 people by the government, had been active in the fighting on December 15. New groups kept coming in from other factories. A large group of workers from the railroad yards appeared, carrying a red-and-white banner. After them came students from a school on Sienecka Street. An eyewitness account describes the ensuing drama:

> I ran out and in a couple of minutes [I was] in the middle of the action. The shipyard workers marched on the police station and prison, both next to the City Hall. Apparently some workers were arrested and their mates demanded that they be freed. In the crowd, I [found] out that the City Hall and the police station were partly taken over. Workers with pickaxes [were] tearing up the pavement on Kalinowski and Huciska Streets. I [reflected] that after this is all over, the state will remove the stone cobbles and cover everything in asphalt. (Here again I turned out to be a good prophet.)

The shipyard workers, slightly better organized and staying together, stood out from the rest. "Some have handmade shields."[86]

On the viaduct stood a detachment of black-clad policemen with protective vests. They fired gas grenades. The crowd replied with stones. At intervals, the most adventurous workers—approximately twenty of them—attacked the police. A participant provided a strategic assessment: "the 'blacks' have the advantage—after all there are about 200 of them. In the crowd of 20,000, I don't see any organization or much fighting spirit. No one leads the struggle. Without organization, there is no chance of forcing the 'blacks' to retreat. What a difference between military professionals and the pathetic incapacity of a commoners' uprising."[87]

The fighting on the viaduct lasted for about an hour. Unable to reach the government building on Świerczewski Street, the crowd attacked the building of the trade unions with cries: "'Where are the unions? Why aren't they leading the workers?' With bars and hooks, the front doors are beaten apart, and the crowd piles in. From all the windows on all the floors, furnishings start flying out onto the street."[88]

The working-class protest shook the party to its roots. The series of escalating responses that followed provided an intimate glimpse into the structures of governance in People's Poland, not only into the party but also into the army and police. At 7 A.M., coastal party officials reported the first assaults in Gdańsk and growing unrest in the three cities. At 9 A.M., Gomułka and nine top members of the regime, including General Jaruzelski, met to review the crisis.

Gomułka set the tone. He proposed to send two army divisions into Gdańsk. Premier Cyrankiewicz further proposed that martial law and a police curfew be declared in Gdańsk. None of those present expressed reservations concerning these proposals. The use of arms was to begin with a warning volley followed by fire at the feet of demonstrators.[89]

While awaiting the army, Gdańsk police struggled to cope with a crowd of 15,000 that stretched over a quarter of a mile from the police station, past the party headquarters, to the railroad station. Pushed away from the police station, the crowd started to attack party headquarters, from which all but a skeleton defense force had fled. Most of the crowd stood mute as a small group threw stones, gas bottles, and gas-soaked rags. Just before 10 A.M., the building finally caught fire. Ten minutes later, another army detachment was sent to defend the building. Almost immediately it fired a warning volley from the upper stories.[90]

This action, described by an eyewitness in the crowd, brings into focus an entirely new dimension of the uprising, one grounded in symbolic meanings that carried deep political overtones: "At that moment, carbines appeared in the upper stories of the party building. Through a loudspeaker we were ordered to disperse or the army would fire on us. The crowd did not react. Then there was a deafening volley and the crowd retreated."[91] Workers lay bleeding, some fatally, on the pavement. Someone began to sing the national anthem. "We sang the first lines, 'Poland lives while we live,' and then we reached the lines, 'March, March, Dąbrowski.' And can you imagine it? With these words the crowd moved forward as if by command—a command to face the enemy. I'll never forget it. There were no more shots."[92]

The defenders of party headquarters had received permission to fire. Possessing automatic weapons as they did, the task of clearing the square should have been an easy one. Instead, incredibly, the army and police refused their orders to fire and began to leave the building, divesting themselves of their equipment as they left. As one worker described this dramatic moment, "After a few seconds, the army came out in gas masks with their carbines above their heads. A captain asked that we let the army through—that the army is leaving the buildings and will not allow itself to be used in a massacre of people. . . . As they went through the soldiers gave their masks away."[93]

In this account, internal security troops cannot be distinguished from the regular army. A second account provides such a distinction: "I saw how a lieutenant of the security troops was quarreling with his soldiers. They didn't want to listen to him, saying, 'We've been lied to. We were told that we were to fight Germans and all there are here are workers.' They didn't want to form up—as they left they threw their carbines into the water."[94] The security officer was helpless in the face of this attitude.

The breakdown in the army and internal security troops extended to the elite police detachments also. On December 14–15, most of the street defense fell to students of the Militia Non-Commissioned Officers' School in Słupsk, who had distinctive black uniforms. As the fighting escalated, more and more wounded were brought to the nearby Gdańsk provincial hospital. One doctor described the militiamen she treated on December 15:

> They were young boys from the militia school in Słupsk. Most were scared and disoriented, suffering from contusions, bruises, and wounds caused by stones. Some had broken bones. I treated one officer of the militia—a captain who had a bruise on his thigh—he didn't need hospitalization. He took me aside and asked me to help him stay in the hospital. He and his father were workers. He said they had not fought during the occupation to shoot at their own. I put a plaster cast on him.[95]

A security officer watched in dismay the breakdown of his fellow professionals in the army and the militia. He called for "reinforcements, more gas," and advised his superiors to remove the army from the streets. "They don't want to shoot and they are going over to the other side."[96]

Information to this effect stunned Gomułka and his cohorts in Warsaw. As Gomułka later recalled,

> I then expressed the opinion that we should use tear gas thrown from helicopters. Comrade Cyrankiewicz relayed the report that the soldiers inside the burning building were refusing to fire and were abandoning their weapons. Comrade Cyrankiewicz transmitted this proposition to Comrade Jaruzelski, whom he also instructed to order an army unit in Gdańsk to come to the aid of those besieged in the party building.[97]

As notorious as Gomułka was for his stinginess, his next sentence guarantees his place in Polish legend. In Gomułka's words, "I rejected the proposition passed on to me by Comrade Cyrankiewicz according to which we should use supersonic aircraft to break the sound barrier over the crowd. I did so because I took for granted that such an action meant a massive beating out and breaking of windows."[98] In the end, the first secretary's concern for Polish windows was not served by his decision to send three armored divisions into the cities of Gdańsk and Gdynia.

As the party quivered from its militia grass roots on the coast to its Politburo in Warsaw, party headquarters in Gdańsk blazed out of control and the crowd savored its movement of triumph. Considering that many workers had been shot, the crowd was remarkably restrained toward militia and security troops as they left the building. As the stairs and furniture inside the building began to burn, someone hung out a white cloth from an upper-floor window and the crowd celebrated the surrender as a national triumph.

> Several militiamen with hands above their heads came out onto a second-floor balcony. A young man in worker's clothing scaled up the window grates, tore down the flag, and hung a red and white one in its place. The crowd began to sing the national hymn. Everyone stood at attention. Workers took off their helmets. Next, the militia standing on the balcony were ordered to throw down their firearms, helmets, and jackets. Opinion was divided whether they should take off their pants also. Some in trousers, some in shorts climbed down the shipyard grates to a truck, and were driven off under guard to the shipyard.[99]

Another eyewitness reported:

> Most pleasant was the moment when they carried out big portraits of Lenin and Gomułka. First they showed them from the upper balconies and then tossed them to the crowd. Everyone burst into applause . . . then "A Hundred Years" [the Polish equivalent of "For He's a Jolly Good Fellow"] and "Poland Lives While We Live"—for the nth time. Nothing could satisfy us more than to see those two portraits falling to the ground. Finally, the workers who had entered the building had to leave too, because the fire was eating away at everything now. The crowd greeted them as heroes.[100]

An apparent protest against a sudden price rise had become an uprising.

The people of Gdańsk had come a long way since the aimless wandering of the previous day. All kinds of mental barriers had fallen as workers confronted the party face-to-face over many hours. Deeply suppressed longings for national independence and freedom of individual action had emerged. For the party, the burning of the headquarters was an unfathomable nightmare; for the workers, it was the realization of an unexpressed dream. Perhaps above all, the workers had created their own legend and had become the heroes of their own epic.

Early in the afternoon, Gomułka's troops began to arrive. In the battle of nerves between the reluctant army and stubborn civilians, even the official account conceded, one troop carrier was captured and driven to the shipyard, where it was set afire. The troops in the transporters "absolutely didn't want to drive into the crowd. People put burning flares into the vehicle vents and the troops had to come out. They couldn't endure it, whether they were in a tank or an armored car."[101] In the course of the afternoon, about five troop cars were burned in front of the rail station. At the end of the day's shift, when a maximum number of people were traveling through the downtown area, a large column of transporters entered downtown Gdańsk. The intent was to intimidate the city's population. Instead, the sight of armored columns sent to fight an unarmed city enraged people. The crowd had started to disperse. In one account, at "the sound of powerful motors . . . such anger filled me that I decided to return to the committee building. But it turned out I wasn't alone, but merely part of a crowd coming from all parts of the city to face the tanks."[102]

In fact, a pivotal juncture had been reached: the massive arrival of the army meant armed conflict on the coast. The angry crowd halted the column in front of the railroad station. In surviving photographs, the armored vehicles seem afloat in a sea of human beings. The agitated crowd alternately lobbied with the soldiers, refused to give way, stubbornly surrounded the armored vehicles on all sides, blocked portholes, stuck flaming rags and liquids into them, and dragged steel pipes to jam the tanks' wheels and treads. When one demonstrator died under the tread of a transporter, his body was taken to the railroad station hall and covered with flowers. As the street fighting grew more and more intense, numerous kiosks and stores and part of the railroad station were put to the torch. The official report of the day's fighting counted 54 stores pillaged, 19 military vehicles destroyed, and 129 people arrested. Many stores were damaged in a wild search for flammable materials.[103]

Although the party press claimed the motivation had been criminal, the main targets during the day—the party building, the union building, city hall, the police station—were political and symbolic, revealing the people's aspirations and perceived enemies. There was vandalism and pillaging, too, but some apparently meaningless destruction, such as that of book kiosks, actually was quite political. A longshoreman explained this central political point:

> The press claimed that books were destroyed in the bookstore—that we workers destroyed national culture. I was there when the bookstore was torn apart, and I saw what was destroyed. I can say that no book of interest to us was thrown into the water, torn apart, or burned. All the books were unsaleable political stuff—Congresses of the Communist Party of the U.S.S.R. and the like. Of course, the kiosks were burned. What did they have for sale but com-

plete works of Lenin? People wanted to destroy them so there would be an end to the propaganda.[104]

After burning party headquarters, many workers returned to the shipyards. The political situation there had changed drastically. On Monday and Tuesday morning, the authorities' main strategy was to use the *kolektyws* (the working groups of party, management and union officials) to force people back to work. After the second march on the city, they abandoned this strategy. In any case, these groups had largely disappeared as union, party, and management fled the shops. As Zenon Kliszko bitterly remarked at the Eighth Plenum, "The entire Lenin Shipyard party organization numbering over 3,000 members and candidates ceased to exist. It melted into the mass."[105] This, along with its problems with recalcitrant police, army, and security troops, explains the central leaderships underlying fear that its great bureaucracies could melt away.

As a last resort, shipyard authorities decided to encourage the formation of workers' committees and the gathering of demands. This was a risky maneuver because both the organization and the demands might veer out of control. It was to be a key element in promoting workers' organization and formulation of demands. This expedient illustrates how local authorities, buffeted by both their superiors and the working population, vacillated as they tried to save themselves and their factories. It shows how the deadly conflict with the party stimulated and shaped the Polish workers' creation of the idea of an independent self-governing trade union. As the shipyard's first secretary described it, "Already on Tuesday, on our initiative, with our participation, with the participation of the party organization and party members, delegates were chosen, discussion started. As a result, order returned to the shipyard."[106] This "order" was achieved by the secretary's issuance of an appeal to create strike committees in the shops and sections. The aim was to establish some kind of structure that would allow the party to get a grip on the rebellious work force. "The instructions came through to create order, to choose delegates, to create some sort of body and keep the work team in some sort of organization so that they won't be acting individually."[107] Shops held elections and then sent delegates off to the occupational safety hall, where a general meeting ensued. Under these conditions, some delegates were essentially self-selected, others were ringers under the direction of the director and party secretary.

A loosely organized general strike committee of approximately 50 members formed in the hall, but its dependent character was signalled by its inability or unwillingness to choose a chairman. Instead, its spokesmen with outside authorities were the second secretary of the party and the deputy director of the shipyard. The committee immediately estab-

lished that there were 5 dead and 40 wounded and set as a basic demand
compensation for the victims, as if there had been a work accident. None
of the demands from December 15 has survived, but there were apparently thousands written down during the delegate elections. In retrospect,
some strikers considered the great number and disparity of demands a
tactical mistake, a "blind alley," in Lech Wałęsa's words. In any case, this
first set of demands was sent to Kociołek and disappeared.[108]

### The Strike Spreads to Gdynia and the Paris Commune Shipyard

With factory strike committees and a general strike beginning to form,
the second day of protest in Gdańsk and at the Lenin Shipyard came to an
end. In the course of that day, the strike had spread to the neighboring
port city of Gdynia. The strike organization and demands in Gdynia
evolved from events that, though often similar to those in Gdańsk, essentially took a different trajectory. The Paris Commune Shipyard in
Gdynia, with its 8,500 employees, continued to work on December 14,
even as reports of the unrest in Gdańsk filtered in. The next morning, following a pattern first established in Gdańsk, workers in the least-skilled
crafts—the hulls—and in the most-skilled—the engine shops—led the
Gdynia strike. A worker stepped through a shop door and cried, "Shipyard workers! To the gates!" The workers numbered about 2,500 when
they reached the shipyard administration area. But, without pausing for
talks with the shipyard authorities, about 1,500 broke through the locked
shipyard gates with cries of, "Out with the scoundrels! Enough lies! Let's
go to the town! All to the committee!" Others shouted, "Gdańsk is striking—let's help them."[109] As they left, party leaders in Gdynia were ordered to leave their headquarters and take refuge in the command post
of the Polish Navy.[110] The march wound through the port dock area,
the repair shipyard, and the fishing enterprise, Dalmor. The throng of
workers, now swollen to 5,000, entered the city, passed the city council
building, and continued to party headquarters. At the news that the Paris
Commune had marched on the town, about 1,500 workers at the radio
factory, Unimor, left their work posts and also marched to the party
headquarters, arriving at the same time. Two leaders emerged—Stanisław Słodkowski, a 26-year-old hull worker in the Paris Commune, and
21-year-old Edmund Hulsz of Dalmor. Here also the protest immediately
took on a patriotic cast as workers drew on the rich storehouse of Polish
national symbolism. A worker's volunteer security service with red-and-
white armbands stood in a line in front of the modern glass headquarters
to prevent vandalism by overzealous protesters.[111] A delegation entered
to try to find some party officials to talk to and was astonished to find
only an elderly janitor, who told them that the party authorities had vanished. The workers asked, "Where are they? Why don't they want to

speak to us?" As the workers' delegation came out to the crowd, someone yelled, "The beloved representatives of the working class have fled."[112] According to Gdynia legend, the party secretary fled the building as the crowd came up, concealed in the trunk of a car. Unprepared, with resources stretched thin, the party deliberately chose to avoid a confrontation in Gdynia that day.[113]

When the first secretary of Gdynia, Hugon Malinowski, arrived as he had been ordered to do at the naval command on Kościuszko Square, he found it defended by marines standing behind coils of barbed wire. Events that followed were not reassuring. He had begun the morning by telephoning Provincial Headquarters in Gdańsk and, disconcertingly, got no answer. Then he received instructions from the navy command to evacuate the party building in Gdynia. The dumbfounded Malinowski listened as the commander of the Polish Navy received a call from no less a personage than Józef Cyrankiewicz, the premier of Poland, who wanted to know what was happening. Admiral Janczyszyn was apparently appalled by the performance of local and national party leaders. He told Malinowski that the party had ceased to exist, and announced, "I am taking command."[114]

It was now 10 A.M. The provincial party building had begun to burn in Gdańsk. Edmund Hulsz proposed to the Gdynia crowd that they return to city hall. Cries went up: "To the Presidium! To the city president." As the marchers went up and down Gdynia's principal street, Saint John's, workers sang the national anthem and the patriotic religious hymn "Rota." Bystanders took off their hats or sang. One of the marchers noticed a tall youth with a broom on his shoulder. He explained, "This isn't a broom, it's a symbol," for Poland needed a "good cleanup."[115] The remark signaled the emergence of a new mood on the coast. In the course of 25 years of Communist rule, the Polish people had developed a general attitude of resignation, a pragmatic acceptance of the fact that they could no more change the patterns of their daily life than they could affect the movement of the planets. In the course of public protest, however, this habit of passivity began to disintegrate. As one worker in the crowd at party headquarters explained, he began to experience "something that can't be written about. You have to have lived it in order to understand how in that band of people we felt our power. For the first time in our lives we have taken a stand against the state. Before, it was a taboo, something absolutely unattainable, unthinkable, beyond us."[116] A second worker observed: "I didn't think I was protesting just the price rise, although that is what sparked it—it had to do with an overthrowing, at least in part, of everything we hated."[117]

In Gdynia, the authorities played for time. While the universally despised police were kept off the street, armed detachments of marines and officer candidates were sent to the party committee, the police station, the prison, the court, and the procuracy. At the same time, City Council President Jan Mariański received telephone instructions from the party first secretary to speak to the crowd, which continued to grow as new groups broke out of their factories to join. Holding a megaphone, Mariański stepped onto a balcony overlooking the square and was met, in his words, with "yells from every direction and demands made in a less than courteous manner."[118] For Mariański, an obscure and powerless official, the operative historical precedents were Poznań and Hungary in 1956— that is, murders of Communists in the streets. Courageously, he went down into the crowd and proposed that a delegation come into the building to talk. When workers immediately named their representatives, Mariański realized that they were more organized than they appeared.

Together with a worker delegation of seven people, three from the Paris Commune, two from Dalmor, and two from the port, Mariański returned to the balcony and promised he would present the demonstrators' demands to Vice Premier Kociołek. He also promised he would try to persuade Kociołek to reply over television and radio. The workers' delegation and Mariański then went back into the building. As they talked, new delegates selected by their workplaces joined the original group.[119]

Apparently Edmund Hulsz already had a list of prepared demands. The main focus was on the issue of massive wage inequality. Organized around the premise that rewards in Poland needed to be equalized, with a differential in income no greater than 2 to 1, the complete demands were reminiscent of English levelers. As Hulsz put it, "In a land calling itself socialist, there cannot be large disproportions [of reward] such as existed in Poland. For example, the director of the Paris Commune Shipyard earned 120,000 złotys. The difference was 150 times [between the director and an average worker]. It was the same in other workplaces."[120] Workers greeted these proposals with delight. "Now things would be like in China, everything equal."[121] "Red" egalitarianism well shows how complex relations were between the party and the working class they had created. It was not a simple rejection of the party and its ideology. On this issue, it turned out the workers were more Communist than the Communists.

Beyond the matter of fairness in substantive economic issues, the Gdynia workers proposed a structural change: the election of new officers to lead the trade unions. Finally, there was a central tactical ingredient: the sit-down strike would continue until demands were fulfilled.[122]

The demands were typed out, and Mariański and the delegates signed them, thereby recognizing the worker delegates. Mariański kept advising the delegates to remain calm and preserve the peace. Nervously he pointed to the bay and said, "The Soviet navy is there. The U.S.S.R. is nearby. They know how to shoot, so control yourselves, for God's sake."[123] Though Mariański's initiative had the effect of keeping workers off the streets for another day, higher party authorities reacted with fury to his implicit acceptance of another side with whom the party should negotiate.[124] The party in theory and in practice represented everyone as the leading element of the working class. Even simple discussion with the delegates implied recognition of social groups not represented by the party. In one way, the list of demands was meaningless—a naive scrap of paper to be later ignored. Still, no public document like it had appeared in decades in the communist world. The negotiation document was totally alien and subversive to the system.[125]

After the rallies in the port area of Gdynia, several hundred workers moved to the Port Recreation Club, which had been lent to the strike committee to use as a headquarters. In the late afternoon, workplace delegates elected 26-year-old Stanisław Słodkowski, a hull worker in the Paris Commune, as the chairman of the committee.[126] The structure of worker representation was uneven. Of 31 delegates assembled in the hall that night, some were essentially self-selected. Others were sympathetic hangers-on who had wandered in, and some were authentic representatives of workplace committees. In spite of talk of a sit-down strike, there was little effort to organize within workplaces before the day's shift ended. Słodkowski, for example, returned to his hullworking shop on the Paris Commune, gave a short exhortatory speech, and then left for the recreation club.

The recreation club stood outside any factory perimeter. As night fell, the Gdynia Strike Committee stood isolated, unprotected by a striking factory work force. When a curfew was announced on radio and television, the strike committee decided that most people should go home for the night while a smaller group remained to prepare a manifesto and plan for the next day. Even the volunteer security guards were sent home, because the committee felt it was acting legally and had been recognized by the state authorities. After all, members told themselves, they had not engaged in violent protest or vandalism. They even thought their plans for a general strike the next day were legal and approved. They were reassured by visits from the port director, as well as by Mariański. But in fact, Mariański engaged more in a reconnaissance mission than a visit. He came at the instruction of naval commanders, who asked him to verify rumors "that the repair shipyard was planning to march in the streets," and whose attitude clearly revealed their anger at the agreement Mariański had signed.[127]

As the Gdynia Strike Committee continued to prepare its manifesto and the Gdańsk shipyard workers met in the recreation hall, the overall

coastal situation escalated toward more violence. The Warsaw representatives of the party leadership, who had flown in to the coast, reacted to
the events of the day with anger and something approaching hysterical
outrage. Deputy Premier Kociołek went on coastal radio and TV with a
remarkable tirade.

> Our streets have been the scene of banditry and assault. Agents of the Citizen's
> Militia, the Volunteer Militia, soldiers and officers of the Polish Army are
> wounded—some gravely and in hopeless condition. Who did this? Gangs made
> up of criminals and blackguards. This is why troops and militia were brought
> in and a police curfew declared.[128]

Kociołek stated that no dialogue or compromise was possible. All the
workers could do was return to work. "The most disparate suggestions
and demands—often in the form of ultimatums—have been put forward.
I want to make it perfectly clear—most of these demands are impossible to fulfill. Yes, just as it is impossible to revoke decisions already
made." Finally Kociołek attacked the patriotism of all those who differed
with him. The speech did not contain the slightest hint of compromise.
Not surprisingly, workers were enraged that he had labelled them as
criminals.[129]

At this point, the party leadership hoped to wind up the entire affair as
rapidly as possible by uncompromising use of superior force. At the very
moment Kociołek's address was being drummed into the ears of coastal
workers, Gomułka's personal representative in Gdańsk, Zenon Kliszko,
was venting his wrath upon the provincial party committee. He accused
the provincial secretaries of incompetence and foot-dragging and even
suggested their deliberate connivance in the disturbances. "Tomorrow
should see an end to all disturbances and the restoration of order," he
said. "As for pay raises, no demand can be fulfilled and we have to say
that openly."[130]

Kliszko damned the provincial secretaries for their acceptance of demands. "What kind of petitions are you accepting?" he yelled. "By what
right are you carrying on some kind of discussion?" The Lenin Shipyard
party secretary tried to explain that this was an authentic protest of the
working class. Kliszko went wild with fury. "I will throw you out of the
party. I'll take your party card away. This is a counterrevolution and all
methods to put it down are permissible!" He added, "Even if 300 workers die, the revolt will be put down."[131]

Kliszko then embarked on a series of decisions that virtually guaranteed violent confrontation. Night arrests of workers who had attracted
police attention in the street and factories continued. Not only was all
possibility of discussion publicly refused, arrest orders were issued for the
Gdynia Strike Committee. Above all, Kliszko ordered a military blockade

of the Gdańsk and Gdynia shipyards. Two armored divisions were ordered to take up positions in front of the shipyards, surround the gates, and prevent workers from leaving.[132]

This was a fantastic decision. The Gdańsk workers were expected to come to work through lines of armored vehicles with cannon muzzles and machine guns pointed at their shipyard, work a nine-hour shift, and then go home. With their strike committee in jail, Paris Commune workers were expected to do the same.

## December 16

### Repression and Resistance

Exactly at midnight, members of the Gdynia Strike Committee heard vehicles drive up to the Port Recreation Club. Breaking down the door (which was not locked), armed police ran up the stairs and began beating everyone at hand. The 31 people present were lined up against the walls, hands in the air, then handcuffed in twos and passed through a gauntlet of police, who beat them with batons and literally kicked them down the stairs and out to police wagons.[133] During the rest of the night, police arrested other workers at home. In Gdańsk, most workers had gone home for the night, but the strike leaders had remained. By 4 A.M., two hours before the beginning of Wednesday's shift, armored detachments were in position around the Lenin Shipyard. Lech Wałęsa and other strike leaders woke up in the shipyard to an astonishing scene—they were surrounded by tanks.

> They were really there! I couldn't believe my own eyes. It was impossible to sleep now. We waited for daybreak. Arriving workers confirmed that the army was everywhere, at all the shipyard gates. All the neighboring streets were also occupied. Tanks had taken up position at every corner near the regional hospital, the railroad hospital, the regional Ministry of the Interior.[134]

In order to reach the shipyard, as Wałęsa later recalled, workers had to pass through the army blockade and pass in front of the tanks and other armored vehicles. "All wondered, 'Are they really going to fire on us?' Something broke within us. What people felt is difficult to describe—a desire for vengeance, but also something of hopelessness and a diffuse sense of immunity from punishment."[135]

The army units included the elite blue-beret division of marines stationed in Gdańsk. One soldier was actually a shipyard worker serving out his conscription.

> We were given 120 rounds of ammunition in case people attacked us, with the order to first shoot to frighten, then to fire into the crowd. Our commander, a

young man of 25, gave us the order in a strange singing voice. I felt that he was saying it because he had to, that he was afraid of his own words: Only one boy from our unit said that he'd fire into the crowd. We cursed him out. Someone asked him, "And what if I shoot you in the neck?' "[136]

This was the nightmare of any army facing unarmed civilians.

The military occupation provoked a general strike in most factories of the three cities. In the Lenin Shipyard, a crowd 5,000 strong gathered in front of the administration building and insisted on reply to the demands they had given shipyard authorities the previous day. But some of the younger workers wanted to do more. At 8 A.M., the boldest of them issued out of Gate no. 2 and advanced upon the army. They were met with a volley of fire, and within seconds, about fifteen workers lay shot in front of Gate no. 2. Four of them were dead.[137]

In this desperate situation, workers called on ritual and symbol. Like an antique chorus in a Greek tragedy, they turned the massacre into a kind of national rite in which the dead workers were the human sacrifices. They picked up the bodies of their dead and wounded from the rubble and retreated. As they did so they sang the national anthem, "Poland Lives While We Live."[138] In retrospect, it may be said that the Polish workers' movement took on a permanent organized form at that instant on December 16, 1970. The event served as a focus for political action over the next ten years. For the decade that followed, politics in Gdańsk revolved around the political symbols of Gate no. 2 and the workers who fell there.[139]

The gates were closed behind the retreating workers, and a bitter assembly of thousands convened. The strikers set up loudspeakers aimed at the surrounding army. As the crowd chanted, "murderers, murderers," the national flag hung with black crepe was hoisted to half mast. Helmets and black crepe were hung on the gates while the crowd observed a minute of silence—ending again with the national anthem. The rendition included the lines banned by the government in People's Poland because of their suggestion of a country under foreign rule: "What alien force has taken, we at sword point will restore."[140]

Now workers dissolved the "official" strike committees inspired the day before by the party and management in the Lenin Shipyard and convened their own creation—"the Council of Striking Workers." It was a wholly worker-led entity, one stripped clean of party officials and workers of doubtful militance. A presidium was elected, composed of Zbigniew Jarosz, Jerzy Górski, Lech Wałęsa, and Ryszard Podhajski, which organized security and provisions for the sit-down strike. Significantly, although the council entered into agreements with the Northern and Repair shipyards, no wider interfactory council was formally set up.[141]

The newly formed strike committees collected and wrote strike demands. The first manifesto of an entire factory that has survived—from the Gdańsk Repair Shipyard—called for rescinding the price hikes, stabilizing wages and prices, withdrawing the army, ending privileges for the party and military apparatus, and publishing of the demands. But there is one demand that leaps out from the page: "We demand that trade unions be freed from control or interference by the PZPR and the workplace management . . . [and] elections to union offices at all levels."[142] Here, six years before the appearance of intellectual opposition in Poland, which is almost universally held to have taught the Polish workers the demand for a free union independent of the party, is the first point of the 1980 Gdańsk Accord, the fundamental demand of Solidarity.

An essential alteration in the workers' relationship with the party-state is here evident. On the first two days of the marches, Gdańsk workers acted as petitioners and supplicants. The form seemed dramatic—a march of thousands to party headquarters—but the workers were fearful of having any structure, any representatives. When the party proved unresponsive, the petitioning moved to retaliation—the burning of the party building. But despite the violence, there was still no positive alternative proposed. The workers were angry at the party not because it had usurped jurisdiction, but because it had not exercised it properly and fairly.

But on December 16, forced by the party's intransigence and escalating use of violence, the workers shed their role as petitioners and metamorphosed into a source of authority, becoming actors on the stage of decision-making in Poland. The workers now understood that the trade unions had to be purged of party influence if they were to achieve true independence. Beyond this, the autonomy of workers could not be maintained if activists were arrested for speaking up for workers. Immunity from prosecution was therefore demanded as solidarity against the state developed. Finally, a symbolic protest was replaced by a new form of association—a round-the-clock sit-down strike that was institutionally autonomous and maintained over time to force a government response. This, then, was the new plateau of self-perception and perception of their enemy that Baltic workers had fashioned for themselves.

The Gdańsk workers now settled into a sit-down strike under conditions that amounted to a state of siege. Cut off by sea by patrolling naval vessels and by land by a cordon of armored troops with tanks, the strikers decided to create an official posture for themselves—and every protection it might afford—by conducting their negotiations with the army and the party through officials in the shipyard. With these arrangements in place and the shipyard shops silenced by an occupation strike, the workers of Gdańsk mourned their dead and settled in for a trial of strength.

*In the Paris Commune Shipyard*

In nearby Gdynia, workers at the Paris Commune Shipyard were evolving through similar stages of insurgency on the first shift of December 16. Attempts by loyalists to start work proved futile as production workers milled around or sat by their machines and discussed the latest rumors of the bloody events in their sister city of Gdańsk. The discussions soon took an emotional turn when workers observed the militia and the army taking up positions by the shipyard. Around 10 A.M., workers marched out of the hull divisions toward the shipyard director's office near the gates.[143] Helicopters circling overhead dropped leaflets appealing for order, but as the disappointed director later reported, "Most of these leaflets were burned or otherwise destroyed." Soon thereafter, news that the workers' strike committee had been arrested began to spread through the shipyard.[144]

These events contained a certain cumulative power: the party officials in the shipyard were equivocating; leaflets dropped from the sky were full of pious or threatening disinformation. The tanks of the Polish Army suddenly appeared outside the shipyard gates, and finally came news that the legitimate voice of the workers—their strike committee—had been arrested. Though each ingredient was far from unprecedented in People's Poland, the effect was to fill the workers with a profound impatience, disbelief, and finally collective outrage. By 11:30 A.M., the throng of workers numbered 4,000. The mood had become insurrectionary. "Put a noose on the director and hang him! Take the party committee and directors as hostages until the strike committee is freed! Don't trust anyone. They arrested the strike committee even though they guaranteed their safety."[145]

As tension mounted, the party decided on a parley, but it proved difficult to find anyone with whom to negotiate. As the shipyard director ruefully recalled, "People were afraid to choose a second committee. The example of the first didn't encourage it."[146] Nonetheless, a dozen or so workers eventually came forward. The crowd bound its delegates to two points: withdrawal of the army and freedom for the first committee. The short and angry confrontation with the shipyard authorities ended in an ultimatum. "Free the strike delegates by 2:00 P.M. or no one will be able to stop the destruction of the director's building."[147] Responding to this cue, the party's first secretary in the shipyard, W. Porzycki, accompanied by four workers, left to present the shipyard demands to Gdynia authorities. Meanwhile, Director Tymiński and other officers remained in the shipyard, effectively as hostages, until the safe return of the delegation.[148]

The workers received a startling welcome from Admiral Janczyszyn, who, in the words of one of the delegates "told us that artillery are trained on our shipyard and not a stone on a stone would remain." He said, "We won't allow anyone to attack our system. If you throw a stone or let out a shout, the armed forces will shoot."[149]

In the shipyard, when the deadline had passed and the delegation had still not returned, the crowd invaded the administration building. Just as it appeared that the building would be burned, the workers' emissaries telephoned that they were on their way.[150] When the emissaries arrived at 2:15 P.M., with no answer to their demand to free the prisoners, the tumult reached its climax. As Shipyard Party Secretary Porzycki recalled, "One of the delegates yelled, 'Mates! Negotiations are in progress. Let's disperse. Tomorrow morning we have to march on the town. We'll assemble at 7:00 A.M. and these two'—he pointed at me and the director—'will be in front.' And in five minutes the crowd dispersed and everyone went home."[151]

*The Party Prepares a Lesson*

The initiative now passed to the party, whose officials, as it turned out, were of two minds. Shipyard managers and local party functionaries in Gdańsk and Gdynia thought a formal process of negotiation was a necessary step toward defusing the situation. Toward this end, they favored freeing the arrested strike committee members. But the Warsaw party contingent led by Zenon Kliszko had not budged from its initial analysis that the coastal working class was engaged in a "counterrevolution." Indeed, at a party strategy meeting that night, Kliszko coldly informed one and all that Gdynia was going to be singled out for special attention. The shipyard would be formally dissolved and all the workers fired. Troops would insure that no one would enter the Paris Commune Shipyard the next morning. Stunned, the shipyard managers asked that radio and television announcements be made so that the workers would not come to the factory. As Michał Tymiński, the Paris Commune director, later reported, "We were told that it was impossible. Then we asked that the commuter rail lines be shut down. We were refused. 'Let the trains not stop at the Gdynia station.' Again, no!"[152]

Ominous as this all was, the party soon made it worse. At 8 P.M., Politburo member Kociołek addressed the people of Gdańsk and Gdynia over radio and television for the second consecutive night. In his speech he held to the same political line as the previous night. He enumerated the costs of the "criminal," "destructive," and "bandit" actions in the streets of Gdańsk and then added unctuously that everything was "returning to normal." In the name of the people of the three cities he thanked the militia and the army for their "selfless service, and their well-carried-out duties."[153]

Kociołek repeated that the demands submitted by the workers were "mostly impossible to fulfill!" He added: "The refusal to return to work is accompanied by the formulation of demands in an atmosphere of nonstop chaotic assemblies. I told you yesterday and I tell you today, it is impossible to repeal the decision for price rises! . . . There is nothing to discuss with you." He then attacked the shipyard workers directly on the issue of their pay. Their wages had "kept ahead of inflation" and their average pay was 1,000 złoty more than the average workers' pay in industry. He repeated his claim that the shipyard was uncompetitive with other shipbuilding industries in other countries. He had already told them earlier in the year that the shipyard should be closed down. "I've heard your claim that if the militia and army are withdrawn you will return to work. Well, the army and militia are in the streets because you have stopped work, and the results are riots, banditry, and pillage. And shipyard workers were not only participants but instigators, and you bear the moral responsibility."

But Kociołek's closing words proved to be the most ominous of all. "I appeal one more time—return to normal work . . . so that we can peacefully observe the holiday period and greet the New Year."[154]

As these words came over the radio and TV, Director Tyminski knew he and his workers were trapped. First, the highest party and military officials closed the shipyard and blockaded it with troops; then they refused to announce publicly that they had done so; finally they called on people to return to work. The rulers of People's Poland had planned an ambush and were now going to teach the workers of the coast a bloody lesson.[155]

After the fact, the party was essentially defeated by the truth— i.e., it proved unable to construct a post facto cover story that was internally consistent. In the Central Committee Report and other official accounts, this situation is explained thus: "While militia forces and army detachments blocked entries to the shipyard . . . Stanisław Kociołek, who from the very beginning acted with great prudence, not knowing of the decision made by Zenon Kliszko, made a television address in which he appealed to the workers of the coast to return to work. Between his appeal and Z. Kliszko, there was a contradiction. When this was realized in the early morning hours, energetic actions were undertaken to inform people that the shipyard was closed and that it was necessary to return home."[156]

As we have seen, the decision was made hours before Kociołek's speech at 8 P.M. Moreover, there were many people privy to the decision-making process and to the content of both Kociołek's speech and Kliszko's order: Premier Cyrankiewicz; First Secretary Gomułka; the minister of national defense, General Jaruzelski; the Army chief of staff; the vice minister of national defense, General Grzegorz Korczyński; the admiral of the Polish Navy; the commanders of the Gdańsk military region, Generals Kamiński and Baryła; and two vice ministers of internal affairs, General Franciszek Szlachcic and Henryk Słabczyk. The situation was complicated even more in that factional infighting may have added to the chaos. Of the three factions in the Polish leadership, all held positions of leverage: the Partisans, through General Słabczyk; Gomułka, through Kliszko and Korczyński; and Gierek, through General Franciszek Szlachcic, who had served under him in Silesia for ten years. One rationalization that emerged after the fact was that Kociołek had taped the appeal to return to work before the decision to blockade the shipyard was made. But in an interview given after his return to high party office as Warsaw first secretary in 1980, Kociołek admitted that the speech was given live. He claimed that after learning of the blockade, he realized what was going to happen and did "everything possible" to warn people not to come to work.[157] Unfortunately for the persuasiveness of this explanation, Kociołek's speech was repeated over the radio and TV at 11 P.M.[158]

As for the alleged lack of coordination among the decision-making "centers," there are three arguments against it. First, the chronology is wrong. Numerous witnesses agree that the decision about the blockade and lockout was made in the late afternoon. Kociołek's speech came hours later, at 8 P.M., and then was repeated at 11 P.M. Second, the shipyard officials conveyed their alarm both to the military police command under General Korczyński and to the political command under Kliszko. Third, Paris Commune Secretary Porzycki adds that he saw Korczyński with Kliszko that night, at the very moment that military planning for the blockade was proceeding.[159] Beyond this, all subsequent "explanations" assiduously avoided the operative fact: the possible consequences of the decision were forcefully pointed out to Kliszko by the shipyard managers. The internal log of the Paris Commune managers and the testimony of Gdynia officials dismantle the party explanations.

Two very unusual—and eventually contradictory—situations had now developed on the Baltic Coast. In Gdynia, a work force that had gone home for the night slept in ignorance of an elaborate armored ambush that awaited them in the morning. In Gdańsk, by contrast, the work force had tied up the Lenin Shipyard in a sit-down strike. As party hostility against them mounted throughout the night, they appeared to be the most immediately imperiled workers on the coast. But in fact, as events were soon tragically to show, it was the peacefully sleeping workers of Gdynia who were destined to endure "the December massacre."

## December 17

The bizarre and dangerous confrontation in the early morning hours of December 17 in the Lenin Shipyard took place in a strikingly lighted setting. The workers' strike committee—in its fear of a provocation that would serve as a pretext for the military to enter the shipyards—set up lighting systems in the work areas. Workers also prepared stocks of explosives and flammable materials for defense of the shipyards against an assault by the army. Around 10 P.M., First Secretary Pieńkowski informed strike leaders that the army had issued an ultimatum for workers to leave the shipyard in four hours or be attacked and bombed. They promised that the worker demands would be fulfilled, but only after the strike ended. After a vote at 2 A.M., the strike broke.[160] Over the next three hours, thousands of defeated workers exited from Gate no. 3 between long lines of police and army and then through Gdańsk, past troop carriers and tanks stationed in the deserted streets. As a crane operator Anna Walentynowicz said, "We had the feeling we were going into captivity like prisoners with lowered heads."[161] No one could possibly have suspected how the surrender of the Lenin Shipyard that winter night would be followed by an extraordinary triumph ten years later. One of the strike leaders remembered: "That is how December ended for me: as an enormous and destroyed hope."[162]

Earlier in the evening, Gdynia First Secretary Malinowski and City President Mariański had driven to Gdańsk to plead with Kliszko to free the arrested strike committee and preserve peace in Gdynia. They were bluntly told that the decision to blockade the shipyard had already been made. "Shaking with anger, his face livid," Kliszko told Malinowski: "No concessions. I will not give the order to free the committee!"[163] Two hours after this ill-fated peace mission, large armored detachments entered Gdynia and took up positions in and around the principal public buildings and factories. Startled onlookers saw "one after another tanks, armored transporters, and heavy trucks headed toward the port and shipyard."[164] Conscript troops rather than specialized internal security troops were sent to the coast. In account after account of civilian contacts with soldiers three elements appear: the improvised chaos of the operation; the fear and disorientation of the soldiers; and their faith in the explanation for their mobilization given to them by their political officers and commanders. "They were disoriented. You could tell by their boots and their haircuts that they were new recruits. They seemed to have been sent straight out of boot camp."[165] A Gdynia woman asked soldiers taking up positions in the Gdynia downtown just after midnight where they were from. "Kraków. We drove all night because Germans are endangering our land."[166] A doctor from the Gdynia City Hospital met soldiers as they jumped out of their vehicles in the hospital parking lot. "Their first words were, 'Where are these Germans?' That was what they thought, these soldiers who are also our soldiers."[167] In another hospital, soldiers who had taken up position came to beg for food. "They said there had been an invasion, that they had been on the road for days and 'we're hungry and where in hell are we anyway?'"[168]

Thousands of commuters piled off the trains of the Gdynia shipyard station in the final predawn blackness of December 17. They encountered a frightening situation. A jumble of sounds hit them as simultaneous loudspeaker announcements competed for their attention. The cacophony came from the station itself and from a nearby military communications unit with a giant loudspeaker. Worst of all was the blocking of movement away from the trains themselves. The Gdynia station consisted of two long parallel quais connected by a narrow pedestrian bridge that collectively funnelled the workers out of the station toward the adjacent shipyard. On the morning of December 17, all movement toward the shipyard and port had been blocked by military and police detachments. Workers became aware of instructions over the station loudspeaker announcing the closing of the shipyard. A gravelly voice appealed to the workers to return to their homes. It was a fundamentally disorienting situation, as there was no way for the blockaded workers to carry out such orders.[169]

A second announcement was no help. "Because of the situation which has arisen in the shipyard, it is absolutely forbidden for anyone to enter. Persons who do not respect this order may incur serious consequences."[170] The announcement was utterly confusing. The railroad timetable for the delivery of 6,000 workers for the first shift was designed so that trains arrived in a steady sequence only minutes apart. With workers unable to move, each new trainload disgorging passengers simply forced earlier arrivals forward—closer to the armored troops who blocked the shipyard. In this manner, the workers "advanced" on the troops in a milling, reluctant jam of people. Suddenly, a tank cannon boomed, followed by a burst of automatic rifle fire. Workers collapsed on the cobblestones in front of the station. Loudspeaker announcements provided a macabre backdrop: "The defense subdetachment was forced to use its arms and will continue to use them in case of forcible attempts to enter the shipyard."[171] Inexorably, the loudspeaker chronicled the event.

> To those taking part in the march! The command of the shipyard and port orders that you halt and disperse. . . . Citizens! In this sad and tragic situation you should not allow yourselves to be governed by momentary emotion. . . . The commanders of the shipyard and port defense absolutely and unconditionally order you to leave the area around the Gdynia Shipyard station. . . . We want to make it clear that the army is not guilty for the bloodshed. . . . Soldiers simply carried out their orders. We warn you that if further provocations occur, we will continue to fire on you. . . . We will carry out our orders to the end. To reduce the numbers of dead and wounded, we ask you to withdraw. . . . The entry to the port and shipyard will be defended by us with all necessary means.[172]

Twenty-three-year-old Jacek Węglarz, a worker of the Paris Commune, had taken part in the march on Tuesday and the strike on Wednesday.

> I arrived at Gdynia Shipyard as another train arrived from the other direction. Both platforms filled with people. Everyone went up on the bridge and down to the viaduct. The atmosphere was tense because people who had gotten there earlier knew about the tanks and the militia. We didn't quite realize what was going on as we took our normal way to work. Then the shots stopped us. I was in the first or second row—anyway, in the front, and that's when I was wounded. Personally, I didn't hear any warnings and I swear that there were none. Maybe there were before I arrived. Well, with the first shots I fell, wounded in the leg.[173]

What workers saw depended on when they arrived and exactly where they were when the firing began. Wiesław Kodzik, a young apprentice in the Paris Commune, preceded Węglarz into the station. When he descended onto the cobblestones, six or so militiamen were standing by the stairs. As more people arrived, the militiamen were forced back onto the viaduct and into the cordon of tanks and troops. The crowd continued to move forward and the soldiers fired. "They did not fire on those in front but fired into the ground, straight into the cobblestones. This was even worse than direct fire because it was like shrapnel ricocheting through the crowd. Whoever has been in the army will understand it."[174] Zdzisław Ślesarow arrived by bus and moved toward the shipyard gates amid a group of twenty:

> We were just level with the beginning of the Gdynia shipyard station when we heard an explosion. It definitely wasn't a rifle. It was too powerful—from a cannon of some kind. After a couple of minutes or even less, we heard and saw a series of volleys from machine guns. We could see their tracers pass over the viaduct. A few seconds later I heard screams from the station and cries: "Murderers! Gestapo!"[175]

On adjacent roads, workers commandeered cars and loaded them with dead and wounded. Adam Gotner, who eventually survived despite seven bullets through the chest, remembers how his car was stopped by soldiers at a roadblock. As he lay there half-conscious, an officer screamed at them in German.[176] Now violent clashes alternated with periods of calm where civilians would converse with officers and enlisted men. "Why was this happening?" inquired a citizen? An army political officer explained, "Because the Kaszubs and Germans are killing Poles."[177] Mothers and grandmothers brought food and hot drink to the units guarding buildings and crossroads. They may have done more to undermine the morale of the army than any other force. A differentiated picture of an army under strain emerges from the accounts. In one incident, in front of the Public

Procuracy, a worker went wild with rage and jumped on an armored troop transporter. "'Shoot—you sons of whores!' The officer and crew stare[d] off into the far distance."[178] In other incidents, the army dragged its feet. "A march of workers on its way to the city hall met an army blockade and refused to give way. The officer [gave] the order to shoot us but the soldiers shot in the air."[179]

Throughout Gdynia, workers found armored troops, police, or militia blocking the entrances to major factories. These workers now converged at the center of town in accordance with the decision of the preceding day, which had specified a unified march on city hall at 7 A.M. After the shooting at the shipyard, at around 6:30 A.M., the growing crowd in the center of town began to attack the building that housed the public prosecutor, the local symbol of justice on the coast. Protecting troops fired, and more workers fell. As the fighting at the Gdynia Central Station and the public prosecutor's office died down, the crowds began to march toward the city hall, where 5,000 people attacked with such determination that the front line of police was forced behind the solid rows of tanks. The army fired again, killing four people.[180]

In at least two and possibly as many as four marches demonstrators picked up the bodies of the dead and carried them to city hall, site of the phantom "agreement" signed between Mariański and the strike committee two days before. It had been shocking enough to workers that their strike leaders had been arrested; now there was the ultimate betrayal of the party killing workers.

The meaning of the epic December is contained in one scene repeated several times—workers marching through Gdynia's streets carrying their dead on makeshift biers (Ill. 1). As a participant in one of these emotional marches recalled, "At first we carried him [a dead worker] on our hands, then we took a door out of the rail barracks and carried him on it so that the people of Gdynia would see that the army is killing people."[181] A sobbing woman covered the body with the red-and-white flag of Poland. People repeatedly suggested that the crowd go to the Swedish Consulate "so that the whole world would know."[182] That is, workers appealed the actions of their own government to other governments and peoples. As one marcher remembered, "On the way we chanted 'murderers.' I remember how the echo rebounded in the rail tunnel. People stood and looked at us in shock. Women cried. I cried. We were all in such shock from the shooting."[183] When they reached the Church of the Sacred Heart, a priest came out with a cross, which was then nailed to the front of the doors. The body was covered with flowers.[184]

Here, as at the shooting at the Lenin Shipyard the day before, workers reacted symbolically as Christians, treating the dead as martyrs whose sufferings and deaths would be followed by a resurrection. They politi-

1. Workers' march to the Gdynia City Hall, December 17, 1970

cized the Christian mystery. In their ritual action, they said that ultimately, the fallen workers would arise and triumph over their socialist
masters.

The extent of the gap separating the party and the people is illustrated
by the official "explanation" of this clash in Gdynia.

> Today, firearms were used against soldiers of the People's Army and the citi-
> zens' militia. The threat of destruction of the shipyard made for two days
> turned into an attack by a several-thousand-person crowd against detachments
> of the army and militia guarding workplaces and city buildings. Provocateurs
> used firearms, and shots were fired on the soldiers and militia from the
> crowd. . . . There could only be one answer—a firm suppression of these acts
> of terror and a speedy restoration of public safety and order.[185]

All this, of course, was fantasy. But it was not too far from the original
premassacre interpretation offered by the party leadership in Warsaw.
Zenon Kliszko, acting for Władysław Gomułka, had envisioned, and
then enacted, a "counterrevolution." The party leaders had wanted to
teach the workers a bloody lesson, but it turned out that the workers had
learned an unintended lesson: that they possessed the capacity for hero-

ism, and, most of all, self-organization. In fact, the workers of the Gdańsk region had achieved some long-term breakthroughs in internal organization and ideology and leadership. The culmination of these breakthroughs lay far in the future, but the tradition of resistance and martyrdom was now in place.

At a symbolic emotional level, Gdańsk and Gdynia remembered those terrible days in December as a massacre of the innocents by perfidious traitors acting for a foreign power. This became part of a hidden oral tradition on the Baltic Coast. It was most visible in the cult of the dead. While families and friends visited graves on the December anniversary, stories circulated of hidden graves with their many hundreds of victims who had been killed and secretly buried.

A mass for the dead celebrated in the parish church of the Paris Commune Shipyard, the Sacred Heart of Jesus, made all these connections visible. It occurred just as the bloody events were drawing to a close on December 21, 1970. As recorded in the parish archive, the victims were described as unarmed "workers, women, and children peacefully and honorably defending the right of working peoples to daily bread. . . . The sermon brought the crowd of faithful gathered in the church to tears and lamentation. Full of pain and inconsolable sorrow, they committed to all-merciful God the souls of the heroes of Gdynia."[186] The assembly first sang the hymn by Kornel Ujejski, "Z Dymem Pożarów":

> Through fiery smoke, through brothers blood and ashes.
> To Thee, O Lord, our fearful prayer rings out
> In terrible lamentation, like the last shout.

The sermon by Father Roman Tadrowski contained an interpretation of the events and a wish for the future. "Shaken with these sufferings, we endure these tragic events, tragic not only for our city, but for all Poles, for our whole poor fatherland." The priest had difficulty reconciling his own sense of the sanctity of being Polish with the raw fact that the Polish police and army had committed civic murder. "Persons pretending to be Poles committed a public criminal act, shooting completely unarmed and innocent brother Poles simply because these poor Polish workers demanded—for themselves and their families—bread."[187] The sense of nationhood embedded in the sermon was so great that the object of worship explicitly became "Poland":

> O Poland, are you not able to feed your sons who work by the sweat of their brows for you and your glory? They did not regret living for you, Poland. They did not regret dying for you, but it should have been on the field of honor, in the defense of their fatherland, not on the streets of their native city, defenseless and innocent and hunted down like rabid dogs. This innocent Polish blood

spilled by cruel executioners, enemies of Poland, calls out for vengeance to the heavens![188]

The reappearance of the Saviour in the sermon did not soften the call for righteous vengeance on those who had dishonored Poland: "To You, Almighty God, we raise this terrible accusation, full of piercing pain. Punish the hand that wielded the sword and not the blind sword. With Your just hand, O Lord! Punish them!"[189]

# The Three-Day Worker Republic:
# The General Strike in
# Szczecin

POPULAR ACTION revealed that workers conceptualized their country as divided between incompetent and traitorous rulers who monopolized political and economic privilege, and deserving working families who were kept poor by this illegitimate state. As the workers were subjected to force and fraud, patterns of obedience, rooted in a pragmatic acceptance of a reality that previously seemed impossible to change, dissolved. The dictatorship of the proletariat revealed itself as a pure military police state, while society organized itself as a legitimate democracy. Workers developed new forms of association and programs that were partly strategic, as they answered the need to oppose the state, and also deeply aspirational, as they answered repressed desires for democratic association and social and economic equality.

Gdańsk and Gdynia had carried out general strikes, formulated demands, elected delegates, and attacked the hated symbolic seat of Communist power, but the full development of organizational and ideological forms had been cut off by overwhelming force. Now resistance emerged in the other major shipbuilding city on the Baltic Coast—Szczecin, with 350,000 inhabitants, and the Warski Shipyard, which employed 10,000 workers. There, events were as bloody, but the development of forms of resistance and democracy reached their highest level. The interfactory strike committee—a territorial union of all employees against the state—was to be most fully worked out in the ensuing days in Szczecin. The demand for free trade unions independent of the Leninist state was the core of the Szczecin workers' program.

On December 12, prior to the upheaval in Gdańsk, Szczecin's primary party organizations held meetings to read the letter from the Central Committee concerning the proposed price hikes. The reaction was so dramatic, the anger evoked by the announcement so great, that it was finally ended only by the hysterical cry of one member who took the floor: "Twenty-five years of work and we have nothing to show. Nothing. How is it possible?"[1]

This agonized reaction by a party member underscored a reality that millions across Poland felt the instant the price rise was announced. It seemed to them that most of the gains in living standards achieved by all their labor since the end of the war were instantly jeopardized. On Monday and Tuesday, December 14 and 15, news and rumors from the Gdańsk region began to filter into Szczecin. Because the Szczecin industries belonged to the same ministries and the same associations for ports and for shipping, shipbuilding, and ship repair, they worked in cooperation with Gdańsk workplaces daily. Despite the government blackout on news, reports of the strikes rapidly reached the people of Szczecin by word of mouth. In a diary kept during December by a port manager, the note for Tuesday, December 15, read: "A colleague couldn't make it to Gdańsk. He was stopped on the road. I now know that there are disturbances in Gdańsk."[2] The entry for December 16 is remarkably accurate: "We already know that serious riots have occurred in Gdańsk, that there are dead and wounded and that many buildings were burned, including the provincial party headquarters, the rail station, the provincial militia headquarters, and others. But the local press has completely unrelated articles. People are becoming infuriated."[3] The press, which usually merely irritated people with its party-defined reality, now enraged them.

Beginning Monday, December 14, the provincial militia in Szczecin pulled in reinforcements from the entire province. A noncommissioned militia officer described how they arrived "from the country stations and smallest posts. The boys didn't even know why or what for."[4] In the Warski Shipyard, on Monday, some workers already knew that a strike had broken out in the Gdańsk Shipyard. On Tuesday, "People weren't working normally but [were] discussing the situation in Gdańsk," and on Wednesday, December 16, "Some made [strike] preparations for the next day."[5]

On Tuesday night, shipyard authorities established a special group to stand night watches to keep order and prevent sabotage. On Wednesday, First Secretary Walaszek and other leaders of the provincial party met officials from the leading factories of Szczecin. During the meeting, Walaszek predicted that the Gdańsk disturbances would not spread to Szczecin. He thought this was so because the Warski Shipyard had had a very successful year and the end-of-the-year premiums would outweigh discontent about the price rises. But that same evening, the party received information from a shipyard informer that the workers were preparing a strike for the next day.[6]

On the evening of December 16, Polish radio and TV finally carried the first national news of the disturbances in Gdańsk, condemning them as the acts of hooligans and criminals. The first articles about the events in

Gdańsk appeared in the national and provincial press on the morning of December 17 as people were on their way to work. These reports said nothing about the sit-down strikes that were still in progress. The Polish state had been racing against time, moving to crush workers in Gdańsk and Gdynia before news spread by word of mouth or through foreign radio broadcasts. In this event, the foreign radio's first fragmentary reports came on the evening of December 16—that is to say, not ahead of the official press, as they often were in a crisis.

## A Day of Fighting: Another Party Headquarters Burns

But then Szczecin stepped into the place of Gdańsk and Gdynia and wrecked Gomułka's hopes to crush all opposition quickly. At 5 A.M. on December 17, Stanisław Rychlik, the regional party economic secretary, went to the Warski Shipyard in Szczecin for a meeting with party activists, who assured him there would be no strikes. Just in case, the party decided to hold mass meetings in the shipyard that day in order to forestall strikes. Professional party workers from the provincial committee were assigned to reinforce this ideological work in the shipyard.[7]

That same morning, two Warski party activists with reputations as internal party critics—Lucjan Adamczuk, the shipyard sociologist, and W. Adin, a secretary of the factory committee—were called in by higher-ups and questioned about the strike. "Who's going to start it, in what shops, and what form will it take?" Adamczuk was asked.[8] He could provide no information, for he knew of no preparations for a strike or demonstration. Back in the shipyard, he soon sensed something out of the ordinary was happening. "The ear of a ship welder is used to the sound of welding torches. When you don't hear that sound, you know immediately that something is up. Even without seeing the gathering crowds, I knew that it had started."[9]

As was the case in Gdańsk and Gdynia, the "pariahs," the hull workers, were among those who led the strike. Around 10 A.M., hull workers appropriated an electric wagon and rode around the shipyard, calling for a strike. Workers from other divisions responded. They moved to the director's building and demanded that party officials explain a few things. The shipyard's director, Tadeusz Cenkier, came out of the building. Like the Gdynia mayor and the Polish admiral, his answer to industrial conflict was to threaten Soviet armed intervention: "Don't march on the city or we'll have another Czechoslovakia, another Hungary."[10] He was whistled down.

In Szczecin, the first slogans shouted and written on the walls in chalk were "Solidarity with Gdańsk."[11] As they had in Gdańsk and Gdynia, workers demanded that the first secretary of the provincial party come to the shipyard to speak to them. When the shipyard's director called, First Secretary Walaszek replied that he wasn't going to discuss anything with "rabble." Walaszek thus held to the general line that had been followed in Gdańsk and in Gdynia, refusing discussions.[12]

Szczecin workers, meanwhile, reacted to the party's refusal to negotiate by preparing to march downtown to party headquarters. Józef Kasprzycki, who emerged as one of the strike leaders the next day, was opposed to marching on the city. "I remembered what happened in Poznań in 1956 all too well. My opinion was that if the state did not want to talk in the shipyard, it wasn't going to talk downtown either."[13]

But Kasprzycki did not prevail. Some two to three thousand "marched into the city via a circuitous route past other factories to let other factories know that we're striking."[14] The crowd was calm while strike monitors confiscated clubs and pipes from the more combative workers. Szczecin workers sang the national hymn, the "Internationale," and two other songs of the Polish revolutionary worker's movement, "To the Barricades, Working People," and the Communist "Workers' Guard March" with its first lines, "We from the burned villages, we from the starving cities; the time of revenge for our hunger, our blood, our tears has come."[15] At Grunwald Square, the militia appeared and attacked the crowd with gas grenades, driving workers to retreat in disorder almost all the way back to the shipyard. The march broke up into groups, part remaining by the shipyard as part fled up the hill to the old city wall, while about 200 broke through to the city center.

By 11:30 A.M., the militia had driven the workers to Famabud, a building-machine factory near the shipyard. Workers there climbed to the roofs and pelted the police with steel and iron fragments. As a participant, Antoni Kij, remembered, "For our part, we had ample ammunition from the metals port. I remember how the militia fled back on their hill like battered cats under the rain of stones and metal. But once there, they received reinforcements and attacked again."[16]

Soon, downtown Szczecin was drenched in tear gas. People in nearby houses threw out wet clothes so workers could wipe their eyes. "We didn't want to let the militia into the shipyard, and so we defended this area. Two police vehicles—an armored transport and a paddy wagon—were burned."[17] After two hours of fighting, the news came that workers from the Szczecin Repair Shipyard in Gryfia were on the way. "My spirits rose," said Kij, "because I was quite worn out by then."[18]

Gryfia's march was led by women reacting to the government's version of the news. They carried a banner that read, "We are shipyard workers, not hooligans."[19] Because Gdańsk workers, not Szczecin workers, had been labelled "hooligans," the banner expressed Szczecin's response to party propaganda—disbelief. The arrival of the Gryfia workers from their island in the Oder River turned everything around. Again, as in Gdynia, the primary impulse driving workers' actions was solidarity.

Warski workers had gone into the streets around 10 A.M. Said a participant from Gryfia, "We assembled in the marine division to decide what to do. The shipyard director, Pustelnik, advised us not to go into the streets because it would only lead to bloodshed. 'If you want to strike, then strike inside the shipyard.' But the young workers were determined to join Warski. When they started off, all of us went."[20] The first ferry to reach Warski carried 800–900 people. Workers waited for the second and third ferries so that they could march all together. Just as they started to move out, the Warski workers returned in full retreat, scattered and bloodied. "Our fresh forces of nearly 3,000 turned the situation around."[21] Now all converged and advanced on party headquarters. "Gryfia went in front, Warski in back," one marcher recalled.[22] The militia responded with more tear-gas grenades and nightsticks, but the crowd moved forward toward the party headquarters, scattering the police. Early in the afternoon, the workers broke onto the main square and massed in front, yelling for Walaszek to address them, but "he didn't show."[23] Armored transporters stood on the square with young Poles scrambling all over them. As their soldier crews passively watched, workers stripped the armored cars and tanks of their pickaxes and smashed in the doors of party headquarters.

From the party's standpoint, the problem was that most of the army troops and police on the coast had been dispatched to Gdańsk. The sole force available was the Szczecin-based 12th Mechanized Division. While considered an elite force for fighting capitalists, it was also a garrison division intimately acquainted with the people of Szczecin whose loyalty was first with the people, not with the officials. Neither the party nor security police could induce the soldiers to defend party headquarters aggressively. A vivid exchange between ranking officers illustrates the depth of the impasse—indeed, the trauma—within the army. The defense of the party building was entrusted to 150 soldiers of the 12th Division under the command of Lt. Colonel Henryk Ziemiański. When the division's political officer, Colonel Drewnowski, was informed by radio that the party building had started to burn, he ordered Ziemiański to open fire on the crowds of workers. Ziemiański replied, "Citizen Colonel, I refuse your order." Then, he added, "You son of a bitch, who am I going to shoot! There are women and children out there!" With this breakdown in military discipline, the party building simply burned.[24]

Enlisted men also refused to obey orders. Workers in front of the burning building refused an army lieutenant's order to evacuate the square, eliciting from the officer a threat to shoot. But the officer's soldiers abandoned the armored transporter in which they were riding, leaving him stranded in a sea of workers.[25]

As the fire died down at party headquarters, some in the crowd called for freeing those arrested in the morning's street fighting. Part of the crowd now left to attack the prison, and another part moved to the regional headquarters of the militia. The militia was prepared for defense, having been reinforced by detachments of soldiers. When the crowd of 15,000 used battering rams in an effort to break into the police station, the army and police forces received orders to fire. According to militia sources, the order to shoot came from Premier Cyrankiewicz over long-distance telephone from Warsaw.[26]

The shooting was described from outside the station by a doctor who was in an apartment overlooking the crowd. "There were many boys and girls around 17 years old. They began to try to smash in the doors of the commissariat on the Starszyński Street side. It was then that the first shots were fired."[27] The crowd vanished in an instant. On the square, "All that was left," said a participant, "were bodies."[28]

Soon after this bloody turn of events, the party secretaries were evacuated to army headquarters. Walaszek ran through the corridors shaking hands with everyone. Then he collared the division's commander and said, "Comrade Colonel, this is all your fault. Your army was too soft. They just stood on the side pretending."[29]

After the shooting in the square, groups of demonstrators attacked the city prison on Kaszubska Street, the press building, the city hall, and the Provincial Council of Trade Unions. All but the prison were set afire. Marchers also attempted to burn the public prosecutor's office building. There were more dead and wounded. A large number of shops and delicatessens in the area of Aviators Square were pillaged. Despite an emergency 6 P.M. curfew, street clashes between groups of demonstrators and the police continued until late that night.[30]

As night fell, police began arresting workers in their homes—a total of 200 to 300 during the afternoon and night. As in Gdynia and Gdańsk, a general pattern of beatings and running of gauntlets between rows of police prevailed. The account of a Warski worker, Andrzej Ostapiuk, is typical:

> I was arrested 17 December at my home around 8:00 P.M. Two militiamen and several soldiers entered our apartment, took our papers, and demanded to see our hands. Stećko had slightly dirty hands and immediately was struck with a nightstick. As we were being taken out, the militiaman asked Zagła or Stećko if he'd served in the army. When he gave the answer no, he was immediately

beaten all the way to the station. I was hit in the shoulder. By turns, they beat all of us. At the entrance to the station, militia stood in two lines. We were beaten and kicked. Around two that morning, we were transported to the prison on Kaszubska Street. Again the prison guards stood in rows and beat us with black batons.[31]

At 7 P.M., Premier Józef Cyrankiewicz provided his first public reaction to the coastal strikes. Cyrankiewicz was still remembered for his threats to the workers of Poznań fourteen years before. He had said then: "Every provocateur or madman who dares to lift his hand against the power of People's Poland will have that hand chopped off."[32] In his December 17 speech, he resorted to the major argument sustaining party legitimacy in Poland: that Poles had no alternative. "The coastal disturbances provided an opportunity to scum, adventurers, and enemies of the homeland for vandalism, looting, and murder," he said. "They are exploited by anarchist hooligans and criminal elements and by enemies of socialism, by enemies of Poland."[33] As in Kociołek's two speeches in Gdańsk, Cyrankiewicz offered no empirical or rhetorical concessions to the workers. He made it clear that price hikes would not be revoked. Within the existing civic, trade union, and party organizations, he said, there were no issues that could not be the subject of a "business-like discussion."[34]

He failed to mention the bloody events in Gdynia and Szczecin the same day. These disasters were passed over with the phrase, "Gdańsk and the coast." When Cyrankiewicz concluded his speech, the state radio and TV announcers read a national decree on security and public order giving full powers to "the forces of order" to suppress demonstrations. The announcement specified that the organs of the militia and security services had been instructed "to exercise all legally available means of compulsion, including the use of arms against persons making violent attempts on the life and health of citizens, looting, and destroying property and other facilities."[35]

In short, there is no evidence to suggest that Gomułka ever wavered in his decision to crush the workers' protest. In effect, the decree proclaimed martial law on the evening of December 17. From the shadows of the structure of power in Poland, the regime pulled out the little-known KOK—the Committee for the Defense of the Country—whose function was to run a militarized Poland in case of internal revolution or invasion.[36] In addition to military and police commanders taking over on the coast, contingency plans were set to militarize all work forces and thereby hold the workers in check.

As fighting died down in Szczecin, an awed party member described the city police station. "They were in full alert, prepared for an attack at any minute. The corridors and stairs were filled with armed police. The windows were all removed or kept open for security against stones. The sight and the atmosphere reminded me of films I had seen of the October Revolution."[37]

Executive reinforcements in the form of two generals of the army and police arrived by air from Warsaw to direct operations. The army general was Tadeusz Tuczapski, vice minister of national defense, a deputy commander of the Warsaw Pact armies and chief inspector of training of the Polish army. He was the number three man in the military hierarchy, after Minister of Defense Jaruzelski and Chief of Staff Chocha, who was already in Gdańsk.[38] The police general was Ryszard Matejewski.

Among the Baltic working class, a new world had come into focus. A Warski Shipyard worker named Stanisław Wądołowski was one of those whose sense of Poland changed fundamentally on December 17. "Up until then I wasn't interested in politics," he said. "I returned home that night tremendously upset. My mates, my friends had already come over. All spoke up, one after another. We knew we had to do something."[39] (Ten years later, Wądołowski would be a strike leader in the Polish August and emerge as a vice chairman of national Solidarity.) Throughout the night, armored units entered Szczecin and took positions in key points of the city, including the gates of the Warski Shipyard. Wądołowski was by no means alone in his awareness of the implications. Józef Kasprzycki recalled: "I was living on Park Street near the shipyard. All night I heard the rumble of tanks moving toward the shipyard. I deduced that the conflict had grown sharper. The next day was going to be dangerous."[40]

## The Szczecin General Strike and the Interfactory Strike Committee

Friday, December 18, the fifth day of fighting in the coastal cities, was a turning point for the Szczecin workers in their unequal struggle against the party-state. In the short run, they were defeated like their fellows in Gdańsk, Gdynia, and other cities of the coast. But in the long history of workers' struggle since the Communist takeover in 1944, this was the decisive step toward organization and a program that would underlie the victory of Solidarity ten years later.

One of the workers fated to play a key role that day, Józef Kasprzycki, headed for the Warski Shipyard as usual that morning. As in Gdańsk, the Szczecin troops were told that they were being called out to repel a German Fascist attack on Polish territory.

> Trolleys weren't running, and there were tanks everywhere. As I was passing the building of the city newspaper, *Głos Szczeciński*, the turret of a tank standing there opened, and out jumped one of my army mates, a fellow officer, a

lieutenant. He recognized me and yelled, "Joe, what's up? Where are you going?" "Well," I said, "I'm going to work in the shipyard." He replied, "But there's a counterrevolution there. Those western sons of bitches." "Well," I replied, "You fool. You know me, don't you. We've served in the army together, haven't we? Do I look like a western bandit?" "Well, no." "All right then, in the shipyard, there are 10,000 people just like me!" "Oh, God," he said, hitting himself on the head. "They've been lying to us. They've sent us out here like to a war."[41]

The shipyard was now surrounded by dozens of tanks, soldiers, and militia. The show of force was calculated to frighten and quell the unarmed workers of the Warski Shipyard, but the workers' reaction was even more aggressive and angry than in the Lenin Shipyard two days before. The work force was allowed to pass through the militia and tank detachments. Then, as it began to sink in that workers were expected to work under the gun barrels of the tanks, they began to seethe. "It was not the compulsion, the use of force so much, but the moral element, the element of honor."[42] This comment illustrates how revolt in Poland or elsewhere can escape from rational calculations of the balance of terror and the chances for success.

Almost immediately groups of workers gathered in their shop sections and then moved to the main gate and out to the administrative building, where they demanded to speak with Director Cenkier and First Party Secretary Muszyński. Some more combative workers simply attacked the tanks standing at the main gate. Two tanks were put out of action when workers put steel rails between their treads and their wheels. (The rails were there for repair work.) The tanks then stood immobilized, firing their machine guns into the air. More tanks drew up to the main gate. Workers continued determinedly to try to demolish the first two tanks. First they brought bottles of gasoline, then a ten-liter barrel, which went off with a blast. In an attempt to rescue the tank crew, several score soldiers sent warning volleys into the air and advanced. When they were about 40 meters from the tanks, they fired a long volley directly into the crowd facing them. At least two workers died, and several were wounded.

Gas and smoke were everywhere, making the day even more dark and misty. Clouds of tear gas drifted through the shipyard. Police marksmen were stationed on buildings overlooking the shipyard. Whether workers were deliberately shot by marksmen is impossible to establish; in any case, some people were wounded within the shipyard.[43] An assembly of workers in front of the shipyard director's building grew more tumultuous. Director Cenkier advised his workers to return to work, but many wanted to march on the city. The return of the dead and wounded from the smoke and gas clouds, a scene whose drama was heightened by the first volley of machine-gun fire, spurred the workers to send emissaries under white flags to warn the army to withdraw from the immediate vicinity of the shipyard or face an attack.[44] The army withdrew, and workers pondered their next move. "It became absolutely hellish," a worker recalled. "Two emotions struggled in all of us, fear for our lives and a fury that had been building up from the day before. The result was determination to begin a hopeless battle. I remember people saying, 'We'll go against these tanks. 5,000 of us will die, but maybe something will change.'"[45]

Groups of workers trying to break away through the gates were held back by other workers. Through a microphone brought out on the street, a technician and party member, Mieczysław Dopierała, proposed that they choose a strike committee in the shipyard, hold elections in the shops, write up demands, and negotiate with the state. The workers would meanwhile occupy Warski in an around-the-clock strike. Other speakers—Jolanta Jakimowicz, Ewa Zielińska, and Józef Kasprzycki—supported Dopierała and also proposed contacting the Szczecin Repair Shipyard in Gryfia for support. Dopierała's description of what they did, though given ten years later, still carries his sense of discovery: "When we gathered, we were doing something that had never been done or discussed in our public or social lives. It was a conflict of the people with the state. We had to open negotiation with them. Who they represented and who we represented, of that there wasn't any doubt. But how to do it, how to organize all this, we had to do ad hoc, with no previous schemes, patterns, or instructions."[46] A free association of workers against the state was now being created.

The striking workers returned to their shops. Each shop or section—there were almost forty of them—elected three delegates and chose a set of demands. At midday, these delegates gathered in the shipyard's main conference hall, where they elected a shipyard-wide strike committee consisting of ten people: Kazimierz Wojtow of W-7; Mieczysław Dopierała of W-6; Józef Kasprzycki of production direction; Kazimierz Szmurło of K-4; Urbanowicz of TR; Tadeusz Sokołowski of W-3; Malczak of K-1; Jola Jakimowicz of Malmor; Ewa Zielińska of W-7; and Podzielny of W-4. A key role was also played by a delegate from an allied firm, Józef Fischbein. This was "the first association chosen by the free will of the people that had ever appeared in the shipyard."[47] Society had now ended its alienation from its own government through autonomous democratic participation, the antithesis of the autonomous dictatorial state. This organization of society was a condemnation of the state.

Kasprzycki was chosen to go to the director and announce over the public-address system that the strike committee had been formed and what it planned to do. The committee divided responsibilities as it began to organize the occupational strike for the 5,000 workers who were in the shipyard. According to Dopierała, "Everyone who had a task was fully responsible for it. From the beginning to end it was a military system and everyone knew what they had to do, even though we'd never had any strike experience."[48]

Throughout that afternoon and evening, the strike committee organized a security service, which called itself the "commandos," to guard the gates, explosives, food, and alcohol stores and to make rounds to prevent arson or sabotage. Workers took command of communications, which included the shipyard public-address system and a network of messengers to and from the shops. They also took control of the factory print shop. Medical service was assured by the regular shipyard staff. Employees of a bakery adjoining the shipyard simply handed bread over the shipyard walls, thus circumventing the army blockade. The shipyard engineer advised on technical questions and hazards. Again, party actions were turned against the party as Franciszek Wilanowski, who had been trained as an "express" judge in the Stalinist period, became the workers' legal advisor. One of the first announcements made by the committee over the public-address system was a request to all women in the shipyard to return home. The explanation was that the workers "knew how the strike had ended in Poznań. On the other side of the shipyard we could see the lines of tanks, and it was reasonable to expect that anything could happen. The majority left; some stayed."[49] Because he had proposed the entire plan of action, Mieczysław Dopierała was chosen strike chairman. Józef Kasprzycki became vice chairman.

Why was the Warski Shipyard so successful in forming a determined leadership? A crucial factor was that Fischbein, Dopierała, and Kasprzycki were reserve army officers who had met by accident during army maneuvers two months before. They trusted each other, and they were accustomed to leading large groups of people. In fact, Dopierała said that the majority of the strike committee were army officers. They were also party members.[50]

The strike committee immediately sent emissaries by boat across the river to the repair shipyard in Gryfia. The strike in Gryfia was well advanced when the emissaries from Warski—Stanisław Wądołowski and a young woman—arrived.[51] In a tempestuous meeting, Gryfia workers had decided on a sit-in strike, with every division electing three representatives who were in charge of collecting and agreeing on their strike demands. Every division elected one representative for the seven-member Gryfia strike presidium. The strike presidium had just been elected and had agreed on 30 demands common to the entire shipyard as the Warski emissaries arrived.[52]

By 2 P.M., the two shipyards had agreed on a common front for joint negotiations with the state. The combined strike committees now worked on a joint list of demands. Ten years later, even the most courageous intellectual oppositionists in Poland, such as Jacek Kuroń and Adam Michnik, gasped in shock when they heard that the first of 21 demands of the Gdańsk Strike Committee in 1980 was for free trade unions independent of the party. As Kuroń put it, "I thought it was impossible, it was impossible, and I still think it was impossible."[53] The demand seemed outrageous, outdistancing the range of possibilities in the minds of politicians and scholars. But ten years earlier, the little-known demands of the Warski and Gryfia workers were also 21 in number, and the first was that the Central Trade Union Council step down because it had never defended the working class, and that its place be taken by "independent trade unions dependent on the working class."[54] This demand was the product of twenty-six years of experience in party-led institutions, including the trade unions. It was the centerpiece of the Gdańsk Accords of August 31, 1980, which Adam Michnik hailed as "The Great Charter of the Rights of the Polish Nation." But it turns out the charter had been written ten years earlier.[55]

A profound sense of cooperation and dignity pervade the demands from the opening sentence: "The work forces of the shipyards, in solidarity with the workers of the coast, support their justified demands and announce a sit-in strike and the following demands."[56] Of the 21 demands, 3 concerned wage issues, 2 focused on the special privileges of the apparat, 3 related to the dignity of workers, three bore on the need to control the forces of repression, and 2 were systemic. Among them, "We demand continuous and reliable information on the country's economic and political situation in the mass media and on national programs."[57] Another protested unearned privileges, demanding "the levelling of the pay of employees in the party and government bureaucracies to the average earnings in industry."[58] Another demanded "an apology for calling workers hooligans on the press, radio, and television and the punishment of those who did so. Working people were forced to demonstrate for their right to exist."[59]

The 21 demands were the program of the strike, which immediately circulated to other factories. As more and more factories joined, a general strike spread throughout Szczecin. To the 25 workplaces that struck on Friday, December 18, were added 39 workplaces on Saturday, 2 on Sunday, 25 on Monday, and 3 on Tuesday, for a total of 94 striking workplaces in Szczecin province. Gdańsk and Gdynia had had general strikes that week also, but they were shorter and less well-organized among factories. In Szczecin, the strike groped toward a union of factories.

On the first night of the general strike, delegates of ten striking factories met in the Warski Shipyard and formed an interfactory strike committee, which they called the Citywide Strike Committee. Every workplace was to have a delegate on the committee, which was to be based in Warski. The delegates also agreed that, to protect the public interest, certain Szczecin workplaces, such as food stores, food-delivery firms, bakeries, and clinics, were not to strike.[60]

As workers of Warski and Gryfia settled into their sit-in strike, the government propagandized. A government leaflet gave its version of the situation: "Behind the backs of disoriented but honest workers, hostile and criminal elements, in fact bandit elements, have burned public buildings, plundered stores and social property." Another leaflet, issued by the Provincial National Council, appealed to youth: "If you love the *Fatherland*, be calm and alert. Do not be pulled into actions against the *Fatherland*! . . . Show that your hearts and minds belong to Poland, which needs you today and tomorrow."[61] In its extremity, the government had nothing left now but force, the threat of Soviet invasion, and blind nationalism.

Between 3 P.M. and 6 P.M., street fighting went on all over Szczecin. As the government put it, "Groups of up to 200 persons plundered the city. There were clashes with the police. Crowds with many adolescents among them tried to attack the party building [already 80 percent burned] and the city hall."[62]

At Elbląg, on the opposite end of the Baltic Coast, a crowd attacked and tried to burn party headquarters and was repelled by the police. Another group destroyed a tank guarding the city prison. In the city center, militia guarding the bank and the post office fired, killing one person. Police procedure was quite similar to that used in Szczecin, Gdynia, and Gdańsk. Police arrested passersby, shot tear-gas grenades into lines of women shoppers, and beat arrested people, who were forced to pass through gauntlets of police on entering the militia station.[63] When asked about these police procedures, a militia sergeant later admitted to "a kind of psychosis created by our chiefs," one of "fear and hatred."[64] He explained: "We were told that many militiamen and their families had been murdered in Gdańsk. They told us terrible things in order to arouse us. Other things went on too; for example, night arrests and dragging people out of their homes. But those were the plainclothesmen."[65] The police and military were kept as isolated as possible and deprived of information. A siege mentality was successfully fostered as militia and army families were evacuated in face of the supposed threat to their lives.[66] Despite all efforts at disinformation directed at security troops, the party's cover story about Germans and Fascists broke down as workers talked to soldiers and policemen. The army controls in the streets of Szczecin from the evening of December 18 were perfunctory or nonexistent. From December 19 on, people gathered around the tanks, and children climbed up on them and into them. As a party observer conceded, "Soldiers conversed with the people and flirted with young women. I doubt that the soldiers could have been used against the people or especially against the workplaces that were striking."[67]

With the ring of tanks around the shipyard and the navy blockade on the Oder, strikers prepared to defend the shipyard against an assault by army, navy, and police. On the river side, workers set up searchlights as naval and police motorboats began to venture too close to the shipyard installation. Shipyard engineers built radio tracing equipment to capture police informers reporting from within the shipyard with walkie-talkies. At Dopierała's request, an appeal to the soldiers was prepared. The strikers also readied two long-range radio transmitters so that people outside Szczecin and Poland would know "if they attacked, we'd call the world for help."[68] The inner leadership also kept secret some of their preparations for the defense of the shipyard. Stores of bottles, rags, and gasoline were readied for use as Molotov cocktails.[69] As one worker put it, "Like in the Warsaw uprising, we prepared as best we could. In the end every second worker in the shipyard had been in the army and knew what to do. Even if the time had come to die."[70]

Although both Vice Premier Kociołek and Premier Cyrankiewicz had said there was nothing to discuss, Szczecin authorities took a different tack that night. In a radio speech, Provincial Council President Marian Łempicki placed all the blame for arson and pillage on young hoodlums and promised that the authorities would do everything possible for worker victims and their families.[71] Every resident of Szczecin knew that the issue was not arson or pillage by young hoodlums, but on the other hand, Łempicki did not attack the workers and did offer material solace to the victims.

## The Fall of Gomułka

The next day, December 19, it became clear that the strike had spread up and down the coastal provinces, engulfing every major city and involving workers in most enterprises. Indeed, the sheer energy of the coastal workers stimulated fears in Warsaw of a nationwide uprising. Flights to Kraków and Poznań were cancelled. Wrocław's central square was cordoned off as army units began to patrol the city. Demonstrations or strikes took place in factories in Wrocław, Poznań, Kraków, Warsaw, Lublin, and Białystok. In Katowice, 50 tanks took up positions in the city center.[72]

By now General Jaruzelski had ordered mobilization of the army; and in addition to sending 25,000 soldiers into the coastal cities, divisions were massed in the Kraków, Poznań, Wrocław, and Warsaw regions. Others remained on full alert in the central region. Military sources later reported that the army directly engaged in more than 100 operations involving 61,000 soldiers, 1,700 tanks, 1,750 transporters, air transport, a large number of helicopters and several dozen warships.[73]

The mobilization of the Polish Armed Forces was a response to the labor situation across the entire country. This was summed up in the report to the Central Committee at the Eighth Plenum in 1971:

> Although the most dramatic events occurred in the Baltic Coast cities, the political crisis affected the entire country. The number of strikes and work interruptions increased from day to day in various Polish cities for the same reasons and with the same demands that emerged on the coast. Workers' strikes occurred in other industrial centers although they were not as extensive or dramatic.[74]

Throughout the week, Gomułka attempted to put down the workers as rapidly as possible while avoiding political consultation with other members of the Politburo and Central Committee. As the strikes threatened to spread across Poland, factions within the Politburo began to maneuver. Early that week, Piotr Jaroszewicz, a candidate Politburo member, left as planned for a scheduled Comecon meeting in Moscow. He returned on Friday. That same evening, the Soviet ambassador to Poland delivered a letter from the Soviet leadership to the Polish Politburo. This letter apparently advised the Poles to seek a political and economic solution under the phrase "strengthen ties with the working class." It was therefore an implicit repudiation of Gomułka, Kliszko, and their closest associates, who had staked their leadership on a quick military and police suppression of the workers.

The background to the Soviet decision is relatively clear. Three factors were likely to have influenced their attitude toward Gomułka and toward the Polish crisis. First, the Soviets were already heavily engaged in Czechoslovakia and China. The Czech situation after the August 1968 invasion was winding down, but the occupation forces were committed, and now the Soviets faced a dangerous and uncertain conflict with the Chinese. In August 1969, large-scale clashes between Soviet and Chinese troops occurred on the Ussuri River, and in the same year Soviet diplomats tested American reaction to the notion of a Soviet nuclear strike at China. Second, throughout the week, the Soviet general staff had closely monitored the state of the Polish population and the Polish army forces through close consultation with the Polish general staff. The fragmentary evidence presented here on the civilian-military interaction suggests that a forthright account of the situation by General Jaruzelski would have alarmed the Soviets. Finally, as suggested by Z. A. Pelczynski, the crisis was in one way fortuitous. The Soviets were already unhappy with Gomułka's unseemly independent plans to cut out two of their key defense industries in Poland—shipbuilding and aircraft manufacturing. A change of leaders was not only a cheap way out of the crisis, but also it rid them of an irritating client.

According to Gomułka, he had already called a Politburo meeting for Saturday morning, December 19. The Soviet letter was delivered around 9:00 P.M. on Friday. Just before the Saturday meeting started, Gomułka had an alarming private conversation with Politburo member Józef Tejchma, who alluded to the breakdown in the army. "If you want to save your reputation," Gomułka was told,

> you should resign. . . . You don't know what is going on in this building and Warsaw. The party [activists are] is against you and your policies. . . . Women and children may go out onto the streets. The army will not fire on them. Children of officers are being spit on in schools. The defense minister of the Soviet Union, Marshal Grechko, spoke with the commanders of our army and told them that the Politburo of the U.S.S.R. has met and discussed the situation in Poland many times. They fear that the disturbances will spread to the entire country. If it comes to that, the Soviet troops do not plan to intervene. The only solution is a change in the leadership.

Gomułka continued: "Not long after Comrade Tejchma left, Comrade Cyrankiewicz came to me and gave me the letter of the Soviet leaders to the Politburo of our party. After reading the letter, which speaks of the necessity of political and economic measures to defuse tension in Poland, I understood the determination with which Comrade Tejchma had spoken to me."[75]

The lineup in the Politburo was such that Gomułka and his close associates were able to control any vote. Given Gomułka's extraordinary force of character, if not stubbornness, it seems likely that he would have survived any vote if not for the fortuitous circumstance that in the course of the week he had begun to suffer from circulatory problems. Taken ill, he now left the Central Committee for the hospital. In his absence, enough of his associates defected during a bruising twelve-hour session that he was replaced by Edward Gierek, who outmaneuvered opponents on the platform of political and economic measures to strengthen ties with the working class.[76]

## The Split in the Warski Shipyard

Brezhnev was not the only one approaching the Polish army. The strike continued to spread through Szczecin on Saturday, December 19. As a strike leader summed up, "Ninety-three workplaces joined us. We know others struck in solidarity, but we don't have any documents from them.

The ninety-three joined in writing and sent their delegates."[77] Because telephone lines had been cut, a constant stream of messengers flowed between factories.

The Szczecin strike committee now issued a leaflet, addressed to the army, defending the patriotism of the striking workers. The appeal seems especially noteworthy: "We are not acting against our fatherland and its system. But we cannot agree that the working class of our land . . . be treated by a group of irresponsible people like an unconscious mass fit only for submission to decrees." The workers thanked the people of Szczecin for "their support and solidarity," called for order in the streets, and asked parents to keep children at home and out of trouble. But the workers also agitated for the extension of the strike: "We are not in danger and we don't need your physical assistance. We thank all Szczecin workplaces that have gone on strike!"[78] The appeal to the Polish army was signed "the strike committees headquartered in the Szczecin Warski Shipyard."[79] As the strike progressed, workers continued to clarify the nature of their self-organization in action and theory.

At 1 P.M., a delegation of twelve people, six each from Warski and Gryfia, drove to the Shipbuilding Technical School adjacent to the shipyard to negotiate with government officials. The first meeting lasted three hours. On the government side were the economic secretary of the provincial party committee, the president of the provincial council, the president of the city council, and the secretary of the provincial trade union council. The government committee worked in consultation with Warsaw. News of formal negotiations between workers and the party was so explosive that they were not referred to in the mass media outside of Szczecin. As in Gdynia and Gdańsk, attempts at worker organization, formation of demands, and negotiation in December 1970 were concealed by the state and were practically unknown in Poland or abroad, even to the political class of party activists, the intellectual opposition, or Polish and Western academics.[80]

The opening negotiating session was inconclusive, though from the party's point of view it had the helpful result of wearing down the workers' delegates somewhat. The second meeting, which began at 8 P.M. and continued until after midnight, involved a change of venue. Instead of the neutral ground of the Technical School in the vicinity of the shipyard, the meeting was held on party territory at the provincial council building in the center of town. The pressure upon the strike leaders was tremendous. In a city under military occupation, the delegates' bus wound its way among tanks and armored cars that ringed the provincial council. Soldiers and policemen swarmed everywhere. The army presented arms to the workers' strike committee as they arrived, a formal reminder of the enormous advantage the state had obtained. In the provincial council, what began as a negotiation of opposing sides turned into a coming and going of "anonymous" observers possessing the countenances of policemen. All the conversations were recorded, but the recordings were made by one side—the authorities'—and remained in their possession.

On Sunday, the front page of one of Szczecin's two daily newspapers, the *Kurier Szczeciński*, carried news of the sit-in strikes and the negotiations with the authorities. The most spectacular item was also on the front page—an announcement by the workers of the Szczecin printing shops that they had struck on Saturday in solidarity with the Warski work force. This was an unprecedented break in control of the party press. In view of the importance of the printed word, said the printers, they had decided to produce the Sunday issue of the *Kurier Szczeciński* with its unusual contents. Their decision was hailed with an expression of sincere thanks from the editorial board.[81] No such workers' pressure on the party press existed elsewhere in Poland. In Warsaw's *Trybuna Ludu*, for example, an information-starved public could read in an article entitled "The Situation on the Coast" that all was normal. In the last line came the key sentence: "In Szczecin, on the other hand, immediately after the events on the 17th, the tension maintained itself, although no further events have occurred."[82]

Throughout the crisis in the Warski Shipyard strike organization, the big hall in the shipyard, where more and more delegates from striking factories moved in and out in a steadily increasing stream, was long on hope but perilously short on information. Warski's original ten-person committee diminished to four when six delegates were dispatched to the downtown negotiations with high party officials. With Dopierała and Kasprzycki occupied by the latter duty, only Fischbein among the inner leadership was left in the shipyard to receive and pass along information from the down-town negotiations. After the first two marathon sessions on Saturday, December 19, ended without discernible progress, the level of anxiety in the shipyard mounted. Ironically, and fatally for the workers' cause, this tension spread, even as the degree of organizational solidarity reached unprecedented heights for postwar Poland. Each newly striking factory signaled the increasing sense of assertion and incipient autonomy that was the greatest visibly maturing political change in Szczecin. The declarations and actions of the printers provided the most tangible evidence of this worker determination, but similar signs were everywhere observable. Messages of support for striking factories promised the Warski leadership that "we will support you to the end."[83] Despite the fact that Sunday was a day of rest and workers could not meet on shop floors, workers from plants not yet on strike met all over the city and formulated plans for work stoppages at the first shift on Monday morn-

ing. A region-wide general strike was, in fact, in the final stages of organizational completion throughout the Szczecin province.

While the strike was growing stronger across the region, it was collaps-
ing at its center. The worker negotiators downtown were isolated from
the nerve center of organization in the shipyard. Instead of taking on re-
newed strength and resolve from each bit of incoming news of worker
support, the workers' delegates were subjected to a torrent of party promises, evasions, and threats. At the end of the third negotiating session at
4 P.M. on Sunday, Warski strike leader Dopierała and his small band of
associates caved in to a lopsided agreement. Though the party made a
number of concessions concerning the security of all strikers and compensation to the families of wounded and dead workers, most substantive
issues were shrouded in vague promises. On the central issue of independent unions, the party won out completely.

The first point—that the Central Trade Union Council should step
down and new unions dependent on the workers take their place—was
changed into a simple promise to transmit to the central authorities the
workers' wish that the trade unions concern themselves more with the
problems of the working masses. The document vaguely asserted that
"compromised officials at all levels must step down."[84] The provincial
authorities also promised to pass on the demands for wage increases and
a return to the old price levels. The strike leaders promised to strike again
in three days if their wage and price agreements were not implemented.
With Christmas approaching, that seemed most unlikely. The authorities
agreed to pay wages during the strike and compensate victims of state
violence and their families. The government agreed that participants in
the strike would not suffer repression and that martial law would soon be
lifted.[85] It also made promises regarding the bureaucracy that were so
sweeping that they edged toward impossible farce. For example: "The
administrative apparat must be cut to the maximum. Starting in 1971, the
administrative apparat will be reduced by around 30 percent."[86] Or: "Irresponsible and incompetent officials will be removed from their posts.
Responsible ones will be kept."[87] On one point the workers agreed to an
outright falsification: "The workers' demonstration demanding improvement of the economic situation was not directly fired on. Direct fire was
opened only on the bands trying to free criminals from prison."[88]

The agreement allowed for suspending the strike rather than ending it
and suggested that the protest resume in three days if no satisfaction were
forthcoming. This was a face-saving reservation, on paper only. As a
means of defusing the crisis and coopting the strike leaders, the authorities signing the agreement were in favor of the strike leaders taking office
in the existing union structure.

The agreement made no mention of the matter of strike committees continuing as autonomous workers' structures after the strike. This was the heart of the defeat. Two sides signed, but the strike committees ceased to exist after signing. The workers' delegates became individuals; the authorities remained as overseers and executors of the agreement.[89]

Crucial structural flaws in the workers' organization were revealed by this pathetic conclusion—hazards the Szczecin workers would spend the next three weeks correcting. At the center of the problem was the dominance of party members like Dopierała and Fischbein. Though dedicated to the idea of worker autonomy, Dopierała remained a believing party member. He received from high party officials a number of private assurances that changes were imminent at the highest levels of the party and that sweeping policy initiatives were also in the offing. A member of the strike committee, Stanisław Serafin, specified that "Dopierała had some information about the changes at the top because he said so in the meeting hall. He said, 'I can't tell you yet, but when you find out you'll fall off your chairs.'"[90] In effect, Dopierała wagered his integrity that the party would follow through on sweeping reforms. In succeeding months, he did his best to improve conditions in the shipyard as first secretary of a new reformed party, but he would soon be dismayed by the actions of the new Gierek regime and ultimately plunged into personal despair.

For coastal workers, however, the process of self-education continued at a rapid pace. The tumultuous events that followed the December 20 accord were as instructive as the events that preceded it. On the very Sunday night that dismayed workers in the Warski shops learned of their defeat at the negotiations and were angrily planning new strike actions, Edward Gierek, the new first secretary, addressed the nation and presented himself as a new kind of chief executive, one promising sweeping reforms. He not only promised consultation with the working class and intellectuals, but he also asserted that ill-considered economic policies would be reversed, with immediate financial compensation for the least well-off and for working women. He held out a hand to Catholics, asking for their help, and continued the policy of distinguishing "criminal elements" from "honest workers" in the protests. He especially addressed shipyard and port workers, from whom he asked peace, order, and calm work. Together, he promised, "We will draw the bitter lessons of this past week."[91] The Warski strike now began to waver and break. Following Gierek's address, approximately 1,000 party members in the work force quit the strike, marching out through the gates for home. Scuffles and disputes and a general breakdown of the strike organization and security ensued as the party members forced their way through the gates, past the majority of the work force, which rejected the agreement and wanted to continue the strike.

## Two Strike Committees and the Defeat of the Strike

That night and early morning, the original strike committee broadcast a communiqué announcing its dissolution and the end of the strike and handing back control of the shipyard to the administration. Similar announcements were made by the commander of strike security in one shop and by the shipyard director.[92]

Despite the split in their ranks, Warski workers now moved toward taking control of their own organization, independent of party influence. Four workers with reputations for autonomous conduct were elected to an enlarged strike committee. Their leader was a 40-year-old former seaman named Edmund Bałuka. Strongly supported by young nonparty hull workers concentrated on the Vulcan slip, the reorganized committee took over the shipyard loudspeakers, reestablished security patrols, and closed the gates.[93]

On Monday morning, contrary to the government's fondest hopes, the strike expanded its reach in Szczecin province as another 25 factories and workplaces stopped work. The army's withdrawal from the streets left the city in an open general strike that continued to grow on Monday and Tuesday despite the internal collapse of the original Warski strike committee. After temporarily fading out of sight with calls to end the strike, Dopierała's group competed with Bałuka's for control of the work force. Both committees were unable or unwilling to heed the appeal from the other striking factories for a single provincial strike committee. When, in desperation, their delegates in the Warski assembly hall finally formed such an interfactory strike committee on Monday morning, the new committee immediately collapsed for lack of support from Warski.[94] That day and evening, Piotr Jaroszewicz, the new premier, and a new Politburo member, Jan Szydlak, visited key Szczecin factories to try to stop the strikes. In the Warski Shipyard, the minister of heavy industry, Franciszek Kaim, and the shipbuilding association director, Stanisław Skrobot, tried to persuade the divided committee and workers to end the strike. The de facto existence of two committees facilitated their task.

Near midnight the city's dock workers decided to end their strike. As one port administrator subsequently reported, "Phones began to ring as other factories wanted to know if it was true. Some silently hung up. Others angrily [called] us strikebreakers. A garment worker called and asked if it was true and then chewed us out."[95] During the night, thousands of militiamen surrounded the shipyard, blocking all entry and exit. Naval and militia patrol boats closed access on the river side. With the promise of safe conduct from Minister Kaim, the shipyard workers left that morning. As leaflets scattered by helicopters floated down to the empty shipyard, the two opposing strike committees announced the end of the strike. The original committee ended with a declaration of political loyalty and confidence in Gierek: "We believe that the new Central Committee will repair the economy of our country. We declare full support for the new leaders of the Central Committee of the party."[96] The new co-opted committee led by Bałuka described the situation quite differently. Rather than announcing the end of the strike, the committee, together with committees from Parnica, Gryfia, the steel mill, and others, announced it was suspending the strike for the Christmas holidays.[97]

The Szczecin strike had ended in confusion, frustration, and defeat. As the workers' legal advisor for the strike summed up the prevailing mood, "The nonparty workers came out of the strike extremely dissatisfied. They accepted the suspension of the December strike, but only because the strike committee did not answer up to its obligations. It was too soft. That was the universal opinion among shipyard workers."[98] Nonparty workers suspected a deal among party members behind the back of the striking work force. Simply stated, party members of the negotiating committee were more impressed by the change from Gomułka to Gierek than was the work force. Their readiness to place their trust in Gierek was therefore an expression of party psychology, a last gasp of the 1960s "revisionist" impulse in party circles. The mistake became vital to the maturation of the strike leaders who were largely party members, but the rest of the shipyard's work force was already well ahead of them.[99]

## The Second Strike in the Warski Shipyard

The hollowness of party gestures during negotiations with workers became evident straightaway all along the coast. In the immediate aftermath of the strikes, security forces began harassing known worker advocates. On Christmas Day, the police in Szczecin beat a Warski worker to death.[100] With each passing day, meanwhile, the diminished standard of living that was the direct product of Gomułka's price hike was underscored, because despite Gierek's rhetorical offensive, the new prices remained intact. The new year was five days old when the Lenin Shipyard workers struck again. The event triggered what one beleaguered party functionary called "rolling waves of strikes," which buffeted the entire coast throughout January 1971.[101]

The party's policy of containment involved two strategies. The first was to defuse resentment by sacking prominent local figureheads whose previous actions in carrying out party policy had engendered bitter resentment among the population. The second was to orchestrate the appearance of serious consultations with the working class by authorizing a sanctioned demand-gathering campaign.

These strategies did not work. In the face of repeated worker strikes and stoppages, party officials were sacrificed in Szczecin, Gdańsk, and Gdynia between January 11 and January 22, including the hated Antoni Walaszek, the first secretary of Szczecin province. Yet the morning of January 23 found the coast's two largest ports, Gdańsk and Szczecin, in the grip of citywide general strikes. The demand-gathering campaign succeeded merely in affording workers an opportunity to reflect on the state of Poland. Despite the constraints implicit in public discussions conducted under the close supervision of the party, worker demands of January 1971 bore an amazing similarity to the demands of December 1970. A wide-ranging debate and discussion now went on in the factory shops. In the words of Szczecin's new worker spokesman, Edmund Bałuka, the Warski Shipyard became an "enormous Hyde Park of discussion."[102]

Gierek's national campaign for increased productivity turned discussion into confrontation. The campaign itself was a reprise of an exotic custom found in socialist countries, one that may be characterized as voluntary compulsion. In such a campaign, the party leadership, having increased production targets without increasing capital or labor, would gather workers in selected plants and pressure them to pledge voluntary overtime. A normal dictatorship would have issued orders to work. A socialist dictatorship wanted workers to say they agreed wholeheartedly. Gierek approached this task with a certain nervousness. He instructed the party to begin agitation in his own regional power base, Silesia. After some effort, the party was able to extract suitable pledges from the relatively well-paid miners. Gingerly, the party tiptoed across Poland toward the volatile workers of the Baltic Coast. On the pages of major newspapers and in all the mass media on the coast, factories pledged to work overtime or on Sundays to help Gierek and Poland. But the Warski Shipyard remained glaringly absent from the daily reports of new pledges. For the purposes of the production campaign, the regime desperately needed to produce a very large trophy—support by Warski workers—for the national mass media. On January 19, the party dispatched Polish radio and TV to the shipyard. In an empty meeting hall decorated with banners and posters supporting the voluntary overtime campaign, technicians filmed a handful of party activists who pledged that the thousand workers of Shop W-4 would work that Sunday. Above them hung a banner that proclaimed, "With a production feat, we support the new party leaders."[103] That night the Warski workers, to their utter bewilderment, saw themselves on national television cheering for Gierek and promising to work the following Sunday. As Edmund Bałuka said, "For a moment I didn't know what planet I lived on or who I was." The government had spliced old footage of a festive meeting in the shipyard from three years before with footage of the banner and the party activists.[104]

In this surrealistic fashion, the most combative and irreconcilable workers in Poland saw themselves cheering for Gierek on national television at the very moment they were agitating for a strike. The next day, local and national newspapers noted that Warski workers had come out in support of Gierek. That same morning, enraged workers from all over the Warski Shipyard converged on Shop W-4 to demand an explanation. After a day of unmerciful hazing from co-workers, the fitters of Shop W-4 left their work stations and converged on the administration building. This moment marked the beginning of the second general strike in Szczecin. It lasted three days and brought Gierek, Premier Jaroszewicz, and General Jaruzelski to the Baltic Coast. During the strike and a nine-hour meeting with Gierek, the shipyard workers consistently returned to their demand of factual information in the mass media and insisted on the punishment of those responsible for the fabrication of the Warski "production feat."

This elaborate propaganda fraud was significant not only for its role in triggering the January strike, but also for its foretaste of the basic tactic of the Gierek regime over the next ten years—a period when many Western governments and academics perceived the regime as more "liberal" and "technocratic" than its predecessor or the other regimes in East Europe. In his speeches to Warski workers, Gierek disclaimed any personal responsibility for the television fraud. But he also refrained from promising punishment of local officials who had perpetrated it. He implied that the affair was a mistake rather than a conscious deception. Indeed, several days later, Szczecin party propaganda secretary Wiesław Rogowski, who had been placed into the post in early January, was removed. Warski workers could not know that Rogowski was not being punished, but rather promoted to editor-in-chief of *Głos Pracy* (The Voice of Labor), the national newspaper of Poland's trade unions. He remained there for the next ten years.[105] This incident illustrates the degree to which Gierek and his associates were contemptuous of workers and how, under a veneer of technocratic competence and prosperity based on Western loans, party politics in Poland continued as before.

Gierek's nine-hour marathon meeting with Warski workers was followed the next day by a similarly exhausting and adroitly handled meeting with Lenin Shipyard and Paris Commune workers in Gdańsk. In both places, Gierek appealed to the workers' patriotism. He emphasized Poland's desperate economic plight and his own background as a coal miner. He affected candor and earnestness and even shed tears. He asked the coastal workers for assistance. "Will you help me?" was his repeated question. Edmund Bałuka and others said "yes" in Szczecin; on January 25, Lech Wałęsa and others said, "We will help" in Gdańsk.[106]

## The Textile Workers of Łódź Confound the Party

Personal appeals by the new leadership restrained workers on the coast but failed to stop the waves of industrial strikes fueled by the party's attempt to hold to the price rises of December 13. In early February, low-paid textile workers in the central Polish city of Łódź staged a successful city-wide strike and finally forced the government to retreat, thus flatly contradicting Gierek's own statement to the Szczecin workers, "There is no possible way of going back to pre-December prices."[107]

The sociology and organization of the strikes in Łódź offer some contrasts to the pattern established on the coast. In Łódź, women, not men, formed the majority of the work force engaged in direct production, although men dominated the more highly skilled and better-paid technical posts. Whereas both skilled and nonskilled manual workers on the coast were among the most well-off in Poland, wages of the female textile workers of Łódź were about 40 percent less than the average Polish industrial wage. Their situation was exacerbated by serious water shortages, which often meant long lines by water trucks added on to their factory work over three shifts and the normal trials of shopping and child care. For many, the time budget was at the limit of mental and physical endurance. In Łódź, the strike started on February 10 in the 8,000-person Marchlewski Textile Plant and the rubber factory Stomil. As it spread, most work crews struck on their shifts and then went home. A leading role seems to have been played by the mostly male technical workers who serviced machines and shops, and who had a strategic role in the political geography of the workplace. This was the case in Marchlewski and Defenders of Peace Textile Plants. White-collar workers, although sympathetic, did not join. In Defenders of Peace Plant, they "stood on the side and waited to see what would happen."[108] In some cases, ordinary party members or shop-floor party committees passed over to side with the strikers and sometimes were among the most radical. No city-wide strike committee was established, but even after the regime gave in by annulling the price rises of December 12 on the morning of February 15, the strikes in Łódź continued for two days, with marches on the city starting from the Marchlewski plant.[109] These worker-based strikes are evidence for the Piven and Cloward thesis that organization and leadership are costly to radical movements and that an unorganized, spontaneous movement is more likely to win real concessions.[110]

When Premier Piotr Jaroszewicz and Politburo member Jan Szydlak arrived in Łódź to meet a 3,000-person assembly of strikers, they surely expected to wheedle, charm, and wear out the women workers of Łódź just as they had done in Szczecin and Gdańsk. But when Jaroszewicz entered the Grand Theater in Łódź, the largely female multitude burst out in a song from the Polish revolutionary tradition:

> Thanks to you, Lord Magnates
> For our servitude and our chains
> Thanks to you, earls and prelates
> For this our land stained with our brothers' blood
> We insurgents do not enter into pacts with the Tsar
> But beat the Muscovites and hang the Magnates.[111]

When Jaroszewicz tried to speak, the women refused to hear of anything but food prices. "Your wife, Mrs. Jaroszewicz, loads ham on her sandwiches, while my children eat dry bread."[112] What could the premier say? On the following day, the government media announced an immediate return to the food prices of December 12, 1970. The women of Łódź had stepped ahead of the shipyard workers of the coast in rejecting patriotic appeals by officials of the privileged state for sacrifices that would be made by the least privileged.

Outwardly, then, all was static in the Poland of 1970–71. Gierek was in and Gomułka was out, but otherwise things seemed to remain pretty much as they were before the ill-fated price increase of December. To the outside world, including other Poles, the memories of December 1970 pivoted on a massacre. But there were also memories of an organizational and ideological nature that coastal workers had internalized. Outside the Baltic factories, no one knew of this new political consciousness.

A turning point had been reached in the political life of the Polish working class. After 26 years of party rule, the Baltic workers had forged four significant new weapons of self-assertion: the rediscovery of the sit-in strike; the development of the interfactory strike committee as a way to unite all citizens against the state; the demand for trade unions independent of the party, as a nonviolent alternative form of struggle; and, perhaps most important of all, the self-confidence and sense of autonomy that came with the knowledge of what it had accomplished.

# Gierek: The Road to Confrontation

ON THE SURFACE, remarkably little had changed in Poland—nothing more than a reshuffling of leaders at the top and a rollback of food prices. And yet all the major actors in the country had revealed something about themselves in the crisis and thought that they had learned important lessons for the future. Like generals, they all prepared for the next war on the basis of what they had learned in this one. These "generals" were the Polish church, the Polish security forces (the army and police), the party, the opposition intellectuals, and the workers. Much of what happened in 1980–81 was foreshadowed by actions taken in the 1970s by each of these important elements in Polish society.

## Primate Wyszyński

In explaining why the regime was able to defeat the workers in the 1970 crisis, the editor of the Paris-based *Kultura,* Jerzy Giedroyć, suggested that one reason was the lack of support from other sectors of the society—"there was no reaction, no assistance from the intellectuals or the emigration. Meanwhile the church in the person of Wyszyński pacified the situation. It did not stand by the side of the workers."[1]

This assertion deserves discussion. Historically, by Polish political doctrine, the primate of the Church was the *Interrex,* the regent, when there was no legitimate ruler in Poland. And indeed, from 1944, there was no legitimacy of rule in Poland, and the church attempted to play the role of regent. Such political duties can be perilous. On those occasions when the church judges resistance to be hopeless, it faces a decision as to how far it should use its spiritual and institutional power to support the state and defuse an insurrectionary situation. It then risks losing its ties with the nation—as happened in 1795, when the church's prelates in Warsaw were hung by the insurrectionary crowd for their collaboration with the Russians.

It was in 1956 that the disintegrating Communist regime first called on the church for help. Seven days after First Secretary Gomułka took power, he released the primate of Poland, who had been imprisoned since 1953. In his first sermon to a nation teetering on the edge of revolution, Primate Wyszyński advised his faithful: "Poles know how to die magnificently . . . but, beloved, Poles also need to know how to work magnificently. A man dies but once and is quickly covered in glory. But through work, he spends long years in trouble, hardship, pain and suffering. This is a greater heroism."[2]

The initial appeal was swiftly followed by an agreement on church-state relations that brought an end to direct Stalinist repression of religion. The church received autonomous control over its internal affairs. Catholic laity were given small but important roles in the media and public life; a small lay Catholic press, the Clubs of Catholic Intellectuals, and lay Catholic deputies to the Parliament also became steady features of Polish life. In exchange, the Episcopate "expressed full support for the work undertaken by the government aiming at the strengthening and development of People's Poland . . . and for the implementation by the citizens of their responsibilities towards the state."[3]

The church and party entered into a symbiotic alliance during the 1956 crisis. Although enemies, they had a common interest in preventing a popular uprising and probable Soviet invasion. This shared purpose did not prevent difficult moments in their relationship. Relations swiftly deteriorated after the high-water mark of 1956. In 1959, the regime declared that "Polish atheism had to fight with the Catholic hierarchy for control over the souls of the whole nation."[4] Religious instruction was banished from public schools and building licenses for new churches were denied. Church-state relations in the 1960s were further poisoned by a struggle to define Poland's one-thousand-year anniversary. The church preached Polish history as 1,000 years of Christianity, while the state defined it as 1,000 years of statehood. An even more bitter campaign opened in 1965, when the Polish bishops wrote an open letter to the West German Episcopate, trespassing on the government's monopoly of foreign policy and its constant stimulation of anti-German feeling for domestic purposes.

The workers' protests in 1970 were remarkable for the virtually total absence of the institutional church. Although the political religion of Polish nationalism pervaded the meaning given by the strikers to their actions, the strikes, the diaries, interviews, songs, poetry and workers' demands demonstrated little concern with organized religion. Only one demand in 1971 was in any way church-related. It asked for the building of a church in a Gdańsk suburb. In August 1980, the symbolic and institutional presence of the church was much more visible—in the images of the Polish pope tacked up on the factory walls, and in the cross that the strikers erected in front of the Lenin Shipyard. It was also visible in one of the 21 demands—for Sunday masses on TV and radio. In 1970, the clergy stayed away from the striking factories and appeared on the scene solely to perform burials. Only in one case, at the Sacred Heart, the parish church of the Paris Commune Shipyard, did priests bless the protesters. Significantly, this same church was apparently the only one on the coast to have a memorial mass for the dead in December. Again, the contrast between the church's absence from the scene in December 1970 and its institutional role as a political sanctuary for the society in the late 1970s and today was striking. Through the decade, the church became more active on the human rights front but in crisis the primate acted as he had in 1956 and 1970.

In 1970, the workers' protest on the Baltic Coast revived the church's rickety alliance with the state. In his first appeal to the nation on December 20, 1970, Gierek called for support of all citizens, "believers and nonbelievers." In the context it was a clear peace offering. The new premier, Piotr Jaroszewicz, was more explicit three days later at the session of the Parliament. "We shall be aiming at the full normalization of relations between the state and the church, expecting at the same time that the efforts of the government will meet with proper understanding among the spiritual and lay Catholic centers."[5] The regime's appeal for help was answered by the primate in his Christmas Eve sermon in St. John's Cathedral in Warsaw. In a situation where everyone awaited new strikes after the holidays, he said, "We beg of you, do not accuse. Show understanding. Forgive! Put your hands to the plow so that there can be more bread in the fatherland."[6]

In its New Year's message to the nation, the hierarchy revealed what it expected in return for the support it would offer the new regime. "We are full of sympathy for the families and people who suffered and with deep sorrow commend to God those who perished. After these terrible losses, we have but one wish, one prayer, not to provoke further suffering. It is necessary to do everything possible so that everyone feels safe and respected in his fatherland. We trust that the promises of the responsible public authorities will be carried out." The bishops condemned the use of force by the authorities as "not conducive to social peace particularly, when it does not spare the innocent—even women and children. The life of the nation cannot develop in an atmosphere of fear."

Here the bishops made the fullest statement of their conditions. They proposed a program, "revealed by the Baltic strikes," which called for rights

> to freedom of conscience and religious practice, to autonomous cultural activity, and social justice satisfying people's legitimate demands, to free expression and truthful information, to material living conditions befitting individual and family dignity, and to state behavior such that no citizens feel humiliated, wronged, or persecuted.[7]

After the second general strike, which culminated in the meeting between Gierek and the Warski workers, Szczecin returned to work, but the force that drove the strikes—the price rise—was still in effect, and it was clear that the crisis was not over.

At this point, as in 1956, the government received even more support from the ultimate spiritual authority. On January 27, 1970, the Polish

Episcopate announced that February 14 would be a day of prayer for the
fatherland. In its communiqué it pointed out the "necessity to maintain
peace and calm at this time in order to guarantee the independence of our
fatherland." As a political document, the bishops' letter, to be read in all
Polish churches on February 15, was, like the strikers' agreement with
Gierek, an act of faith. It appealed to the "healthy national instinct of
self-preservation rather than national suicide." It recalled the December
dead, and it called for work united with prayer, including a prayer for

> those who have taken the responsibility for order and peace in the fatherland,
> of justice for all, that in this difficult economic and social situation, they may
> find the right road to calm and healthy development; that they be faithful to
> their promises and respect the fundamental human and civil rights of citizens.[8]

With this prayer for Gierek and his team, the church had done all it could.
The next few days brought a lull as the Central Committee held a long-
awaited and long-postponed plenum on February 7–8. The party decided
to stand pat on the price increase. Four days later, the textile workers of
Łódź responded with a general strike. After three days of strike militance,
the party, despite its help from the church, was forced on February 15 to
rescind the price increase.

In light of this historical evidence, an estimate of the church's role in
Polish society and politics must differentiate between the laity, the lower
clergy, the bishops, and the Primate Wyszyński and his successor, Cardinal Glemp. Summary conclusions must also take into account the presence of a nationalist ideology, in which the ultimate object of worship, the
nation, is intertwined with religious symbols and rhetoric.

Primate Wyszyński revealed his motivation and much of his understanding of Poland's situation in a 1971 letter to Father Hilary Jastak, the
parish priest of the Sacred Heart Church in Gdynia.

> Considering the situation caused by the careless actions of the local authorities,
> we felt it was essential to do everything to quell quickly the rising discontent in
> the land. I personally greatly feared Szczecin—that some foreign powers might
> take advantage of the disorders with irreversible harm to the Polish State. For
> after all, it is well known how many enemies Poland has, and how they watch
> our presence in Szczecin. . . . It was necessary to do everything possible to
> quickly restore peace. That was the reason for my appeal of Christmas Day. I
> was ready to protect everyone, in order to have peace prevail in Poland. . . . I
> am convinced that the December sufferings opened the eyes of many Poles to
> the problem of rule in Poland.[9]

Wyszyński's policy in 1970–71 was the same policy he followed in the
successive crises in 1956, in 1976, and finally in 1980, when he asked the
strikers on the coast to return to work. This policy has been followed by
Primate Glemp, who equated the violence by the state and by Solidarity

in December 1981. It was followed again by Cardinal Glemp when he negated Solidarity's call for a general strike on November 10, 1982.

It is not easy to form a conclusive judgment of this policy. In Eastern Europe, no one seeks a suicidal confrontation with Soviet armies. But in 1970–71, who was to say that further waves of strikes with church and intellectual support could not have forced more lasting concessions? Such concessions were, in fact, obtained in 1980. Primate Wyszyński's February letter is of capital importance in assessing him as a politician because it reveals many of the assumptions on which he based his broad policy in 1971. These assumptions are not reassuring. The primate elected to see the crisis as the result of heedless decisions of local authorities, even though it was clear on the coast and in Warsaw that the sustained repression was run by top party and military officials. When he wrote the February letter, he could hardly have been unaware that the new regime was made up of persons such as Generals Jaruzelski, Tuczapski, and Szlachcic, who played direct decision-making roles in the events.

Wyszyński's reference to Polish enemies and his fear for the Polish-German border illustrate his failure to grasp the new political landscape that Polish workers understood immediately—that the Polish-German treaty removed the fear of dismemberment from the West and opened new opportunities for internal resistance. Wyszyński was much too quick in bringing up the question of Poland's national survival—almost as quick as the Polish regime itself. In the circumstances, one is encouraged to speculate to what extent the primate became the victim of "self-serving" information relayed in confidence by the Polish regime. On the whole, the primate's letter to Father Jastak and his other actions do not show a sophisticated political mind at work.

Finally, it seems prudent to note that in their efforts to preserve peace at any cost, the primate and the bishops compromised not only politics, but religion. The sentence "we beg of you do not accuse, show understanding," from the primate's sermon on Christmas Day, and the prayer for "those who have taken responsibility for the fatherland," can be read as washing away the political, criminal, and moral responsibility for the dead and wounded of 1970. Primate Wyszyński and the Polish bishops seemed to have fallen into the trap created by the political function of the church in Poland. Though dressed in religious garb and speaking a language of religion, they became entirely political. Under the circumstances, the ethical basis of the church's teaching becomes difficult to see.

## A Rhetoric of the Security Forces

In a sense, the public pronouncements of Primate Wyszyński and First Secretary Gierek were compromised at their core. A more honest language is found distilled in the sermon for the dead preached by Father

Tadrowski in Gdynia. Soon after Father Tadrowski preached his sermon, the chiefs of the police of Szczecin province sent a letter of thanks to the families of their militia and security personnel that was honest in its own way and showed the depth of the civil cleavage in Poland:

> To the mothers, wives, daughters, and sons of agents of State Security services and the Citizens Militia of Szczecin Province.
>
> Together with all the inhabitants of Szczecin, we have lived through painful, tragic, and bitter moments when asocial and criminal elements disturbed the peace on the streets of our city—destroying shops and setting afire public buildings. Thanks to the energetic action of your sons, husbands, and fathers, law and order were restored.
>
> The self-sacrificing and courageous action of the agents of State Security and Militia were the result of their high moral and political engagement and also their awareness that their actions were approved by those closest to them— their wives, children, brothers, and sisters. It was especially the quiet support of their wives, those faithful companions in the difficult daily life of a militia-man and agent of the State Security, which permitted them to carry out their obligation to restore order in our city.
>
> Your justified anxiety for the safety of those dearest to you did not prevent you from understanding the obligation which rested on your husbands, sons, and brothers. We warmly thank you for your support in creating an atmosphere that allowed them to fully carry out their work in those difficult days.
>
> We take this occasion to also send you warm greetings and best wishes for the new year to all the members of our large militia family.
>
> *The Party and Professional Direction of the*
> *Szczecin Provincial Citizens Militia.*[10]

The security forces were brave, law-abiding, just, and above all, had served the highest good—Poland. This was the authentic language of the party and police, backed up by an extensive system of privilege and isolation from the society at large.

## The Myth of Jaruzelski and the Polish Army

After the suppression of the workers' strikes on the coast by the army and police, the Polish regime simply changed a few leaders at the top. As part of the rhetoric of conciliation, it was important to load the odium for the violence upon Gomułka and a few associates and to protect the armed forces from public disapproval. Immediately after the bloody events, rumors spread in Polish society that General Jaruzelski, Admiral Janczyszyn, and other members of the high command had resisted their orders from Gomułka. The violence was blamed on the police, and in some versions it was widely reported that General Jaruzelski and Admiral Janczys-zyn had even been placed under house arrest until Gierek came to power. The myth continued at full strength through the rise of Solidarity and played a certain role in the unpreparedness of Solidarity for the military crackdown of December 1981. It received a powerful stimulus in the 1976 crisis when it was widely reported that General Jaruzelski had said at an emergency meeting of the Politburo that "Polish soldiers will not fire on Polish workers." Although widely quoted, no one could find a source for this dramatic statement by the Polish minister of defense.[11]

The origin of the myth can be located precisely. At the January 1971 meeting with the Warski workers, Gierek replied to worker recrimina-tions about the repressive use of the army with a direct lie. General Jaru-zelski, he said, "was cut out of the decision." Gierek also went on to exclude Cyrankiewicz and other key officials. All decisions "took place behind Cyrankiewicz's back. Only a small group of people, two or three, made the decisions." This, confided Gierek to the workers, "was not for public knowledge, but that's the way it was."[12] While it was clearly very much in the interests of the party to have such rumors circulating widely in the society, it was a special bonus that such disinformation subse-quently affected the political judgment of Western academics and intelli-gence analysts. Instead of seeing martial law in December 1981 as an action in the best interests of the Soviet Union, Western analysts' view of Jaruzelski and the Polish Army caused them to see martial law as a re-grettable but patriotic act of a high command dedicated to saving the Poles from themselves. Moreover, they built elaborate theories of the autonomous role of the Polish military on this basis. A careful review of the evidence from 1970 seriously undermines this romantic view.[13] Al-though Jan de Weydenthal, Teresa Rakowska-Harmstone, and Andrew Michta have questioned the traditional Western academic view,[14] it has continued as a remarkably successful case of an authoritarian regime's disinformation.

The contrary evidence is derived from a number of sources. Dozens of civilian accounts leave no doubt that the regular army played a principal role in the shootings in Gdynia. Three divisions were sent into Gdańsk and Gdynia, and another, the 12th Division, was deployed in Szczecin. These four divisions were responsible for the majority of the deaths and woundings. The relevant historical evidence ironically reveals both the power of the myth of the "good" army and the fact that the myth was a double-edged sword. On the one hand, the faith that the army would "be with the people" provided a strong incentive for workers to fraternize and to go forward in the face of levelled guns in the expectation that the soldiers would not fire. On the other hand, rank-and-file soldiers and lower-grade officers on the scene are distinctly different from the generals who issue the orders. Not only were military forces directly involved in all the major clashes on the coast, but their actions turned out to be only the most visible aspects of the massive preventive mobilization carried out by the Polish General Staff and General Jaruzelski. The Gomułka letters, the Kubiak Report, and the Central Committee Report of 1981 confirm the numerous civilian accounts assembled and cited in Chapters Two and Three of this study.[15]

In Jaruzelski's speech to the Party Plenum in February 1971, available in the West at the end of 1971, he explained his actions on the coast straightforwardly. The December decisions on repression "were made by the first secretary in the presence of the premier." "Therefore," Jaruzelski continued,

> these were decisions which had full binding force, both in actual fact and from a formal legal point of view. I cannot imagine a situation in which, either then or at any other time, the command of our People's Army could fail to carry out the decisions of our party-state leadership, especially when such a decision is justified by a threat to the socialist social order.[16]

General Jaruzelski himself also contradicted a key element of this myth—namely his purported statement that "the Polish Army will not fire on Polish workers." When he came to prominence in 1981, no one could find a direct source for the sentence, which was quoted everywhere. But in an interview in the *Christian Science Monitor*, General Jaruzelski clarified matters by saying bluntly, "Workers who strike are not Polish."[17]

### Refurbishing the Army and Police

The realm of myth served an important repressive function. Also important was the realm of institutional performance. The Baltic Coast operation had been a display of incompetence by the military and police. It was a story of force applied too little, too much, or too late, of improvised operations with joint units of army, police, and security troops breaking under the pressure of events and, in the end lapsing into passivity and openly fraternizing with the population.[18]

The major lesson learned by the Polish army in December 1970 was to avoid engagement in direct suppression of civilian protest. In the planning for martial law in Poland in 1980–81, this was the main principle that the army held out for in its negotiations with the Ministry of the Interior—namely, that the direct attack on striking workers or street crowds would be made not by the army but by special police units, which would be greatly expanded. The army would serve an administrative command function, and its units would be restricted to a demonstrative terror function. Only in the last resort would the army enter into direct action. In an even more desperate stage—if Czech, German, and Soviet units had to be invited in—certain elite divisions were designated for joint actions. Ironically, given the strength of the earlier anti-German propaganda, in 1981 it was planned that Jaruzelski's 12th Mechanized Division would, in that event, work in a joint operation with an East German division.[19]

The disastrous experience in December 1970 implied a need for a quick expansion of troops specialized in suppression of civilian discontent. At the start of martial law in December in 1981, security units, although faced with a new general strike involving many hundreds of workplaces and factories, were able to break the movement in the course of a week. With motor vehicle and helicopter transport, relatively small units traveled from factory to factory across entire provinces, putting down the sit-in strikes.[20]

Immediately after the 1970 debacle, organizational upgrading of the internal security function occurred within the Polish army. General Korczyński, the hammer of Gdańsk and Gdynia workers, was retired as head of the internal security troops. His successor was General Tadeusz Tuczapski, the military commander in the Szczecin strikes who, as chief of training for the army, indicated the newly enhanced status for internal security when he was moved into this post. Soon after, Tuczapski also became the secretary of the Committee for National Defense (KOK), a post he held in 1980-82. The KOK can be described as a standing martial-law government in case of civil unrest or war. In 1980–81, it became the planning body and then the main executive organ of martial law. The Military Council of National Salvation (WRON) was a screen created to divert attention from the KOK. The army, then, had learned many things from the 1970 experience.

The Soviet Union also went to school in 1970. In 1953, Soviet troops had to be used in East Germany to crush popular protests. There was no native German force capable of facing the storm. In 1956 in Hungary, Soviet officers immediately scattered the Hungarian army and set it wandering across the countryside. Hungarian troops, whether officers or enlisted men, joined the revolution as individuals, and occasionally small units. In Poland on the other hand, Gomułka and Ochab were backed by the commanders of the KBW, the internal security troops, the air force, and the navy in successfully facing down the Soviet leaders and the Soviet and Polish troops that were sent to Warsaw.

By the time of the 1968 "Prague Spring" in Czechoslovakia, the Czech troops remained in their barracks as the Warsaw Pact armies invaded. In 1970 in Poland, in spite of unambiguous orders given by Gomułka and his minister of defense, Jaruzelski, the armed forces rapidly became unusable. On the other hand, no units or individuals turned against their superiors. Rather, they became passive, or merely pretended to follow orders. Even with the limitations on the use of the army in 1981 and quite un-promising personnel, the technical progress seems noteworthy.

## The Party's Policies

Behind a rhetoric of national reconciliation and technocratic competence, the Polish Communist party embarked on a series of actions that ulti-mately led to its downfall. In labor policy, there was a pattern of co-option and discreet repression. Mieczysław Dopierała, the Warski party secretary, failed to achieve substantive reforms, and resigned. The secu-rity chief of the January Warski strike, Adam Ulfik, narrowly escaped being murdered in his apartment by security thugs who tried to force his head into a kitchen oven. A young worker named Gołaszewski who led a Warski shop in the January strike was found dead, gassed in his kitchen oven.[21] Stanisław Słodkowski, the leader of the Gdynia Strike Committee, spent ten years under police surveillance far from Gdynia.

Immediately following the December 1970 mobilization, the party fired a number of shop activists, even as it nominally raised some of the more visible militants to union posts, where they were surrounded and stalemated by dependable party loyalists. These symbols of the worker resistance were then subjected to varying degrees of pressure until they were, in one way or another, totally insulated from influence. As Wałęsa described the process, "Little by little the shipyard got rid of those who had shown themselves as the most active. I, for example, found that I always received the worst work. Any raise or promotion was closed off to me."[22]

The regime's policy toward workers in general was twofold. Its pri-mary strategy was to maintain direct lines to the one hundred or so lead-ing factories in the country, taking them out of direct supervision by their provincial party committees and placing them under a department of the Central Committee. Factory directors and first secretaries were in the central nomenklatura. This policy involved buying off workers in large factories and favored branches of industry. If trouble ensued anyway, experience showed that the way to handle it was to go to the factory, negotiate, promise, and, if necessary, buy off the workers. The weakness of this policy was that it reinforced the lessons workers thought they had learned from the 1970–71 strikes—that strikes did pay and the conse-quences were not inherently suicidal. Throughout the Gierek era of the 1970s, hundreds of "work interruptions," as the party called them, re-inforced this lesson. In fear of worker protests, the government continued huge subsidies of basic food staples. The 1976 government attempt to raise food prices, which was rescinded the same day when strikes began up and down the country, was only the most spectacular instance of the veto over government policy that the workers had acquired.[23]

Gierek's policies toward industrial workers were relatively successful in the short run. His regime co-opted, neutralized, and suppressed workers. Such tactics defused a given crisis, but in the long run fueled the workers' movement. His policies over his ten-year rule reveal a clear portrait of a weak state. Gierek's regime was unable and unwilling to guard the general interest of the Polish party or the Communist state—even to the limited extent Gomułka had once achieved. Poland became more subject to the contradictions implicit in its status as a semi-industrialized country in the capitalist world market and a society trapped in the Soviet socialist empire.[24]

These circumstances had a fatal impact on the Polish economy. After Gomułka, economic policy was hostage to particular industrial and party lobbies, to peripheral and self-interested advice and direction from Western banks and corporations, to the veto of Polish workers, and finally, to the investment priorities established by the Soviet Union. The party's administrative performance—erratic, incompetent, and corrupt—exacerbated these maladies.

Gomułka's "selective development" scheme and economic squeeze of Polish workers, as politically maladroit as it was, had attempted to face the real problems of Poland's backward industrialization. It did attempt to deal with particular industrial and political lobbies, and it partially threatened to thwart military industrial priorities set by the Soviet Union. The two industries Gomułka had selected for elimination as a part of selective development—aviation and shipbuilding—became favored industries under Gierek. This was a firm step backward. Other investments, such as the building of the hugely expensive Katowice Steelworks, deepened the imperial costs precisely where Gomułka had tried to draw a line. Instead of a transition to intensive advanced technology, Gierek invested in even more dinosaur steel projects at the behest of the Soviet Union.

Agricultural policy also illustrates the shortsightedness characteristic of the Gierek decade. By the measure of gross national production, Poland was said to be the world's tenth or eleventh largest industrial power in 1980. In the real world of the competitive global market, Poland could only sell primary products and agricultural goods produced by its harassed and capital-starved private farmers. But of $21 billion borrowed from the West in the 1970s, fully $6 billion were siphoned off to pay for food imports, despite the fact that 25 percent of the population was engaged in food production. While this temporarily assuaged popular discontent, the policy was a classic example of a government mortgaging a society's future. It was claimed that Poland would borrow to pay for whole plants and technologies and eventually sell products from those plants on the world market, but this never came to pass. Whole plants and patents were bought in the West, but they were frequently inappropriate, or came into production so late that they were already out of date.

In the first half of the decade, wages and living standards rose precipitously. As Poland's economic situation materially worsened in the mid-1970s, the party blithely maintained a steady drumbeat of "success propaganda" for popular and foreign consumption. The result of the June 1976 food price increase merely underscored the self-defeating nature of Gierek's governing style. Worker reaction was both broad and deep across Poland. Literally hundreds of strikes erupted. Poland needed belt-tightening and new investment, but with incompetent and corrupt state leadership, workers no longer believed any rationale for sacrifice.

## KOR and the Intellectual Opposition

The opposition intellectuals believed that the lesson they had learned from 1970 was clear—that Polish workers were a social force that required guidance in proper aims and methods. To these intellectuals, who were almost entirely unaware of the organizational and programmatic achievements of the coastal workers, the 1970–71 events seemed to be blind riots focused on economic "bread issues" with an unarticulated existential but programless protest against Communist power.[25] The task for the Polish intellectuals was to ally their organizational and programmatic leadership with the force of the working class. For the Polish political class and Western specialists, the period 1976–79 was "when Michnik and others were formulating the plan and vocabulary that led to the radical changes of the year 1980 to 1981."[26]

The party's response to the 1976 strikes was so vindictive that a group of Warsaw intellectuals formed the Committee for the Defense of Workers (KOR), which raised funds for medical and legal assistance for victims of the state's repression.[27] After a year of such support for workers, the group reformulated its aims and adopted a more comprehensive title—the Committee for the Self-Defense of Society, KSS-KOR. The number of nominal members rose to 25, but the number of activists rose to several hundred. Associated with the committee were numerous social self-defense groups: Peasants' Trade Unions, the Free Trade Union of the Baltic, Student Solidarity Support Committees, and several dozen unofficial bulletins, journals, and book-publishing ventures. Supported by the Catholic Church, KSS-KOR succeeded in creating a broad front for human rights. Other opposition groups soon emerged: the Movement for Defense of Human and Civil Rights (ROPCiO), the "Flying University," the Confederation for Independent Poland, and Young Poland.

KOR's intervention bureau, under the direction of physicist Zbigniew Romaszewski, documented police brutality and legal repressions against Polish citizens. KOR also founded a news bulletin, *Robotnik,* which reported workers' resistance in factories and propagated workers' rights. In December 1979, *Robotnik* published a "Charter of Workers' Rights," which was widely distributed across Poland.

The Polish economic situation continued to worsen. The regime tried again to raise food prices in July 1980 against a backdrop of social conditions that seemed tailor-made for insurgency. The effect of the Gierek expansion had been to raise living standards and expectations while making inequalities and privileges more visible.

The reaction to the 1980 price hike was a wave of rolling strikes that continued in various parts of the country for 45 days until, on August 14, the Lenin Shipyard in Gdańsk, as on December 14, 1970, initiated a sit-down strike. As in 1970, the Paris Commune Shipyard in Gdynia struck the following day, and the Warski Shipyard in Szczecin followed two days later. In the Lenin Shipyard, the events followed a trajectory that was historically conditioned: a sit-down strike on August 14 and the codification of a set of demands calling for a trade union independent of the party; and the formation of an interfactory strike committee on August 16, uniting 20 factories behind a 21-point program with which 156 factories were affiliated by August 18. The party likewise tried various policies that had worked in the past. On August 22, with more than 300 factories affiliated with the interfactory strike committee, the government agreed to talks in the shipyard. After tense negotiations over the succeeding week, the Gdańsk Accords were signed on August 31. They gave the insurrectionary calendar of Polish history a new date: The Polish August.

The workers of the Baltic Coast had been sustained over ten years by the breakthroughs they had achieved in 1970 and 1971. But August 1980 was not simply a repetition of 1970. The new insurrection was geographically and socially more encompassing. It had succeeded in taking the local experience of a region and a class and making it strategically meaningful to all Polish citizens and all subjects in Leninist states.

Chapters Two and Three have presented the narrative history of the origins of Solidarity. Succeeding analytic chapters will examine the evolution of the organization, ideology, and symbolic politics of Solidarity, as well as the significance of underlying sociological factors, within the overall context of the development of Solidarity.

# · P A R T   I I ·

# The Anatomy of a Democratic Movement

## CHAPTER FIVE

# The Vanguard Versus Workers' Self-Government

SOLIDARITY's internal organization inspires two questions: What were the origin and nature of Solidarity's organizational form, and how adequate was it to the tasks it faced?

On the morning of August 14, 1980, when the strike began in the Gdańsk Lenin Shipyard, the Free Trade Unions of the Baltic had three founding members and several dozen sympathizers. By September 17, there were about three million members in some 3,500 workplaces. By October 10, the members numbered around eight million.[1] By the end of the year, Solidarity neared ten million members not including the organizations forming in its train, such as farmers' solidarities, pensioners', small-business entrepreneurs', police, and student unions. This vast mobilization occurred in a country with an active working population of seventeen million. Among social movements Solidarity is noteworthy for two characteristics: the speed with which it arose, and its eventual status as a majoritarian movement of a country's adult population.

## The Organization and Effectiveness of Solidarity

The foundation of Solidarity was the workplace. Workplaces united in regional associations called "interfactory strike committees." With its statutory emphasis on the decision-making power of its factory locals as opposed to regional and national leaderships, Solidarity seemed a near-perfect antithesis of its opponent, the Leninist party-state. In one sense it was a mirror image of that opponent: it subordinated industries and occupations to the territorial principle and united workers and employees against the employer-state. On the whole it seemed either a throwback to or the ultimate fulfillment of the wildest dreams of the anarcho-syndicalists with their faith in the general strike.

The general consensus is that, like the overall program, the organizational form of Solidarity originated among the radical intellectuals and was transmitted by them to the workers through the worker's newspaper *Robotnik,* through the propagandizing of the Charter of Worker's Rights and support for the Free Trade Union of the Baltic.

The elite account focuses on the actions and manifestos of the intellectuals in order to explain the actions of the workers. Even the report of the research team headed by French sociologist Alain Touraine follows the elite account. The intellectuals

> aimed at the bottom first by supporting the workers imprisoned or otherwise sanctioned . . . in June 1976 and later through the creation of worker's newspapers and the organisation of free trade unions on the Baltic Coast and in Silesia. . . . KOR played the major role. . . . As a result, the workers were able to organise a campaign going far beyond the riots of 1976 and the intellectuals were at long last able to escape their isolation.[2]

In describing the strikes in 1980, Touraine continues the basic dichotomy of the brute force of the workers and the consciousness of the intellectuals. "But the intellectuals were soon to make their voice heard, and their arrival on the scene was crucial in defining the composition of Solidarity over the months to come. . . . These intellectuals, often radical or moderate militants in the democratic cause, constitute the essential link between trade unionism and democratic themes in Solidarity."[3] Thus Touraine and his collaborators support the elitist consensus. Without intellectuals, workers would be capable of only limited economistic aims or "riots" and no democracy. Touraine's methodology is the same—to understand workers, examine what the intellectuals are telling them.

To be specific, although the Polish intellectuals were aware of the bloody events of 1970, they were largely ignorant of the significant steps toward the organization of free trade unions that occurred there. In this respect the regime was quite successful in creating an image of a crowd that fought for bread but was incapable of more reflective self-organization and action. It should be said that this image corresponded to the Polish intellectuals' expectations. The categories of thought determined perception more than did false information or the lack of information.

The character and adequacy of Solidarity's organization is the subject of an ongoing debate and dilemma. The rise of modern professional bureaucracies, which include armies and police, has made it extremely difficult for unarmed civilians to overthrow a determined authoritarian government. Weber offered the view that a strict hierarchical organization had to be created to defeat a hierarchical anti-democratic organization. "Under otherwise equal conditions a 'societal action' which is methodically ordered and led is superior to every resistance of 'mass' or even of 'communal action.' And where the bureaucratization of administration has been completely carried through, a form of power relation is established that is practically unshatterable."[4] In other words, a hierarchical organization can be effectively opposed only by another hierarchical structure. Lenin's party followed that logic, yet Polish workers did not want to create a "good" Leninist structure to oppose the "bad" Leninist structure that headed the Polish party-state. Confounding Weber and Lenin, they built a highly decentralized structure designed to be responsive to its members and grass-roots shops while drastically limiting the power of its central leadership.

E. J. Hobsbawm has implicitly argued for the hierarchical structure of Weber and Lenin in his work on "primitive rebels," who were characterized by local aims and lack of central organization. This typology treated these primitive forms as precursors of the modern revolutionary party with its command relationship between leaders and members.[5] Unlike Lenin, Weber and Hobsbawm, Robert Michels, in his book on political parties, drew attention to the way a leadership hindered and prevented radical impulses of its membership.[6] American scholars Frances Fox Piven and Richard A. Cloward continued in this line, arguing that the less organization and leadership a movement has, the more radical it will be.[7] Centralization versus grass-roots organization, hierarchical leadership versus mobilized member initiative—this dichotomy was confronted in a dramatic and desperate way by Solidarity.

In the summary analysis of organization that follows, the elite account that treats workers as the passive followers of elite leadership is put aside in order to develop a historical context based on a social history of Polish workers. Three steps toward the organization of Solidarity are singled out. Only in the third do the intellectuals appear and affect events. Only at this point does their understanding of what happened and their estimate of the political potential of workers become relevant.

## Three Steps to Solidarity, 1931–1980

The conflict between the Polish state and Polish workers shaped workers' programs and their forms of resistance. Within that conflict, three steps were critical in determining what organizational form Solidarity was to take. During the December 1970 Baltic coast strikes, industrial workers rediscovered the round-the-clock sit-down strike, in which they took control of their own workplace. This was the first step. Almost immediately, the workers extended their efforts and formed interfactory strike committees to unite all factories and workplaces against the state. This was the second step, which involved complex notions of elections, delegation, representation, and unity. The August 1980 strikes were simply a cellular multiplication of these two steps, which were first taken in 1970. On August 31, 1980, the day the Gdańsk interfactory committee signed the accord, it was supported by committees in Bydgoszcz, Elbląg, Szczecin, Wrocław, and Jastrzębie. There remained, then, the third and final step: to create a national structure for the new independent union. This problem was addressed on September 17, 1980.

*The Sit-Down Strike and Interfactory Strike Committees*

The sit-down strike was a refinement of the classic form of industrial protest, in which workers put down their tools and went home. This left them vulnerable to the employer countermove of hiring strikebreakers. The great merit of the sit-down strike was that workers controlled the means of production and strikebreakers became an inoperative factor. It was known among the Poles as an Italian strike, and it had been Italians in the 1920s who first used the sit-down on a massive scale, not merely as a weapon of a labor movement but as a challenge to state power.

Sit-down strikes in Poland started in January 1931 in one factory and expanded immediately to become the major form of industrial protest by 1933. They became more than a tactic for use in one factory as solidarity strikes were common, often with proclamations of a general strike against the government.[8] Ironically, at that time a then-obscure Communist party union organizer named Władysław Gomułka experienced the capitalist tactics against the sit-down strike—sending in police and army and "locking out" or firing the striking workers. The rise of the sit-down strike in Poland had a domino effect on workers in other countries. From May through June 1936, a massive sit-down strike movement swept across France (where it was called a Polish strike). In the United States in December of that year, the sit-down was decisively used in the strike that began in Fisher Body no. 2 in Flint, Michigan. "The Great Sit-Down," as it has been called, brought General Motors to its knees, became the model for the newborn Congress of Industrial Organizations (CIO), and hastened the unionization of most of American heavy industry over the next five years.[9]

After World War II, the sit-down strike disappeared in Poland because of the massive power of the Communist state. More anonymous forms of resistance became advisable, the most popular being slowing down on the job.[10]

Workers tried to use the sit-down strike in those years, but the state ruthlessly crushed their attempts. A multi-day strike of textile workers in Łódź in 1947 in which workers used the sit-down strike was broken by military and police force. In April 1951, at the apex of Polish Stalinism, miners of the Dąbrowa basin organized a three-day sit-down strike, which again was broken by force with the leaders going to prison.[11] Thereafter, the sit-down apparently faded from the memory of most Polish workers. The best-known industrial conflict in Poland before December 1970 did not employ the sit-down as a weapon. In 1956 in Poznań, the 3,000 workers of Factory W-3 in the Stalin Metallurgical Combine tried silent demonstrations in front of the director's and party offices, mass meetings, and short work stoppages. In secret agreement with the

15,000 workers of the combine and other major factories of Poznań, they marched on the city center. This culminated in a city-wide uprising on June 28, 1956, in which the spontaneous violent uprising of the entire city overwhelmed the incipient labor organization.[12]

After the change of leaders in October 1956, many of the most dedicated worker-activists placed their hopes in a reformed trade union and council movement. Typically, Stanisław Matyja, a worker from W-3 in the Stalin (Cegielski) Factory and the outstanding leader of the Poznań workers in 1956, was voted a leader of the workers' council. But in early 1957, the council movement was swiftly brought to heel as the government swamped the movement with "ringer" councils from more passive factories. Workers learned they could not trust official unions and councils; they learned to be wary of promises of reform.

Stanisław Matyja was fired from W-3 and lived a marginal existence until 1980, the year Solidarity was born. The other activists in W-3 also were fired. The attempt in 1956 was only the most dramatic, the most hopeful of attempts at reform. The results not only discredited the concept of reform of existing structures among workers, but they also served as a concrete and highly instructive demonstration of how the party could manipulate a whole movement, creating leaders and factory organizations that they could then shape and take over from within. Such experiences taught workers that they had to have their own institutions rather than accept promises of reform from existing trade union and council institutions.[13]

As detailed in Chapters Two and Three, the sit-down appeared in Gdańsk, Gdynia, and Szczecin in December 1970 along with demands for free trade unions independent of the party. The fullest development of the interfactory strike committee occurred in Szczecin. These developments were stimulated by the government's countermeasures, such as the military blockade of the shipyards and the deliberate decision to encourage formation of strike committees. In the evidence on which this study is based, there is no indication of a historical memory of the prewar sit-down strike weapon. The sit-down and the interfactory strike committee were experienced as new beginnings.[14] Strike leader Mieczysław Dopierała's comment on the organization of the sit-down in the Warski Shipyard on December 18 bears repeating:

> When we gathered, we were doing something that had never been done or discussed in our public or social lives. It was a conflict of the people with the state. We had to open negotiation with them. Who they represented and who we represented, of that there wasn't any doubt. But how to do it, how to organize all this, we had to do ad hoc, with no previous schemes, patterns or instructions.[15]

In this account, which stresses "political opportunity structure and the conditioning of movement emergence, strategy and dynamics by the state,"[16] the open strike would have been mercilessly crushed until 1970. At that time, a desperate crisis made it marginally preferable to fighting army and police on the streets. The succession of Gomułka, an old-line Communist, by Gierek brought to power a regime less willing to use force to put down dissent. Lenin called this condition of opportunity for a revolutionary movement an "elite which does not want to rule this way any more."

In terms of organization, the January 1971 strike in the Warski Shipyard led by Edmund Bałuka added little to the lessons of December. But it was a valuable rehearsal for the future. Bałuka commented that everyone now knew exactly what to do, and what had taken hours and days in December was done with dispatch in January. The January strike was a public demonstration that a determined sit-down strike was not suicidal, that it could force negotiation with the government, that even the first secretary, the premier, the minister of defense, and the interior secretary could be forced to negotiate with workers.

All the structural components that would allow the workers to create Solidarity in 1980 had thus been conceived, tested, and internalized by coastal workers in 1970. The first two organizational tools—the sit-down strike and the interfactory strike committee—had been forged. The central ideological step had also been taken: the articulation of the demand for independent unions.[17] A new frame for worker struggle now existed on the Baltic Coast.

The 1976 one-day strikes in response to a sudden food-price rise were nationwide, but they illustrated the regional character of the workers' breakthroughs and lessons of 1970. Because the price rise was rescinded after one day, a possible organizational evolution was cut off; but over one hundred factories stopped work across Poland. In two cases, workers went out into the streets. They were dominated by immediate economic concerns, in contrast with both 1970–71 and 1980.[18]

On August 14, 1980, workers in the Lenin Shipyard in Gdańsk put down their tools and declared a sit-down strike. Two days later, together with representatives of twenty other coastal enterprises, they formed an interfactory strike committee and, as they had done in 1970, drafted 21 demands, led by a call for independent trade unions. Two days after that, on August 18, they consolidated their movement by solidifying the 16,000-member ranks of the Lenin Shipyard and gaining representatives from 156 factories, who became affiliated with the interfactory strike committee. On August 16, an interfactory strike committee was formed in Szczecin, and as the strike in Gdańsk and Szczecin continued, new

interfactory strike committees emerged in Wrocław, Bydgoszcz, Wałbrzych, and Upper Silesia. Numerous factories struck in support all over
Poland as the sit-down strike and the interfactory committee model
passed into the repertoire of resistance for workers all over Poland.

The "Polish August" culminated on August 31, when the government
agreed to accept the 21 demands. The independent union Solidarity was
born. The organizational forms of protest that sustained the Polish August had implemented the achievements of December 1970.

### Solidarity Becomes a National Organization

The creation of a national structure for Solidarity came on September
17, 1980, and it was the third and final stage in the structural evolution
of the democratic movement. The August victory had legitimized regional
independent structures, but the movement, though independent, was re-
gionally confined. The task at hand on September 17 was to create a
national structure out of these regional bodies.

Hard lessons learned over 35 years made most of the Gdańsk activists
suspicious of an attempt to extend their free unions by fiat or amalgama-
tion across Poland. They remembered the "reforms" and promises after
1956 and 1970. They trusted their own members but feared inexperienced union members who had not waged a successful organizing campaign. They also feared that they might quickly become bureaucratized
and centrally controlled and managed from above rather than from
below by their members. The independent union was designed to remove
party influence. Beyond this, workers wanted a structure in which power
remained with the rank and file and in which tenure for union officers
was limited. Many other provisions were instituted to insure accountabil-
ity to the grass roots. Despite these generalized objectives of internal democracy, the Gdańsk agreement said nothing about the future structure
of the free trade union. Moreover, the agreement made it clear that the
new union was limited geographically to the Baltic Coast.[19]

There is no question that the Polish government hoped to wall in the
Gdańsk workers by restricting the agreement to the coast. Driven by fear
of exclusion from the agreement, factories all over Poland exploded in a
second wave of strikes. The media's near blackout of substantive information concerning the union situation fed the second wave by sparking
rumors and misinformation. In the Maurice Thorez Mine in Wałbrzych,
a routine visit of state security police to check up on a report of labor
trouble provoked the rumor that union emissaries from Gdańsk had appeared, instantly promoting a strike and the formation of strike committees. This second wave of strikes strengthened Solidarity immeasurably
by giving workers collective experience in organized assertion through

sit-down strikes and the confidence that flows from such experiences. Still, party officials continued to resist the strikers' demands tooth and claw, while factory work teams organized not only by territory, but also in unions covering one factory, one craft, or one industrial branch. Adding to the confusion, the government's unions started to withdraw from the national Central Council of Trade Unions, adding the adjective "independent" to their names, like wolves putting on sheep's fleeces.

On September 15, the union's opponent, the party-state, provoked the decisive leap into a national organization by publishing a decree regulating trade union registration. Unions that did not choose to register with the Central Council of Trade Unions could apply for registration to the Warsaw provincial court. The decree spurred a panicked rush to Gdańsk by all new trade unions because no registration deadline had been set by the court and because the court arrogated to itself not only the right to decide whether the negotiated status of a new union conformed to the Polish Constitution, but also the right to cancel a registration whenever it decided union activity contravened any law.[20]

These vague but threatening omissions and caveats provoked dismay and anxiety in the ranks of the new trade unions. Gdańsk surely would be registered, but what about regions in rural Poland or tiny factories in politically insignificant sectors?

## The Conflict: A Centralized or Confederated Union?

The movement had come to a critical juncture. Returning to the problem posed by Weber, Lenin, and Hobsbawm—how to structure a movement in opposition to a "hierarchical anti-democratic organization"[21]— KOR's response was not quite up to the authoritarian prescription of Weber himself, but it did contain overtones of centralization. There was a reasonable explanation for KOR's desire for one union under one statute—namely, the justifiable fear of Poles, intellectuals as well as workers, of the manipulative and coercive power of the one-party state. KOR wanted a united movement to oppose the power of the party. In contrast, the coastal movement and Lech Wałęsa opted for a decentralized structure grounded in many unions and many statutes. These contrasting approaches perfectly reflected the experiences of both groups.

The Warsaw intellectuals, unaware as they were of the ideological and organizational achievements of the Polish working class, assumed that worker activism on the coast was a function of consciousness-raising by the intelligentsia. Consequently the intellectuals believed Solidarity would protect itself against the ravages of the state by being centralized and administered by activist intellectuals. In the formula common in Polish intellectual circles at that time, "Solidarity is the creation of KOR and Wałęsa the creation of Kuroń." A good deal of ignorance and self-delusion entered into this encounter.

In contrast, the Baltic workers had learned, through brutal experience with the party hierarchy, to be extremely wary of centralized reforming institutions. They remembered the experience of the workers' councils after 1956 and the reformed trade unions of 1971. They knew how easy it was for the party to introduce its agents and to tame locals into a central structure and gradually to strangle the independent locals and regions. Also, after 35 years of party rule, Polish workers would not have joined an organization headed by someone other than themselves. They came to the September 17 meeting with a confidence in their own powers that had been verified by their recent triumph in their confrontation with the party state.

An inevitable political struggle flowed from these contrasting views. It revolved around the shape of the union statute. Work on a regional union statute was already far advanced. Warsaw lawyers Jan Olszewski, Władysław Siła-Nowicki, and Wiesław Chrzanowski had brought a draft of a union statute for the coast to the Lenin Shipyard on August 25, and it had been published in the last issue of the Strike Bulletin on August 31. It provided for two tiers in a Baltic coastal union: the workplace local and the interfactory committee.

In addition to these problems of structure, there were problems of an internal political nature. The Gdańsk union did not present a wholly united front. During the August strike, deep conflicts based on personal ambitions and differing policies and temperaments arose between the "upstart" Wałesa and most of the rest of the members of the free trade unions, in particular, Andrzej Gwiazda, Bogdan Borusewicz, and Anna Walentynowicz. These conflicts were kept as far as possible from public view—but they were heated. In Wałesa's estimation, it was a conflict of "the Jacobins against the realists."[22]

Immediately after the signing of the Gdańsk Accords, the Gwiazda-Borusewicz faction within the Gdańsk union attempted to oust Wałesa as chairman. Though no one has written in detail about the nuances of this internal coup proposal, it is probable that this attempt to remove Wałesa was made in consultation with the KOR group in Warsaw. As Wałesa saw it,

> Madame Anna [Walentynowicz] came to see me and offered some friendly advice. "Resign as chairman of the interfactory committee!" According to her, I wasn't big enough for the job and for the tasks ahead. We needed someone of the sort of Andrzej Gwiazda, Modzelewski,[23] or someone else. . . . The candidate wasn't spelled out but the intention was clear. I was too weak, not "revolutionary" enough in my demands, too soft with the authorities. This proposi-

tion didn't come from Madame Anna alone. Behind it there was a small but influential faction of the free trade unions of the Baltic. Were they right? Only time would tell.[24]

Already the main lines of rhetorical conflict—necessarily somewhat simplified and overdrawn for popular consumption—had begun to emerge. Despite countercharges that Wałęsa was not revolutionary enough and that KOR was too Jacobin, all were moderates in their desire for nonviolence and in not seeking to seize state power. In this sense, the struggle turned less on policy differences than on a personal struggle for power. There was, however, one important policy difference, and that was the issue of national structure.

The national meeting of new trade unions occurred in the Gdańsk Solidarity headquarters in the Seaman's Hotel in Wrzeszcz on September 17. The meeting was held in the Klub Ster (the Rudder Club) on the ground floor of the building. The entire event was open to the public, which massed up against the barred windows on both sides of the long, dilapidated club hall.

The transcription of the taped meeting offers a priceless insight into the extension and growth of the new trade unions across the country, the obstacles they faced, and the barriers placed in their path by police and party officials.[25] Here the subject is the conflict over organization.

According to Wałęsa, the maneuvering behind the scenes began immediately before the meeting between KOR centralizers, represented by Karol Modzelewski, and coastal decentralizers, represented by Gdańsk lawyer Lech Kaczyński. Kaczyński returned from the preconference meeting and announced that "the knives were out."[26] Modzelewski had argued for a centralized structure because, as Wałęsa paraphrased it, "If we did not unite, the government would have unlimited opportunities to manipulate the different unions."[27]

In press announcements, it was said that 34 union organizations took part in the meeting, but they varied greatly in strength and sometimes in principle of organization. Wrocław, Szczecin, and Jastrzębie were interfactory committees organized in August. The speaker from Bydgoscz, Jan Rulewski, said he represented 130 factories. Łódź had had its founding regional meeting September 5, Warsaw on September 10. The region of Kraków had come together September 12, but did not include its principal factory, the giant Lenin Steelworks, which spoke separately and was already engaged in an industrial branch alliance with the Katowice Steelworks rather than a territorial alliance. Similarly, the Scientific and Technical Workers of Poland had just had their founding meeting in Warsaw on September 10 and now had to renounce their occupational-craft organizing principle for the territorial basis. The speaker for Częstochowa represented no one. He reported he had escaped from that city, where repression was fierce. Several others of the 34 represented no more than their factory or a group of factories.

In public, at least, the Gdańsk Presidium presented a united front on the position that there should be many statutes and many unions. To carry the policy, they relied heavily on their organizational control of the meeting. All the other regions wanted to unite with Gdańsk for their own safety. Many of the delegates arriving in Gdańsk came from places and regions that had not had a voice in Poland for decades. They hardly knew each other. The delegate from Krosno on the Wisłoka River introduced himself by adding, "That's in the south of the country where you have the Bieszczady Mountains."[28] The Gdańsk Presidium openly used its organizational prerogative and its great prestige as the founding region to try to control the meeting. The KOR group operated as a political faction that had existed prior to the emergence of Solidarity. Most of the delegates from provincial centers were entirely unaware of this. Jacek Kuroń was not there—he was rumored to be in a nearby hotel—but at the meeting the KOR faction spoke in a prearranged order for their policy of one union and one statute. This was a popular position, because all regions wanted to be associated with Gdańsk.[29] The delegate from Krosno illustrated this by ending his report with the emotional warning, "If we don't unite, they're going to roll right over us. We are for a uniform solidaristic front of the independent self-governing trade union of the entire land. [Applause.]"[30]

The dynamic of the long discussion revolved around the Gdańsk Presidium's effort to prevent the centralization issue from being put on the table and KOR's efforts to overthrow Gdańsk's control. When Zbigniew Bujak of Warsaw-Mazowsze, a KOR spokesman, ended his speech with an appeal, "We have one mission: to gather behind Gdańsk and its statute,"[31] meeting chairman Lech Bądkowski ignored him and quickly passed on to the next speaker. When the next KOR speaker, Stanisław Wróbel of Wałbrzych, returned to the issue of the statute, Wałęsa no longer could restrain himself and replied,

> So we won't keep going round and around these statutes, I'll explain something so that we can be done with it. We propose, we say it openly, everyone can adopt our statute, can adapt it whether as a regional or branch statute. . . . For sure, it would not be good if we submitted one statute, because that's not the way to go. . . . We don't want rubber-stamp unions again, we don't want fusions, we don't want a centrally run union.[32]

Another KOR speaker, Lech Dymarski of Poznań, persisted: "Our members rather expect that there will be one statute for all regions. . . . I just want to emphasize, once again, our members are for unity and for a merger, not merely creation of a consulting committee as some have proposed here."[33]

KOR's program finally was openly put on the table, thanks to the intervention of Bodgan Lis from the Gdańsk Presidium. Instead of reporting on the state of organization in Gdańsk, to the astonishment of Wałęsa and the meeting chairman, he suddenly gave the floor to KOR's Warsaw lawyer: "Now we ask Mr. Olszewski[34] to present a proposition for some kind of common action of all interfactory founding committees in all of Poland." Jan Olszewski promptly appealed "that we apply for registration as an all-Polish structure."[35]

Bądkowski tried to regain control: "Honorable Counsel, please let's not jump ahead of the order of the meeting. This is a question for the coordinating commission. Please don't forget this. Now we're dealing with the second point."[36] Olszewski replied as a practiced lawyer: "Honorable Chairman, I received permission to speak and the subject of my address is a meeting to which I was authorized by my board which authorized me to speak of it." His call for "a national structure [which] would be able to apply for registration in one common act for the whole country"[37] ended in another strangled attempt by Bądkowski to stop him: "Thank you. Two and a half hours have passed by. This is an appropriate time to have a break of around twenty minutes."[38]

But KOR pressed on. Modzelewski now stated the controlling fear of the intellectuals: "If as many unions arise as speakers in this hall presenting the situation in the individual regional committees, then we are finished. Maybe the coast will survive longer, but if they finish us off, they will also finish off the coast. It will be the last to go but inevitably it will fall."[39]

Wałęsa had certainly never read Michels or Piven and Cloward but his counterarguments and fears informed by his twelve years of union struggle are as precise as theirs. "After twelve years of struggling I don't want to lose everything with you because of such a foolish decision. That's what I'm afraid of—the defeat and the ignominy." Wałęsa feared a rapid centralization, in which the government would flood the union and defeat it. "What you'll get are ten government unions and only five which really built themselves up from the rank and file, what we wanted to build." He feared a betrayal of the rank and file by a central leadership. "I fear this defeat because of decisions that are not consulted with the ranks."[40]

As the meeting fell out of his control, Wałęsa proposed that they move into executive session to keep the conflict out of public view. One delegate from every union committee now went upstairs to a small room used by the Gdańsk Presidium. There is no transcription of what was said because tape recorders were not allowed. The closed meeting lasted between one-

and-a-half and two hours, and when the delegates came back, they announced that they had taken two unanimous votes: there would be one national union, Solidarity, and its statute would be that of Gdańsk.

The two unanimous votes were contradictory because Gdańsk's statute, even when articles concerning a national consultative commission and many regions were added, left Solidarity a headless national structure.[41] With this statute the National Consultative Commission existed (when it was in session), but it possessed no permanent executive or secretariat and thus had no ongoing presence. The consultative commission and the chairman had no formal power of decision over regions and locals. Essentially the decentralizers had won. In this manner, Solidarity acquired the decentralized democratic form that effectively governed its actions over the next 500 days of its life.

Supporters of the Wałęsa position at the September meeting—such as Krzysztof Wyszkowski, one of the initiators of free trade unions in Gdańsk—said that after the vote they feared Solidarity was going to be like an enormous water-filled mushroom that would appear practically overnight and then disappear just as quickly in a cloud of dust. Wyszkowski felt that all regions needed to struggle for their union, while those who had free unions handed to them would turn out to be uncommitted members of a hollow structure.[42] His fear proved to be overdrawn, in part because local party officials across Poland came to the rescue by harassing the fledgling unions and thereby forcing local groups to unite and organize against the state.

During the 500 days of Solidarity, successive attempts were made to strengthen the central decision-making bodies of the union. In the first stage, the 1980 Gdańsk Presidium effectively served as part of the central leadership and as a permanent executive. On November 19, 1980, at a national commission meeting in Szczecin, it was decided to create a secretariat in Gdańsk, and also to call a cabinet made up of the strongest regions to prepare the order of business for commission sessions. The cabinet was to consist of representatives from Gdańsk, Szczecin, Jastrzębie, Bydgoszcz, Poznań, Łódź, Warsaw, Lublin, Wrocław, Kraków, and Rzeszów.

On February 12, 1981, by resolution of Wałęsa, the national commission elected a temporary presidium composed of the chairman, Wałęsa, and the two vice chairmen, Andrzej Gwiazda and Ryszard Kalinowski, as well as Zbigniew Bujak of Mazowsze, Tadeusz Jedynak of Jastrzębie, Jan Rulewski of Bydgoszcz, Andrzej Słowik of Łódź, and Stanisław Wądołowski of Szczecin. The secretary of the consultative committee, Andrzej Celiński, and press spokesman Karol Modzelewski frequently participated in the meetings, which took place once or twice a week, but rarely with all members present.[43]

One year later, delegates at the First Solidarity Congress faced the same issues of separation and limitation of powers or centralization. The main proposals for decentralization were (1) to limit the chief executive's power by election of two vice chairmen with powers nearly equal to those of the chairman (everyone knew the chairman would be Wałęsa); (2) to prevent cumulation of posts, so that, for example, Wałęsa could not be chairman of the Gdańsk region and of Solidarity at once; and (3) to have the presidium—an executive body within the national commission—be elected by the national commission. Beyond rejecting these limitations, opponents proposed that the chairman himself should select the presidium (a permanent executive body residing in Gdańsk) from the members of the national commission.

In all three cases, Wałęsa's new goal of a strong, more centralized executive leadership won out a goal in vivid contrast to his previous quest for a decentralized leadership. In the year that had passed, it seemed as if Wałęsa had undergone a dramatic change in his concept of a democratic union. In actuality, however, the union had achieved by 1981 the grass-roots participation throughout the country that on September 17, 1980 was restricted entirely to the Baltic Coast. The danger of being outflanked by government-controlled unions was no longer present.[44] Still, at the time of the proclamation of martial law on December 13, 1981, these organizational changes had not been put into effect.

## Summary

These three steps toward Solidarity's organization—the rediscovery of the sit-down strike, the development of the interfactory committee, and the creation of the national structure—reflect the operative dynamics of the organizing heritage that produced the independent union. The round-the-clock sit-down strike was a rediscovery of a form of industrial struggle with capitalism developed before World War II. The second and almost simultaneous creation of the interfactory strike committee uniting all workplaces against the state is more specific to the struggle with the Communist state. Similar council forms emerged during the 1956 revolution in Hungary, where a national meeting of factory councils was prevented only by the action of the Soviet armies.

The interfactory structure is shaped as an antimodel of the state, spreading horizontal structures where the Leninist state erected hierarchical forms of mobilization and control. The development of this form made great progress in Szczecin in December 1970. This sophisticated structural evolution within the Polish working class far surpassed in general relevance and organizational specifics the central ideas that surfaced in the intellectual opposition between 1976 and 1980. Jan Józef Lipski attempts to be much more specific in outlining KOR's causative role than the other observers cited herein, but even his explanation, it turns out, is vague and general. Lipski considers the Charter of Worker's Rights, published in *Robotnik* 35 (December 1979), to be the key document demonstrating the connection of KOR to workers and Solidarity. But this document does not discuss either the specific or the general aspects of worker's organization that have been the subject here. On the contrary, the charter advises workers to form independent trade unions only "wherever there are strong groups of workers able to defend their representatives." This, of course, was precisely the problem that Polish workers had spent all the years since World War II trying to solve and that the specific organizational breakthroughs on the Baltic Coast in 1970 did solve.[45] One conclusion is inescapable: the organizational building block of Solidarity emerged from a popular tradition specific to industrial workers of the coast, who acquired it and passed it on as part of their bloody heritage from 1970. It was a tradition wholly absent from written accounts and unknown to other classes and strata in Poland, most particularly to the intellectual opposition, which developed with force only after 1976.[46]

The final brick in this edifice—the national structure created on September 17—placed the power in the factories and regions; the national organization was a consultative body. This form, however, served Solidarity's basic purpose. Throughout the life of Solidarity, the state maintained the power to create sudden crisis, whenever it or the security services wanted—in October with the registration crisis, in March at Bydgoszcz, or at any other moment. No permanent executive, however centralized, could have changed the outcome of December 13, 1981, when under martial law, the police and army attacked Solidarity. The organizational advice of Lenin, Weber, and Hobsbawm was not pertinent.

Even though the regime imprisoned 10,000 union activists during martial law, the decentralized structure was able to reconstitute itself within months. In eight years of nonviolent struggle, waves of strike protest would sweep along the organizational leadership just as it had begun to despair. As Lech Wałęsa said to the young striking workers in the Lenin Shipyard as he joined them in May 1988, "I am your general—tell me where you're going and I will lead you."[47] A second wave of strikes that summer ultimately forced the government to share power with Solidarity.

As important as he was, and even given his considerable political talents, Wałęsa was not a charismatic leader leading the movement. Elite thought in contemporary culture is so deep that it comes as a shock to realize that "Wałęsa, the charismatic leader" was a creation of the Western, and especially American, media, doing for Poland what the media routinely does in the United States. This aspect of Wałęsa's leadership is discussed more fully in Chapter Seven. As Gerlach and Hine have observed for social movements in the U.S., "If there is no observable bureaucratic organization, a single charismatic leader or a very small elite is assumed to be controlling the movement."[48]

Further, the organization described here comes rather close to the Gerlach and Hine model of movement organization. Rather than "a well-defined chain of organization which is centrally directed and administered in a pyramidal hierarchal pattern" this organization is "decentralized, segmentary and reticulate."[49] These characteristics were found by Gerlach and Hine in a society and state with civil rights and alternate power bases quite dissimilar to Poland's, yet the characteristics were also present in Solidarity. The element of national liberation against an elite perceived as serving a foreign power, which was also a universal employer, gave the movement more natural cohesion, and also gave more power to the national coordinating commission in crisis than one would have expected given the structure.

# Solidarity at the Grass Roots

WHY DID a tradition of workers' resistance develop in the shipyards of the Baltic Coast? Why were the same shipyards the leading force in 1970 and 1980? In 1970, the government's price increase and Gomułka's campaign of "voluntary compulsion" were catalysts for insurgency, but the same causes applied to the whole of Poland, not just to the Baltic Coast. Other Polish industries, such as aviation, were threatened with closure by Gomułka's plan for selective development, but their workers did not revolt. What factors, sociological or otherwise, account for the coast's unique climate of self-assertion? Two general areas merit investigation: first, the objective characteristics of the workers—their age, sex, education, family structure, social origin, associations, and living conditions; and second, the objective circumstances of the workplace—the type of industry, whether it produces for export or national markets, the division of labor, and the relations between workers and their party superiors.[1]

## Characteristics of the Baltic Coast Workers

### Peasant Migrants or Old Working Class

The regional history of coastal workers has received some comment but almost no sustained study. Various sociological factors seem to bear upon this history, and interpreters have a wide choice of possible influences: the presence of immigrants from Poland's *kresy*, or eastern borderlands, with their wounded national pride and their keen sense of Soviet domination; or, in contrast, the greater openness to the world (which presents the opportunity to make comparison) of a coastal region engaged in worldwide fishing, shipping, trading, and shipbuilding; or perhaps the special quality of a new territory—a frontier region settled by rural migrants like Lech Wałęsa, seeking a new life after 1945 in the former German territories. So many of the leaders of 1970 and 1980 were migrant peasants who had found work in the shipyards that it became a widely held stereotype. There are two diametrically opposed theories that draw attention to workers' peasant origins to explain their radicalism or quiescence. One side argues that workers are likely to become politically active only after the first generation of uprooted peasants is succeeded by generations of workers who have had time to develop traditions and institutions. Thus, Zygmunt Bauman explained the Polish workers' apathy in

1968 by "the immaturity and lack of clear political aims of the working class, the majority of which had only recently left rural areas and culturally still belonged to the peasantry."[2] Suggested here is that workers who have recently arrived in the cities will compare their new situation to the even harsher conditions they left behind and remain politically quiescent.

But the same fact can be used to arrive at the opposite conclusion. In 1980 in the coal-mining areas of Silesia, it was not the old established miners with working-class traditions going back over generations who struck, but the new mining area of Jastrzębie, developed with miners recruited in rural hinterlands. It was these new workers who sparked and led the strikes and brought the Polish coal miners into Solidarity.

More systematically, Leon Trotsky postulated that uprooted peasants thrown into factories were more likely to be radical than second- and third-generation workers because they were "without any artisanal past, without craft traditions or prejudices."[3] In other words, they were like blank slates influenced above all by conditions in the factories where they worked.

It seems more likely that when uprooted peasants would come to work in factories, they would arrive with a political tradition favorable or unfavorable to radical industrial action rather than without any political memory at all. The key factor in the peasants' political behavior is likely to be not their social dislocation, but the political tradition they brought with them to the factories. Thus in Catalonia in the twentieth century, members of the radical working class had arrived already possessing an anarchist allegiance from their villages.[4] In Poland, many children of peasant farmers arriving in the shipyards had vivid memories of the intense civil war against the Communists that broke out in many parts of rural Poland after World War II. That civil strife was followed by the state's unsuccessful war on the peasantry during its drive to collectivize, which collapsed in 1956.

In spite of its fragmentary nature, some interesting facts emerge from the sociological background of the coast. Although Poland had an established working class before World War II, the coastal working class is very much the product of migration from eastern and central rural Poland to the new industries in Gdańsk and Szczecin. In Szczecin by 1950, the larger part of the workers (26 percent) came from the most backward, most rural parts of Poland, regions such as Kielce, Rzeszów, and Lublin. Another large group (26 percent) came from the areas annexed by the U.S.S.R. The rest was essentially made up of rural migrants from central Poland. It was thus an overwhelmingly rural migration.[5]

By 1970, the stereotype of the shipyard worker as a peasant who had migrated to the coast to find work was not, statistically speaking, accurate. The massive migrations from the countryside had come to an end, and younger workers were increasingly the children of other workers. In Warski, for example, 68 percent of the manual industrial workers were from worker families, 26 percent were from the peasantry, and 8 percent were from white-collar families.[6]

Still another study in the Lenin Shipyard surveyed 245 students of the shipyard vocational school, all preparing for industrial manual work. Students of these schools seem to have been especially active in the 1970 street fighting. In the Lenin school, 72 percent (176 students) came from worker families; 16 percent (38) from white-collar families; and 13 percent (31) from peasant families. Eighteen percent (45) had relatives in the shipyard. Thirty-five percent (86) had been born and raised in the Gdańsk metropolitan area.[7]

*Job Turnover and the "Flyers"*

The dispute over the radical potential of the established working class versus that of the peasant migrants shades into a concept of social dislocation. Party journalists Dariusz Fikus and Jerzy Urban in February 1971 announced with some flourish their discovery that many of those most active in Szczecin in 1970 were uprooted social isolates or "flyers"—flotsam recently arrived from the countryside, living in workers' dormitories, disoriented, with little or no connection to work and society.[8] Gomułka went one step further and claimed that the shipyards served as dumping grounds for ex-convicts and criminals.[9]

Here it becomes important to make distinctions between the work forces on the coast. In all the shipyards, both highly skilled workers (such as the tool-and-die machinists of engines) with long work stages and relatively unskilled workers with short work stages played leading roles. The shipyards had a high work-force turnover, but it was concentrated among young new workers. Only one in every seven workers survived the first year of employment, when they were frequently pushed into the most unpleasant, dangerous, and low-paying jobs. In a study of 500 people leaving the Lenin Shipyard, 208, or 42 percent, worked in the hulls divisions.[10] Lech Wałęsa, in his vivid description of the shipyards, calls the hull workers and metal workers of W-1 "pariahs" doing work in conditions of forced labor.[11] An aggregate finding for all the shipyards in the Gdańsk area in 1979 found that 30 percent of all workers in direct production left their jobs in the course of a year,[12] but turnover was concentrated among new workers. Most workers had long work stages and were quite stable in their work situation. Comparatively speaking, this is not high turnover. The turnover in the American automobile industry in the 1920s was between 200 and 300 percent a year. It was new migrants from the countryside who worked in Fisher Body nos. 1 and 2 that joined the strikes in Flint, Michigan that unionized General Motors in 1936, while older, more established workers in the Buick plants and women in the AC Spark Plug Plant were so unresponsive that no attempt was made to call them out.[13]

## Age and Sex

Three other characteristics of the shipyard workers—their age, their gender, and the absence of peasant workers—stand out. At the end of the sixties, Poland was near the high point of the postwar demographic bulge. The postwar generation had entered the work force. "More than 50 percent of all workers were less than 29 years old. Two-thirds were under 40."[14] Most of the workers thus had joined the workforce and entered political life after 1956 and, as a generation, had not endured either the war or Stalinism—events that had a demobilizing effect on their predecessors. Although 40 percent of all workers in Poland were women, this percentage was much lower in shipbuilding. At that time, 18 percent of the Warski Shipyard work force were women.[15] Not all of these were in administrative posts; an equal number worked in some of the most ill-paid and onerous physical tasks, such as the cleaning of ships and hulls. But most were discouraged by male workers or chose not to take part in the strikes.

One of the most significant facts about the shipyards' work force is that it was a massive concentration of young workers. This conforms to Marx's thesis that an elaborate division of labor and high concentration of workers would lead to the development of political consciousness.[16] In Poland, workers in the largest factories have been in the vanguard of resistance. The Lenin Shipyard in the 1970s employed about 16,000 people. Of these, some 70 percent were workers, while another 20 percent were engineering and technical personnel. The Warski Shipyard at the end of 1969 had 7,850 manual workers, almost 80 percent of all the employees.[17] Moreover, these large concentrations of male workers tended to be young and unmarried. In 1969, 48 percent of all employees in Warski were single; an additional 14 percent were married with no children.[18] Both single and married workers faced difficult housing conditions. For the past twenty years, Poland has been at the bottom of the list in housing conditions—not only for socialist countries but for twenty-five European countries. As bad as housing conditions were in 1970, they are much worse today, with waiting periods of twenty years. In a 1972 survey of worker opinions about working and living conditions in the Lenin Shipyard, housing led by far in the list of difficulties in daily life. Thirty-six percent named it as their major life problem, compared with the 19 percent who named either health or income. Some 46 percent of those questioned in the sample did not live in their own apartment or house.[19] In 1970, more than 2,000 workers out of a total work force of 10,000 in

Warski lived in rented rooms, usually several to a room. Hundreds more lived in shipyard dormitories.[20] A full quarter of the work force was on a waiting list for housing in 1972. [21] As a Lenin Shipyard worker expressed it, "There's no future here. To receive an apartment you have to wait ten years. A man grows old, he wants to marry."[22] These young workers with short work stages played a major role in the coastal protests.

### Broken Ties to the Countryside

There was one final important difference between the working class on the coast and workers in the rest of Poland. A large percentage—nearly 20 percent—of the industrial work force in the entire country simultaneously worked a farm; hence the term "peasant-workers." Their situation approximated that of many women industrial workers in that they were underpaid, overworked, and often functioned as labor reserves in the most unsuited posts. In times of economic crisis, they could fall back on their farms for subsistence. This group is almost impossible to mobilize because of its long commute times and double workloads.[23] The Baltic Coast was exceptional because of its high urbanization and low percentage of private peasant farmers in the suburbs and hinterlands. Because the state had taken over the formerly German lands, collective and state farms predominated in the coastal region. Even if they had peasant roots in eastern or central Poland, the workers in the shipyards were too far away from their home villages to preserve a working connection with the land. In times of economic crisis, shipyard workers were unable to supplement their salaries with extra work on the farm.

Hence the fate of these workers was directly tied to the factory. This characteristic clearly differentiates the coast from the rest of the Polish workers. Again the elementary social fact needs to be emphasized. In Western economies, the percentage of the industrial manual workers continues to decline year by year with technological changes (below 20 percent in America). In Poland and the Soviet Union and the other countries of Eastern Europe, this social category is occupied by half or more of all employees and is a major feature of the social and political landscape.[24] Industrial workers are numerous, and in terms of political geography, they were exceptionally well placed on the coast.

## Characteristics of the Baltic Coast Workplaces

The three shipyards, Lenin, Paris Commune, and Warski, dominate the industrial and political centers of Gdańsk, Gdynia, and Szczecin. Only a few hundred yards away from each workplace are the centers of state power: the party headquarters, the police station, the jail, the city hall, the trade union offices. This spatial arrangement is reminiscent of Paris in the eighteenth and nineteenth centuries, one very favorable to popular protest because the populace can issue from its neighborhoods or factories and attack the Communist equivalents of the Bastille.

## An Export Industry

What the shipyards produced and for whom also seems to have played an important role in workers' radicalism. All three shipyards were engaged in producing for the export market. By 1970, Poland occupied tenth place in the world in tonnage of ships produced, but it was second in production of fishing vessels and fifth in foreign sales of ships. Most of Poland's production was for export, and most was sold to the Soviet Union.[25] This was the crucial fact that linked the labor question and the political question. Shipyard workers firmly believed that the ships were produced for the Soviet Union under contracts that were exploitative. According to universal consensus, the Polish shipyard industry was forced to buy many ship components with hard currency, but it was repaid in rubles. This view was asserted by the work force, and it formed the political context for the work in the shipyard.[26]

## The Organization of Production and Class Solidarity

As an export industry subject to international competition, shipbuilding necessarily involved frequent and close contact with foreign contractors, many of whom maintained representatives in the shipyards. Occasionally, foreign contractors came to carry out specialized tasks. The shipyard work force routinely made invidious comparisons between the shipyard's own anarchic organization of work and managerial incompetence and the rationalized, orderly methods of Western technicians.

Not only were the inexperienced and unskilled younger workers mobilized in 1970 and 1980, but also the best paid and most highly skilled workers—the tool-and-die machinists of the prestigious "S" shops. To understand this phenomenon, it is necessary to shift focus from the social characteristics of the work force to the subtleties of the work process itself—the division of labor within the shipyard and the functioning system of authority. With a worker spending most of his or her active life within the factory, it makes sense that the character of work, as well as social and political relations within the factory, might be a major determinant of workers' attitudes.

The Gdańsk and Szczecin shipyards were rebuilt from greatly damaged German shipyards. In spite of extensive investment and rebuilding, their technological level and organization had not changed significantly over the years. This problem was particularly acute in the Lenin Shipyard and somewhat less so in Warski, while the Paris Commune Shipyard, which had been extensively rebuilt after the war, was the most modern in technology and organization.

Thus all the Polish shipyards are distinguished by a low level of modernization. In 1970, for example, 60 percent of welding in U.S.S.R. and G.D.R. shipyards was done with modern methods of machine welding, while Poland continued hand welding.[27] Capital investment in Poland was extensive rather than intensive, even by socialist standards. Gomułka ran down capital stock hoping to close the shipyards in the 1960s. In spite of heavy investment in the Gierek era, the shipyards have remained technologically backward. Because of rising technolgical requirements and increasing competition from new producers such as Korea and Japan, Poland's shipbuilding industry was already in decline in 1970. As an example of one of many limiting factors, the Baltic Sea is too shallow to allow passage of the enormous ships to which the entire world industry was rapidly turning.

In the work process itself, there are again some suggestive, though far from conclusive, characteristics. Much shipyard work—70 to 80 percent—can be defined as artisanal and relatively highly skilled in character. Thus a highly qualified work force is required. Some welders could become fully competent after three months, others only after three years, but full competence in many of the direct and indirect production posts could take five to eight years.[28]

In terms of job safety, shipyard work is comparable to work in metal foundries or mines. Many workers were required to carry out complex tasks on temporary scaffolding on ships under construction in all seasons. Tools and power sources, gas and electricity lines, heavy machinery and parts constantly being moved from place to place characterized the workplace. At the same time, the requirements of "storming"—rushing to fill an order or quota at the end of the month, quarter, or year—routinely increased the danger on the job. The work operations additionally created high noise, dust, and chemical concentrations and constant danger of fire. Seventy percent of the work in the Lenin Shipyard was conducted in the open air, irrespective of the weather.

As in most socialist countries (China is an exception), workers in Poland were paid by piecework rather than with a daily wage. Foremen and managers enjoyed considerable discretion in allocation of desirable and undesirable work. Managers, foremen, and political officers also controlled bonuses and other kinds of premiums that were distributed as various objectives reached fulfillment. As a result, the piecework system pitted ordinary workers against the foremen and managers and also pushed them to enter self-protective cliques and combinations—often of the veteran workers against the young.[29] As a carpenter put it, "It's possible to earn good money in the shipyard, but a young man can't."[30] Although this situation would seem likely to split the work force into clientelist vertical arrangements, personal accounts do not show this to have been the case.

The industry had gone through a period of enormous growth since the end of the war; but by 1970 it was marked for closing by rational technical criteria. The relatively highly skilled, well-paid workers of the shipyards fought back, but their struggle was linked with their status as an integral part of the Soviet defense industry, and their understanding of the way their labor was exploited by the Soviet Union made their labor protest against the closing of a rust-belt industry inexorably become a patriotic act.

In the system here described, social relations were established through face-to-face contacts among workmates. The breakfast and lunch breaks held crucial roles in communication. These were the times when work crews came together, and exchanged opinions on issues, and made decisions. In a socialist situation, social spaces such as cafes and bars are greatly lacking. The few such places that existed were monitored by police informers. The workplace and the apartment offered quasi-public spaces.[31]

## The Managers and the Work Force

Shipbuilding was dependent on a vast network of cooperation from other firms, many of them located in the surrounding area, but the "plan" was incredibly inefficient and uncoordinated, a situation that gained no respect for the state's administration. By the shipyard management's own estimates, 40 to 60 hours of every worker's monthly work time was routinely spent looking for or waiting for materials, parts, and tools. The shipyard was a traffic jam of workers searching and bargaining for needed materials. This created a compensatory impulse to hoard materials in order to be able to continue working. Complaints about the organization and distribution of work by top managers were universal. As one worker put it, "The work is so badly organized, they don't even have our time cards."[32] Again, a characteristic of the system was its inefficiency. Capitalists may be exploitative, but they will punctiliously provide and watch the time cards.

The relations between veteran workers and shop-floor foremen were relatively good, for they shared professional perceptions about the source of inefficiency, namely the general organization and management rather than each other. Workers complained about the mindless rushing to fulfill the production plan without proper organization and sufficient supplies. The piecework system meant that bad organization and managerial incompetence cut workers' pay. Management here was so bad that work was being completed and then ripped out several times.[33] One Warski worker complained, "We wear out the shipyard's paths in search for work—wasting our time, for which we're not paid, which is unproductive."[34] Respondents to shipyard industrial surveys most often described their work as "difficult" (89 percent) and "tense" (80 percent). An extremely high evaluation (89 percent) was made of relations with workmates, however. This suggests loyalty to the work team in spite of, or possibly because of, harsh working conditions.[35] Blame was pinned on those in charge, while the difficult working conditions and the need for cooperation bred workers' solidarity.[36]

Underlying all these issues was a profound sense of futility, a sense that one was wasting time and energy and, eventually, life itself. Although shipyard workers were among the most highly paid industrial workers in the country, they achieved this status only through enormous amounts of overtime. It was not unusual for more than 80 percent of the work force to be engaged in overtime. A worker from Wałęsa's shop in the Lenin Shipyard described his ten years under Gierek: "I worked 12 hours a day or an extra half month every month. I earned 15,000 to 16,000 thousand złoty monthly on the average. But I believe that work like that is senseless. I never ate dinner at home. I saw my children on Sundays and holidays. In the end, I had nothing, and Poland is still poverty-stricken."[37]

In spite of promises by Gierek and the temporary elimination of Saturday work by Solidarity, Poland continued on a six-day week throughout the 1970s and 1980s, while the U.S.S.R. had been on a five-day week since 1967. Only Romania and Albania kept pace with Poland. An embittered Szczecin worker summarized matters: "We work 25 years in our trade, but after those 25 years we are like grandfathers no matter what our age."[38] It seemed that work in the shipyard was not only badly paid; in the workers' eyes it was hostile to or did not further marriage, family, even life itself.

In a monolithically structured command economy, with no buffers of capitalist owners, management, labor unions, or other associations between the state and the workers, everything economic and social was also political. This had the effect of dramatizing the party's responsibility for the plight of the workplace. Existing work conditions, of course, clashed with socialist equality propaganda. Because equality was preached by hypocrites, workers who were harassed by campaigns to limit overtime as they struggled to make ends meet became increasingly resentful. Meanwhile, workers saw managerial personnel doing very well, even though on paper their remuneration was relatively low. In Gdańsk, a party investigation of complaints about the shipyard's management essentially confirmed the rumors rampant among workers about the earnings premiums and bonuses enjoyed by the bosses. Nothing was done to redress the inequity, however. As the Gomułka reforms tried to make workers work harder while telling them they were lazy, pay fell for about a third of the work force, even as the pay of the management and directors of the Warski and Lenin Shipyards rose 25 percent.[39] In the following decade, the

Gierek loan-driven economy not only pushed differentiation between workers and bosses to new levels of inequality, but also made that inequality more visible.

## The Party in the Workplace

The Polish United Workers' Party systematically created the objective conditions for the revolt of the working class. Perhaps the most ominous social truth was that even the party's own members were alienated. The mass party organizations in the Baltic shipyards melted away in a matter of hours in December 1970. The sudden disappearance of the party machine prompted Politburo member Kliszko to hint broadly in 1971 at a "conspiracy" to undermine Gomułka.[40] But Kliszko was engaged in a futile attempt to justify his own role in the coastal massacre. A party study of the social and political organizations in the Lenin Shipyard reveals varying stages of decomposition over a 40-year period.

Even before the 1948 fusion of the Polish Socialist Party and the Polish Workers' Party into the Polish United Workers' Party—the shipyard organization—the basic institution of centralized control was characterized as "infiltrated by many persons alien to the working class, by careerists, and persons of low morals."[41] Under the direction of higher authorities, the party committees of both parties carried out a verification of their members, but the official party historian ingenuously noted that it did not achieve the hoped-for result because it was carried out very superficially. In 1945–46, the party was unable to correct the shipyard problems, partly because of the introduction, the party conceded, "of an autocratic style of management of the shipyard by the shipyard party committee which copied the style of the central party leadership."[42] When the Stalinist period ended in 1956, Gomułka characterized Stalinism as a system "violating principles of democracy and justice. It was a system which destroyed human conscience and character. It squashed people, it humiliated their human dignity and honor. Swindles, lies and falsehoods, and even provocations served as instruments of rule."[43] In 1956, the party organization in the Lenin Shipyard was described as being in a crisis situation. The trade union fared no better. Described in 1956 as "a bureaucratized instrument for mobilizing people to heavy work," the trade union in the shipyard did not change significantly over the next decades.[44] Though 98 percent of the shipyard officials were union members in the 1960s, party sources admitted that the trade union became steadily more "powerless" and less effective. "There was a growing disapproval of the party's action for its conscious restriction of the range and competence of the union [and] a sharpening criticism of the union for its spinelessness in the face of the shipyard's political and management authorities."[45] Attempts to resuscitate the party failed abysmally. Although by 1970 its membership stood at more than 3,000—20 percent of the work force—the party chronicles sourly noted that "In its ranks were to be found people not having much in common with the party's ideology, persons who had entered the party thanks to the overenthusiastic activists of some shop organization."[46] In the party's own account, the shipyard union was a prisoner of the shipyard party apparatus, while the apparatus itself served as a powerless instrument of highly centralized power in Warsaw.

## CHAPTER SEVEN

# Sacred Politics

THE WORKERS' strikes in 1970 and Solidarity are connected by four elements: personnel, program, organization, and a local tradition of resistance. This local tradition, with its own songs, poetry, satire, heroes, and legends, lived on beneath the carapace of official People's Poland,[1] and was possibly the most important of the four elements. It crystallized during the strikes in a kind of revolutionary mass performed by workers with the bodies of their slain mates in the rubble in front of the Lenin Shipyard on December 16, and in the processions with the dead in Gdynia on December 17.

The Gdańsk May Day parade in 1971 was dominated by two banners: one demanding the punishment of those guilty for the 1970 killings, and another seeking a plaque to commemorate the dead. The marchers' path on that May Day wound past the state dignitaries at party headquarters to the shipyard wall, where Lenin Shipyard workers had been killed on the morning of December 16. Some workers kneeled at the wall as they deposited wreaths of flowers; others reached out to touch the wall, as if to promise to keep faith with the dead (Ill. 2).[2] These symbolic actions contained a historically grounded aspiration to a "sacred politics" that uniquely combined the European socialist tradition with nationalism. This it accomplished through its eschatology of a martyred proletarian and his imminent resurrection and triumph. It was sacred politics that was to connect 1980 to 1970.

While striking in August 1980, Poles performed ritual acts and created symbolic objects to express their situation. These icons, "ideas that had achieved concrete expression,"[3] offer an entry into the popular ideology of the movement not only as self-expression, but also as a means of communication that transmits the most important facts about the movement to its adherents and opponents.

In spite of considerable theoretical interest in the political significance of symbols, relatively little empirical work has been done. This chapter aims to examine the Polish trade union Solidarity along this neglected symbolic dimension. It sets aside investigation of the movement by more traditional methods, such as analysis of organization (Chapter Five) or program (Chapter Eight), in an attempt to analyze Solidarity through its most widespread, most popular self-definitions—its rituals and symbols. Instead of the classic questions of political discourse—"Who gets what,

**2.** At the wall of the Gdańsk Lenin Shipyard, May 1, 1971

how, when, and where?"—the questions posed here are "What do they want?" "Why do they fear?" "What do they regard as possible?" and even "Who they are?"[4] In this approach, ritual and symbolism become "modes of exercising or seeking to exercise power along the cognitive dimension." They are a "mobilization of bias," a way of being in the world.[5] Solidarity's symbols are analyzed along four dimensions: (1) Who belonged and who potentially belonged to the movement? Who was excluded? What were the ethnic, religious, and political boundaries of membership? To put it sharply—was Solidarity a nationalist movement? (2) What were Solidarity's internal arrangements? Was it a solidaristic total movement? An undifferentiated mass movement? (3) Did Solidarity have charismatic leadership? What was the relation of its leaders to ordinary members, what did this show about its politics or its democracy? (4) How did the movement carry on symbolic warfare with its opponents? How developed was the process of attack, or depletion of the enemy's symbols and rituals?[6]

At this level, the analysis is of popular mentality. In order to explain the movement's dynamism, the strikes are examined using categories derived from anthropological studies of rites of passage.[7] In this view, the

strikes were the moments of creation of most of Solidarity's symbols and
rituals. They were periods of separation and transition engendering new
social, cultural, and political forms.[8] For the strikers, they were life decisions for purification and revitalization, decisions for new lives. In the
schema of the anthropologist Victor Turner, they belong to the category
of human behavior he calls a "primary process," which

> erupts from the cumulative experience of whole peoples whose deepest mate-
> rial and spiritual needs and wants have for long been denied by power-building
> elites, who operate in a manner analogous to that of Freud's censorship in
> psychological systems. . . . A whole hidden cultural structure richly clothed in
> symbols may be suddenly revealed and become itself both model and stimulus
> for new, fruitful developments in law and in administration, as well as arts and
> sciences.[9]

The sacred politics of Solidarity is most striking for its reunification of
the European revolutionary tradition, which was formed during the
French Revolution and then divided in the first half of the nineteenth century into two separate strands—national insurrection and social revolution. The first strand emphasized fraternity, the second equality; the first
emphasized nation, the second universal social revolution. As both traditions developed, they increasingly left out the third element of the French
revolutionary call to arms—liberty.[10]

In Solidarity's new synthesis, the two strands are united, but distin-
guishable. First, there is a current of national insurrection couched in
categories of national captivity, suffering, and ultimate liberation. It em-
phasizes the solidarity of all Poles against their foreign oppressors. It continues the national myth, the political religion elaborated by the nineteenth-century Messianic poets—Poland, like Christ, will die, be buried,
and be resurrected. It is religious in form, nationalist in content. According to the Polish dramatist Gombrowicz's twentieth-century assessment,
"For the Poles, God is a pistol aimed at Karl Marx."[11]

The second current of universal social revolution is derived from the
European Socialist tradition. Its symbols are social rather than national—
workers versus the state, the power of the weak and oppressed against the
strong, the solidarity of all workers and peasants, equality against privilege and hierarchy, direct democracy against democratic centralism.

Solidarity has usually been assumed to be simply a nationalist movement, its symbolism merely a continuation of nineteenth-century prewar
tradition. Such an analysis misses the innovative quality of Solidarity—
the extent to which the dominant symbols were invented during the
strikes, and the degree to which dominant symbols and rituals were lifted
from nationalist and socialist tradition and transformed.[12]

## The Context of Organization and Communication

Several considerations heightened the importance of symbols in the rise of Solidarity and diminished the importance of formal organization, communication, and politics.

Solidarity was a movement that grew from three members of the Founding Committee of the Free Trade Unions of the Coast on August 14, to about 10 million members by the registration struggles in early November. Structurally, Solidarity was a federation of regions and factories. The activities of the "decision-making centers" and their programmatic statements give an important but limited understanding of the movement.

During the sixteen months of Solidarity, the importance of the written word was diminished by government control of the mass media, which was maintained, however imperfectly, to the very end. Government control was more successful in the first months. It was most stringent on television and radio but ceded ground to Solidarity bulletins, newspapers, journals, and books. Although its list of serial titles reached 2,000 by December 13, 1981,[13] the movement was hampered more by government control of paper and printing machines than by censorship or police harassment. For sixteen months, the movement had neither a daily newspaper nor access to radio or television. It did benefit from the daily programs of foreign radio stations, particularly Radio Free Europe and the BBC.

As Solidarity organized under an information blackout, preexisting networks, which were converted for the occasion into union-organizing centers, also became very important. In many provinces, these were made up of KOR activists and sympathizers, the clubs of Catholic intellectuals, or rectories of activist clergy.

In the beginning, Solidarity was a movement of the spoken word—spoken at thousands of strike and organizational meetings, where workers sized up one another and voted. At every meeting, whether local, regional, or national, delegates would record what was said on tape. They would stand in crowds for hours with their recorders in the air. Later, the cassettes would be circulated and copied like expanding chain letters. As first steps in organizing the union, strikers would seize control of factory public-address systems. In their demands they would ask for regular access to the public-address system, the factory information boards, and the telex. Immediately the tapes of union meetings, songs, and resolutions were played over factory loudspeakers.

In the first months, with virtually no press, and with an information blackout in the mass media, the workplace telex was of enormous importance. It linked the union local with the entire country and was less easily tapped or cut off than the phone lines. Solidarity locals ingeniously inserted carbons under a single teletype paper to obtain multiple copies. One plant, having obtained crucial news, would pass it on in prearranged circuits of teletype machines—each with carbons set to obtain multiple copies to post on bulletin boards—thus bypassing the government's lines of communication.

A further type of communication was rumor. Although downplayed by intellectuals, it gave an emotional edge to the conflict. Apart from the many rumors of war and invasion, there was a nearly universal popular belief that the regime was smuggling the food and wealth of the country to the U.S.S.R. For the *lud* (the people), the Lublin strikes in 1980 were said to have begun when a railway man stole a barrel of tar from a train on its way to the U.S.S.R. When he opened it, the rumor held that he found the finest Polish ham. In the Gdańsk region, the people spoke of the continuous air bridge of helicopters between the local military airports and Kaliningrad in the U.S.S.R., which by dead of night delivered Polish wealth to the Soviets.[14]

Very powerful in their emotional and explanatory content, rumors identified the problem and the source of daily misery and constituted the fundamental myths of the state's illegitimacy. Through rumors, people strove to explain why, after decades of hard work with no war or natural catastrophes, there were nearly universal shortages and a corresponding fear of dearth. Whatever the truth of the details—Was there an air bridge between the air bases at Pruszcz and Kaliningrad? Were there vast secret food stores? Did a Lublin railway worker really find ham in a tar barrel in July 1980?—the rumors were metaphoric summations of the Polish state's subordination in the Soviet empire and the ruling party's concomitant illegitimacy.[15]

## The Strike as Political Ritual and Symbol

The strike was the fundamental symbolic action. It was the moment of creation, the place where good and bad were defined. Its universal symbol was the factory gate decorated with flowers and symbols. In August 1980, at the Lenin Shipyard gate, above the wooden cross, the portraits of the pope, the Black Madonna of Częstochowa, and the crowned White Eagle, flew a banner saying "Workers of all factories, unite!" Marginal persons disdained by the state's hierarchy were accepted as their true leaders. An unemployed electrician, Lech Wałęsa, fired from the Lenin Shipyard years before, climbed in over the fence to become chief of the shipyard. In the Paris Commune Shipyard, a young worker, Andrzej

Kołodziej, who began work the day before the strike, was acclaimed chief by the 8,500-person work force. At the Katowice Steelworks, workers searched out an isolated and persecuted activist, Kazimierz Świtoń, and spirited him back so that he would show them how to strike.

During the strikes, workers separated themselves from their political, economic, and familial structures. The factories and workplaces were walled off from outsiders, including the workers' families and the state. General orders for abstinence from liquor were issued to the entire society by the strikers and were accepted in a kind of ritual fasting, purification, and retreat analogous to a religious ritual.

The neophyte strikers developed "an intense comradeship and egalitarianism."[16] Polish society before Solidarity had expressed resistance of daily degradation by holding to elaborate prewar codes of courtesy—kissing women's hands or using intricate forms of address, *Pan,* Pani (Lord, Lady). The strikers abandoned the formal *Pan* and *Pani* for the familiar *ty* for anyone who was a member of the movement. This universal *tutoiement* seems to be a common feature of the euphoric liberation stage of social movements, and is found in the French Revolution and in the early stages of the Spanish Civil War.[17]

Victor Turner notes that "as [the strikers] share common trials and eat and sleep in common, a group unity is experienced, a kind of generic bond outside the constraints of social structure."[18] From a mode of structure involving jural, political, and economic positions, offices, statuses, and roles, the strikers entered into a direct, spontaneous, and egalitarian mode of social relationship, "a bond uniting people over and above any formal social bonds."[19] Their "behavior and symbolism were momentarily enfranchised from the norms and values that govern the public lives of incumbents of structural position."[20] From a situation of multiple personas and social compromise, "they engage[d] in mutual honesty."[21] They opened a period of "scrutinization of the central values and axioms of the culture"[22] in which they lived: "a period of direct human bonds unusually propitious for the generation of new symbols and structures."[23] Ethical categories are so pervasive in firsthand accounts of the strikes that they make it very difficult to fully distinguish categories of religion, culture, and politics. In the accounts, the role of the state as psychological censor emerges very clearly.

In these conditions, political conversion blended into psychological transformation. A dramatic example was Zdzisław Markiewicz, the first party secretary of a factory near Gdańsk. He had been a delegate to the last Party Congress. Now, under the emotion of the August strike wave where "people opened their lips and sincerely began to say what they had been forbidden to say before," he got up before the workers of his factory and bore witness how he had not been allowed to speak the truth at the Party Congress. He then kissed the cross before them as a pledge that he would remain true.[24]

For a Gdańsk dockworker, the August strike showed "how simple people had preserved their child's faith in the victory of good over evil."[25] A strike delegate from the Silesian town of Żywiec commented that Solidarity was not a union or a political party. "We are a movement of truth. We can be described this way. This is a very important factor which people instinctively understand. . . ."[26]

For millions of people, joining the union was the occasion for tapping unrealized reservoirs of energy, enthusiasm, and creativity. This can be described psychologically as a falling away of personas and masks. In deciding whether to join, a worker chose whether to strive or to leave and go home. It was the choice of a way of life—a manner of being a man or woman—which explains why candidates for union office would proudly specify the day they had joined the union as the day they struck. For many people that day was as important in their lives as their birthdays. It marked a rite of passage; and one year after the 1980 summer strikes, union locals all over the country commemorated their strikes with monuments, tablets, or other observances.

During the strikes, individuals rejected social masks. Systems of structure and nomenclature collapsed as workers took control of factories. As they did so, the workers resolved internal contradictions formed because of the pressure of the censor-state. The Leninist state demands at least an appearance of unity of internal beliefs and external behavior. Daily life in a Leninist state implies that everyone must wear different masks in different situations, vote in elections for single lists, remain silent in cafes or when watching the evening news, pay bribes or accept them to survive. The people pragmatically accept what they have no power to change. The necessity for multiple masks and different truths generates internal psychological conflict. In the Solidarity rite of passage, the dissonance between the *pays réel* and the *pays irréel* disappeared. People stopped pretending. Revolution in Leninist societies adds a fourth term to the French Revolution's Liberty, Equality, Fraternity—the Polish *Godność*, which can be translated as "dignity, self-esteem, honor."

## The Emblem SOLIDARNOŚĆ

The universal symbol of the union shared by four major iconographic media—monuments, posters, flags, and badges—was the distinctive SOLIDARNOŚĆ in red letters on a white field, suggesting a marching crowd (Ill. 3). It was created during the August 1980 strike in the Gdańsk shipyard. The title SOLIDARNOŚĆ had been given to the bulletin of the striking

**3.** The SOLIDARNOŚĆ

workers by its editor Krzysztof Wyszkowski, a founding member of the Free Trade Unions of the Baltic (the predecessor of Solidarity). The lettering was designed by a 29-year-old Gdańsk artist, Jerzy Janiszewski, who later joined the strike. He volunteered to aid the bulletin and then thought he could help the strikers by creating a graphic "ordering their emotions."

> I saw how Solidarity appeared among the people, how a social movement was being born. I chose the word [SOLIDARNOŚĆ] because it best described what was happening to people. The concept came out of the similarity to people in the dense crowds leaning on one another—that was characteristic of the crowds in front of the gate. They didn't press or push each other, but they leaned on each other, neither standing by themselves nor falling on others. . . . Finally, I added the flag because I was aware that this is not a regional or group questions, but a universal rising. The letters have a disordered look because that is their strike attribute.[27]

Polish uprisings in the eighteenth, nineteenth, and twentieth centuries adopted the White Eagle or Black Madonna as their signs. Both symbols were culturally limited to Polish lands. Worse, as symbols of identity and sovereignty for Poles, they were signs of resurgent Polish imperialism for Poland's neighbors—particularly the Lithuanians, Belorussians, Ukrainians, and Russians. By adopting SOLIDARNOŚĆ as their emblem, the Gdańsk strikers gave the movement political and cultural resonance through-out the bloc. The badge suggested the national colors, but also the red of social revolt, and the graphic evoked a message of universal revolution. The Madonna in her shrine on the Shining Mountain remained the master symbol of Polish national consciousness. So with the successful conclusion of the August 1980 strike, Lech Wałęsa traveled to the Madonna's shrine and swore an oath: "With a feeling of responsibility for the fate of our fatherland, I repeat the words of the primate, I stake my all on Mary! Madonna, I place not only myself but all Poland into your care. . . . Into your special maternal care, I entrust the independent self-governing trade union Solidarity."[28] But Solidarity now created its own symbols with their own particular emphasis.

## Political Boundaries

While the symbol SOLIDARNOŚĆ adequately expressed a besieged people's struggle against tyranny, it did not say anything about democracy, about the diversity of the movement's members, or about the arrangement of its constituent parts—individuals, factory locals, and regions. In theory, Solidarity could have been monolithic and even antidemocratic. The symbol did not indicate how the movement's participants should associate. Deeply ingrained in the history of Solidarity, however, was the popular desire to reserve the decision-making powers for people gathered in grass-roots assemblies—what Thomas Jefferson would call "elementary republics."[29]

Out of these political drives emerged two kinds of symbols. The universal symbol of the movement was simply the word SOLIDARNOŚĆ, often worn as a lapel badge. But it was complemented by a proliferation of local symbols, including badges representing regions, cities, workplaces, or occupations. These provincial assertions also frequently carried the word "Solidarność." On the regional badges, the standard form combined the seal or crest and the name of the region with the word "Solidarność." The most common use of the eagle was not as the symbol of national sovereignty, but as the historic crest of a region.

More explicitly than the symbol SOLIDARNOŚĆ or the monuments, these badges revealed the movement's internal structure and aspiration. To cite Lévi-Strauss, this kind of drawing of space can be "almost a projective representation of the social structure."[30] The Poles did not simply unite, they divided—drew boundaries in which a political space for democratic participation could exist. Solidarity's Poland became a federation of factories and regions that was symbolically expressed in the proliferation of industrial and regional badges.

In the absence of "elementary republics" and division of powers, the alternative would be uniform solidarity—a general will in which people would "be forced to be free." The most extreme historical example of the opposite tendency among insurgent movements came with the French Revolution, when Jacobins, in the grip of their desire to create a perfect "general will," obliterated all territorial boundaries in an attempt to establish a monolithic France, one and indivisible.[31]

A second aspect of political space was the drawing of sharp boundaries between the state and Solidarity. The strike gate was the first, most dramatic expression of this. Strike gates were not only decked with flowers, portraits of the pope, and the Częstochowa Madonna, but they also projected such messages as "humankind is born and lives free." Where the party-state absorbed and represented everything and everyone, the mere act of drawing a line between the people and the state was revolutionary. It produced situations of unintended self-mockery by party officials. In strike after strike, workers and state representatives sat down on opposite sides of negotiating tables. Party, management, and government officials were unself-consciously joined on their side by the government's official trade unions. The image—a basic "we versus them"—was repeated for the next sixteen months, even on television, which often strongly censored the words, but was unable to censor the image and the message. Even General Jaruzelski unintentionally expressed the new democratic dynamics when he remarked: "Yes, the people do not trust the state, but can the state trust the people?"[32]

The contrast was reinforced by different styles—on one side, workers in their twenties and thirties with beards and moustaches and dressed in turtlenecks and jeans; on the other side, apparatchiks twenty or thirty years older dressed in Stalinesque or tailored Italian and English suits (depending on their level in the apparat). Solidarity's press spokesman, Janusz Onyszkiewicz, was tremendously effective in the battle of styles. He would issue statements for the union while dressed in a turtleneck and jeans. He would ride up to the cameras on his bicycle, on the back of which he carried his briefcase. This direct, understated style and language established the credibility of the movement with the Polish public, and at the same time divided it sharply from the state.[33]

## The Solidarity Monuments

### The Gdańsk Monument

During Solidarity's sixteen months of legal existence, factories all over Poland erected plaques and statues commemorating their strikes. Three monuments—those of Gdańsk and Gdynia to the dead of 1970, and of Poznań to the dead of 1956—are of national and even international significance. They stand today, the first monuments to the victims of Leninist states erected in the Soviet Bloc since 1917.

The most important of these three, the Gdańsk monument to the fallen shipyard workers (Ill. 4), like the logo SOLIDARNOŚĆ, issued directly from the August strike, but its origins reach back to the violent strikes of 1970. The collective memory of the strikes is an essential part of what we may call the foundation myth of Solidarity. Immediately after the bloody conclusion of the December strikes, the demand for a monument to the victims surfaced among Gdańsk workers. In the May Day parade of 1971, workers carried a banner demanding such a monument as they marched past the tribunal of party dignitaries.

**4.** The Gdańsk monument to the fallen shipyard workers of 1970

In 1977, groups that later founded the Free Trade Unions of the Baltic and the Young Poland Movement (RMP) took up the demand. Each succeeding year the crowd grew, from some 800 in 1977 to 5,000 in 1979. In that year Lech Wałęsa told the assembly that the following year on this day, December 16, at this place in front of Gate no. 2 of the shipyard, they would dedicate a monument to their dead. When the strike started in the Lenin Shipyard on August 14, 1980, one of the six demands was the erection of a monument to the dead of 1970. On December 16, 1980, almost 500,000 people came to dedicate their monument—more than the population of the city of Gdańsk.

Immediately after the 1970 strikes, a draftsman in the Lenin Shipyard, Bohdan Pietruszak, secretly began to chart sketches at his workbench for a monument to the dead workers. His sketches tended to be sorrowful in spirit and horizonal in form. A recurring form was a *Pieta*. When the August 1980 strike began, Pietruszak interrupted his annual vacation to hurry back to the shipyard and join the strike. On the first evening, he immediately went to his desk and drew a monument completely different from any he had imagined before. Instead of a horizontal design and a contemplative, sorrowful mood, the monument had suddenly become vertical—four "very high crosses" with anchors suspended from them. Now it expressed unstoppable force. A political strike had generated a new political symbol.

When Pietruszak finished his new design late in the night, he went off to sleep, leaving the sketch on his desk. When he returned the following day, excited coworkers told him how they had seen his drawing, recognized what it was, and immediately taken it to the strike committee, which had already adopted it as the monument the workers of Gdańsk would dedicate for December 16.[34]

For technical reasons, the number of interlinked crosses was later reduced to three, but the design took on more and more symbolic meaning: three workers had died in front of Gate no. 2. The fourth died later. The three crosses had connotations of the three crosses on Calvary. The crosses—symbols of martyrdom, faith, and resurrection—were combined with the three huge anchors, which hang suspended Christ-like from the crosses. The anchors—symbols of hope and resistance—not only had a Christian referent ("They are the hope we have as the anchor of our soul," Hebrews 6:19), they also were a pre-Christian symbol of the people of the coast, a symbol of the 1863 uprising against the Russian tsar, and the sign of the Polish resistance during World War II.

The combination of the 139-foot-high by 18-foot-wide crosses with proportionately huge anchors created an impression of something unexpected, explosive, unstoppable, rather than a feeling of contemplation or martyrdom. On the lower portions of the crosses are abstract designs suggesting steel plates shot through with machine-gun fire. Set on these plates are seven large bas-reliefs depicting the workers at home, at work, and on strike. The strike relief is the most dynamic: "The workers march out of the cross triumphant under the banner of Solidarność."[35] One relief depicts a grieving woman and the words from a poem by Czesław Miłosz:

> You, who have wronged a simple man
> Bursting into laughter at his suffering . . .
> Do not feel safe. The poet remembers.
> You may kill him—a new one will be born.
> Deeds and talks will be recorded.[36]

When the people of Gdańsk assembled to unveil the monument on the night of December 16, 1980, a misty rain began to blow in from the sea. The crowd stood silently, reacting only twice: with soft whistles when the Gdańsk party secretary spoke of Polish gratitude for their liberation by the Red Army, and in reply to the roll call of the dead of 1970 with the refrain, "He is amongst us!" When the bishop elevated the host during the consecration, the entire crowd knelt. From then on, the monument became the object of pilgrimage of the worker delegations from all over Poland, and its image was reproduced again and again in the iconography of the movement. Together with the Solidarność emblem, the Gdańsk monument became a symbolic center of the movement.

### The Gdynia Monument

The Gdynia monument (Ill. 5) is quite different in its mood, association, and design. It is located on the narrow street leading to the Paris Commune Shipyard from the interurban rail station where, on December 17, 1970, the army and militia fired on workers who were on their way to the first shift in the shipyard. The monument is in the shape of a huge set of numbers—1970—and stands on a foundation in the form of a cross. While the other numbers are realistic in form, the numeral seven suggests a worker shot and falling to his knees. He falls, but the other worker-numbers support and carry him. Like the interlocking crosses, the meaning suggested is solidarity in struggle, martyrdom, and ultimate triumph.

The monument was dedicated in ceremonies beginning at 5:00 A.M. on December 17. At three minutes before 6:00, the moment when the troops had begun to fire in 1970, there was a moment of silence observed by the 200,000 people who came to take part in the dedication ceremony. Al-

5. The monument to the workers of Gdynia

though the Polish state grudgingly permitted the monuments to be erected, there was a limit to its cooperation: the party refused to allow two inscriptions. The first read, "On the 17th of December, 1970, from 6:00 in the morning, a massacre of people on their way to work was carried out by order of the state on nearby rail bridges and viaducts. Honor to their memory."[37] The other banned lines were from Adam Mickiewicz's foreword (1832) to the poetic drama, *Forefathers*.

> For half a century past, Poland presents to our view on the one hand such continual, untiring, pitiless cruelties of tyrants, and on the other such unbounded devotion on the part of the people and such stubborn endurance, as has not been seen since the times of the persecutions of Christianity.
>
> It seems as if the kings have a Herod-like presentiment of the appearance of a new light on the world and of their own imminent fall, whilst the people believes ever more strongly in its own rebirth and resurrection.
>
> The annals of martyred Poland embrace many generations and a countless multitude of sacrifices; bloody scenes take place on all sides of our land and in foreign countries.[38]

### The Poznań Monument to 1956

The Poznań monument (Ill. 6) was dedicated on the brilliant Sunday morning of July 28, 1981 on Mickiewicz Square. Twenty-five years before, it had been called the Stalin Square. It was here that the Poznań uprising of 1956 had begun.

The Poznań ceremony began with the sound of sirens and the ringing of bells. Stanisław Matyja, the leader of the Poznań workers in 1956, crippled by his beatings at the hands of the security police, dedicated the monument with the words, "I ask for the unveiling of this monument of suffering, honor, and triumph."[39] With his words, a huge red-and-white flag suspended like a catenary curve in front of the monument was moved to a horizontal position, thus revealing the entire monument.

From a distance, two crosses, one 70 feet tall and the second 52 feet tall, seem to be marching, united by their common cross-arm, which is attached by what appear to be huge rope cables. They continue the theme of human solidarity intertwined with martyrdom and ultimate triumph found in the Gdańsk and Gdynia monuments. On the front of the first cross is the date 1956, on the second the dates 1968, 1970, 1976, and 1980, thus including for the first time the 1968 protest of the intellectuals. (Under martial law, on January 31, 1982, the workers of Poznań were to bring welding torches to burn yet another date, 1981, into this sequence.)

On the right, the third part of the monument consists of the head of an eagle rising out of a formless trunk or egg. The eagle's head is fully formed, adult, alert, and combative, as if to suggest not only the resur-

**6.** Poznań monument to
1956

rected Commonwealth of Poland, but also the conscious will and sacrifice needed to resurrect it. At the eagle's base are the words, "For Freedom, Justice, and Bread—June 1956." The monument exudes a warlike aspect appropriate to the three days of street fighting in 1956, but the inclusion of the eagle, the symbol of the Polish state, imparts a nationalist association that is stronger than in the Gdańsk and Gdynia monuments.

## Wałęsa as Anti-Hero

Solidarity's iconography depicts the movement, its events, its regions, and its occupations, but rarely its leaders or any living person. This absence of charismatic chiefs is congruent with Solidarity's grass-roots democracy. Logically, if the movement had created a charismatic leader (as assumed by the Western, especially American, press), the effect would have been deleterious: it would have been an escape from the freedom and democracy the workers had sought.[40]

The few depictions of Lech Wałęsa suggest the movement's aversion to an overweening leader. They also suggest an alternative explanation of leadership closely connected to the rites of passage. Wałęsa, like many of the union leaders who emerged during the strikes, is, in Turner's terms, a "structurally inferior" type. As the strikers rejected power and hierarchical structure and leaders imposed from above, their leader is reminiscent of characters frequently found in folk mythology, "the holy beggar, the little tailor, or simpleton who strips off the pretensions of holders of high rank and office and reduce[s] them to the level of common humanity and morality."[41]

When Lech Wałęsa was symbolically depicted, he was usually caricatured and affectionately cut down to size, as if the movement feared a powerful chief. A few images are to be found on movement badges, and other caricatures occur in the movement's journals and bulletins. One badge is an extraordinary example of the charisma conferred on the movement (Ill. 7). The pope, dressed in vestments and tiara, holds a shepherd's crook as he blesses Wałęsa. Dressed in a shiny blue suit, Wałęsa holds up his clenched first. The pope and Wałęsa are on the same plane, but the pope is twice Wałęsa's size, indeed superhuman. The image sug-

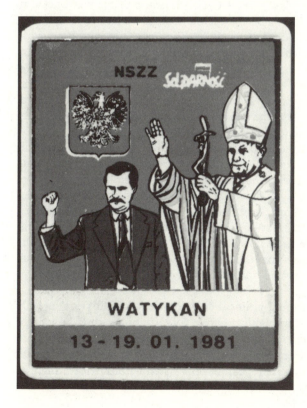

**7.** A movement badge: The pope blesses Lech Wałęsa

gests the powerful effect that the selection of a Pole as the Vicar of Christ on earth had on the revival of Polish messianism in this proletarian form.

Three more images, a badge and two drawings, more strongly presented Wałęsa as an Everyman and a trickster. On one badge, a blue-line caricature on a white field shows a Wałęsa whose head is curiously out of proportion with his trunk and legs (Ill. 8). Wearing an ill-fitting boiler suit, he is shown giving the universal crossed-arm sign of insult—in the Polish context, presumably to the Polish and Soviet leaders.

Like this badge, the two drawings are explicitly caricatural. In a line drawing from a regional newspaper, *Solidarność Podbeskidzka*, the head of Wałęsa is drawn in three-quarter profile (Ill. 9). His moustache is flexed like the biceps of a muscle man. The tips of his moustache end in triumphant clenched fists. The profile and the heavy moustache subliminally recall Piłsudski, who succeeded in pulling Poland out of the ruins of three empires. In a full-page line drawing from a Solidarity regional journal, created at the time of the union's national congress, Wałęsa appears in a comic opera general's uniform (Ill. 10). On his head is a plumed eighteenth-century hat with the word "Solidarność" on the front. He has spurs on his boots and his frock coat has epaulets with the initials NSZZ. His military order is the Madonna of Częstochowa, and his belt buckle is inscribed "Solidarność." In his right hand he grips a cavalry sabre, and in the left a fringed Solidarity banner. Like the other renderings, it is a caricature with a large head and small body. Wałęsa is saying, "I need generals because I'm out to sign a victory and not a defeat."[42]

This kind of leadership requires not elevation above one's followers, but a reduction or stripping away to the most universal humanistic elements of subject peoples. The portrayals of Wałęsa contain two separate symbolic elements. First, Wałęsa is Everyman—one of us—like everyone else who has no voice, no influence, and on whom the costs of history fall as inevitably as rain. The Wałęsa as Everyman theme combines elements of the poor Christian with those of the subject-masses in world history. He remains uncorrupted in the midst of corrupted power. His simple deductions and observations dumbfound the powerful. Second, Wałęsa is a trickster. He is honest, a good Christian, a true worker's chieftain (Ill. 11). But, although he turns down the party's offer of a villa and a car, he also has a peasant-like slyness and capacity to endure and outwit the rich and powerful. He knows his goals and will employ all possible stratagems to attain them.

Wałęsa emerged from a political culture that, after 40 years of daily experience under a nearly perfect nondemocracy, understood how to go about creating as wide a democracy as possible. In other political cultures, people might react in a very different manner at the moment of liberation. The Polish experience can be contrasted with the liberating mo-

**8. (top left)** A movement badge: Wałęsa salutes the high and mighty   **9. (top right)** Wałęsa triumphant, a line drawing from *Solidarność Podbeskidzia* 2 (January 15, 1981)   **10. (bottom left)** Wałęsa as a comic-opera general, a line drawing from *Wryj* 1 (1981)   **11. (bottom right)** Wałęsa as Father Christmas, a circulating Christmas card under martial law ment of the Cuban Revolution. When 1,000 *barbudos* entered Havana rejoicing, the same people who had made the revolution spoke deliriously of the twelve commandante "apostles" and the "Christ" Fidel. Castro's entry into Havana was an "apotheosis." "We all knew that Fidel was the undisputed *caudillo* of the revolution."[43] Although the revolution had been made by a national front, the deeply rooted *caudillismo* fused with the Leninist cult of personality to the detriment of the popular revolution.

## Symbolic Conflict

Symbols "shape political discourse and political struggle is partly a struggle to control such discourse. The relative success of political contenders in determining the shape and the character of the terms of debate has decisive implication for their ability to gain authority or obedience."[44] Symbolic conflict might take place along several dimensions; the enemy might be symbolically dehumanized and vilified. On this dimension Solidarity stands out in comparison with other political movements of the nineteenth and twentieth centuries by virtue of its symbolic disinterest in the enemy. No other characteristic shows as clearly the movement's moral renewal, concerned in an almost solipsistic way with upholding its moral integrity. To hate the enemy, to vilify him, was to risk becoming like him. Violence or its representation is not a creative act. By contrast, the Nazi or Communist movement raised in-group solidarity by arousing hatred of the dehumanized Satanic enemy, whether Jew, capitalist, or kulak. It also prepared its members to kill the out-group. The lack of aggression, the lack of a symbolic portrayal of the enemy is a remarkable aspect of the Solidarity movement. This apparently was an important part of Solidarity's political strategy. By ignoring its enemy, the party-state, it acted as if it were free rather than locked in a life-and-death struggle.

Symbolic warfare between Solidarity and the state occurred on two levels. The first is the level of patriotic religious opposition to national captivity. This included the antecedent national myth of Poland as bulwark of the West against Eastern barbarism. The second level stripped the Leninist state of its own legitimation. The most explicit statement of symbolic warfare was the Message to the Working People of Eastern Europe sent by the Solidarity Congress in the Fall of 1981.

> Delegates of the independent self-governing trade union Solidarity, assembled at their first congress in Gdańsk, send the workers of Albania, Bulgaria, Czechoslovakia, the German Democratic Republic, Romania, Hungary, and all the peoples of the Soviet Union words of greeting and support. As the first independent trade union in our postwar history we are deeply aware of the community of our fate. We assure you that, notwithstanding the lies being spread in your countries, we are the authentic representation of 10 million

workers which has emerged as the result of workers' strikes. We support all of you who have decided to take the difficult road and fight for free trade unions. We believe that soon our and your representatives will be able to meet to exchange our union experiences.[45]

This written challenge to the Leninist revolution was paralleled by symbolic challenges.

Merely by existing, Solidarity entered into symbolic conflict with the party-state. Its symbol—SOLIDARNOŚĆ—its strikes, its worker-leaders, and its monuments to its worker dead undermined the claim of the party to the heritage of the socialist movements of the nineteenth and twentieth centuries. Solidarity's posters, which wove together the Polish messianic tradition and the worker tradition, were exceptionally effective at this.

Particularly devastating was the poster (which was also produced as a badge) for the dedication of the Poznań monument (Ill. 12). A heroic statute of a Stakhanovite is covered with the labels used by the party to describe Polish workers during their strikes and uprisings: anarchist hoo-

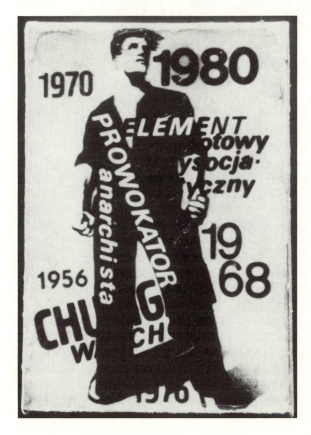

12. A poster for the dedication of the Poznań monument to 1956

ligan, antisocialist element, provocateur, agitator. A second poster, produced for the film "Man of Iron," shows a worker straining to burst an iron band welded around his skull (Ill. 13). Blood flows as he breaks the steel blindfolds and begins to see.

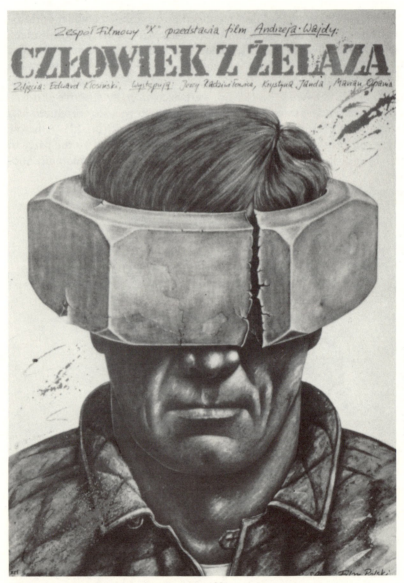

**13.** A poster for the film "Man of Iron," summer 1981

There were areas of even more direct symbolic conflict. Marx and Engels's appeal at the end of the *Communist Manifesto*,—"Let the ruling classes tremble at a communistic Revolution. The proletarians have nothing to lose but their chains. They have a world to win"—is the most appropriate motto for the symbolic conflict at the Lublin Auto Repair Shops. To the surprise of the Lublin party, when the Solidarity local unveiled its monument to its founding strike, a worker stood with arms outstretched breaking his steel chains (Ill. 14). In the months until the declaration of martial law, "persons unknown" would weld the chains together by night and the Solidarity would weld them apart by day. After martial law, Solidarity, now in the underground, welded them shut by night and the state would weld them apart by day.[46]

May Day was the center of particularly intense symbolic conflict. Like the hymn, the "Internationale," May Day had belonged to the entire socialist movement before the Russian Revolution and was progressively appropriated by Communist parties as their exclusive feast.[47] For a worker in the bloc, it was a day to march in serried ranks before the representatives of the state on their tribunals. A graduated series of administrative pressures guaranteed the workers' attendance.

The three members of the organizing committee of the Free Trade

14. LZNS Factory, Lublin, monument to its founding strike: A worker breaks his chains

Unions of the Coast chose May Day with its international labor connotations to begin the symbolic contest for workers' allegiance in Poland. "On the holiday [May 1], which for over 80 years has symbolized the struggle for workers' rights, we form the Founding Committee of the Free Trade Unions of the Coast."[48]

Under martial law, Polish workers continued their resistance through symbolic actions. Meanwhile, the party attempted to return to the pre-Solidarity symbolic order. May Day was reestablished. Tribunal grandstands were set up all over Poland, and workers, by order of their commissars, marched before the party dignitaries standing upon them. One town, Świdnik, which surrounds an aviation plant, succeeded in not marching in 1982. Blackmailed by their superiors to march, workers decided they would, but only in bare feet before the tribunals. The state responded by cancelling the march. To prevent any extemporaneous and barefooted May Day marching, the authorities also ordered the scattering of fiberglass in the streets. Świdnik passed into Polish workers' legend as the only town in the Soviet Bloc not forced into, but rather forcibly prevented from, observing May Day.

Świdnik had already won a reputation for organizing city-wide promenades scheduled at an hour that would serve as a demonstrative boycott of the national evening news. The martial-law government countered by imposing the earliest curfew anywhere in Poland so that the townspeople would stay in their apartments and homes with their television sets. With imaginations worthy of the surrealists, the people of Świdnik responded by putting their television sets out onto open balconies or next to opened windows so that they blared into the winter night.

Other symbolic actions prefigured the country that might have been. To illustrate what a working class could produce, a Wrocław factory held a speed-up strike; like Charlie Chaplins, they worked at double time. Similarly, under martial law, workers in another Wrocław plant marched into and out of their factory as if they were robot soldiers while their military commissars and factory managers watched in dismay.

Do symbols matter? This was really the point of a worker at the Lenin Steel Mills during martial law, who said in despair, "We've got all the symbols, and they've got all the guns and tanks."[49] Symbols are not armies, but they do express identity and serve as vehicles to communicate political messages and emotion. Solidarity's symbolic ritual served as a "mobilization of bias"[50] around which to rally against a state that held the means of compulsion, organization, and communication in its hands. The ten million members of Solidarity received an ideological preparation in democratic and nonviolent behavior. Daily life in Poland gave it to them, and the symbols of Solidarity were the expression of the lessons they had learned.

## Worker Messianism

In terms of substantive content, a most remarkable feature of Solidarity's symbols was the creative reworking and unification in a new synthesis of the Polish national insurrectionary tradition and the tradition of proletarian social revolution. Polish messianism merged with socialist but anti-Leninist revolution (Ills. 15, 16, 17, 18).

Solidarity's spontaneous adoption of symbols gave it a reach and resonance beyond the Polish cultural zone. Most of these symbols came from the social revolutionary tradition. "Solidarność," as the symbol's creator put it, was a universal rising or movement, and the solidarity it proclaimed was potentially an all-inclusive one, extending beyond the Polish nation. This creative synthesis of two revolutionary strands that divided in the first part of the nineteenth century appears to be the reason for the noticeable ideological disarray that Solidarity evoked in the world's left and right. The right liked the anti-Communism but not the workers' egalitarianism. The left liked the union and proletarian aspect but felt uncomfortable with the religious and national elements. Solidarity symbolically attacked the Leninist strands in the European social tradition and induced a palpable paralytic shock in the Leninist state apparatus.[51] Polish workers faced a universal problem—the Leninist state—and went beyond purely Polish concerns in their actions, thoughts, and symbols while trying to solve it.[52]

Much writing on symbolic politics has been pervaded with an explicitly negative model in which political elites manipulate the "masses" with fundamentally irrational symbols. Rational critical thinking is contrasted with mythical symbolic thinking, and it is assumed that reality lies beyond if only the symbols and ideology can be unmasked. The practitioner's integral use of the concept "mass" comes complete with a built-in rationalist and elite political theory. Without rejecting their pessimism about modern politics, the counterexample of Solidarity, with its concern for democracy and its sober rejection of violence or proposed scapegoats (in the relative absence of elites and command structures), all suggest that ritual symbolism should be taken as an essential form of human activity. At present, symbolic politics is usually loaded with an implicit charge of being irrational or antidemocratic. This case suggests that symbolic and ritual politics need to be examined without an implicit negative valuation—as arational rather than irrational.[53]

Symbols are treated here as a form of popular ideology—a supplement to formal ideology, organization, and communication. There is one aspect of Solidarity in which symbols are the key, rather than merely a supplement, to other processes and structures: namely, its role as a "primary process," or group "rite of passage"—Turner's term for the

15. A poster for the tenth anniversary of December 16, 1970: A crown of thorns for the martyred at Gdańsk Lenin Shipyard

avalanche-like movement of millions of people into a different psychological and political condition. It is this aspect of collective enthusiasm and rapid change in social attitudes and behaviors that other methods of social analysis will find hardest to account for.

When the symbols of Solidarity are compared to those of other twentieth-century social movements, the specificity, even the peculiarity, of Sol-

**16.** Decoration for Christ's tomb on Holy Saturday in the Pauline church, Warsaw, 1982. The outlines of the murdered bodies contain the dates of revolts against the state in postwar Poland

**17.** Poster for the film "Man of Iron." A burial shroud for a murdered worker suggests that the workers are Jesus taken down from the cross

idarity stands out. The Communist, Fascist, and Nazi movements produced symbols notable for four features, almost all of which are entirely absent in Solidarity: sexuality, aggression, dehumanization of the enemy, and charismatic leadership.

The Solidarity symbolism lacked a focus on personality, and on leaders. Instead, it was concerned with an entire people in the stream of history. As art, it belonged either to the period before bourgeois subjectivism or to the period after it. As political symbol, it was remarkable for portraying a decentralized land of regions and for not portraying its leaders, or for diminishing them in its portrayals, as if to insure that its Cincinnatus would return to his plough. The "good society" that it imagined resembles nothing so much as Marx's image of a France of freely federated communes, or Edward Abramowski's "concept of ethical anarchy, in which free will of autonomous social groups was given precedence over the claims of the sovereign state,"[54] or Thomas Jefferson's republic of freehold yeomen. Solidarity was distinct from anarchism because of the strong component of institution-building and conscious creation of political space. It was distinct from Leninism because it did not reduce political life to the administration of things. It was distinct from Western liberal democracies because of its emphasis on decentralized grass-roots democracy rather than competing elites subject to periodic elections.

**18.** A Solidarity underground Christmas card

Formally, most Solidarity symbolism was rather abstract. It avoided sentimental Gothic or the genre-realistic style. Although the Western mass media created an impression of the religious and pious and folkloric, a relatively small proportion of Solidarity's symbols were traditionally religious or patriotic. It may be noted that under martial law these religious and patriotic tendencies gained considerably in strength.

The Solidarity movement's symbolic disinterest in the enemy was quite remarkable. According to Georges Sorel, an effective myth that moved people to act in history was the drawing of boundaries between "us" and "them," delineating one side as unjustly oppressed and the other as hateful.[55] In contrast, Solidarity's symbols from 1980 to 1981 not only lacked the aggressive symbols of twentieth-century mass movements—the clenched fist, the bayonet, the revolver and carbine (what was called in Civil War Spain *la dialectia de los puños y pistolas*)—it also did not indulge in demonization or dehumanization of the enemy. Here the comparison is striking. No Jews, capitalists, priests, kulaks, Trotskyites, or imperialists appear. Enemies are not portrayed as spiders, serpents, skulls, vultures, mad dogs, lice, or pigs. Fascist art, of course, is relatively well known for such attributes, but the interest of Western "high culture" in the production of the modern tendencies in Russian art, such as the Primitivist, Futurist, Cubo-Futurist, and Constructivist Schools, has obscured the fact that the main production of the Communist movement was precisely of this kind: aggressive, dehumanizing, and increasingly drawn to the sentimental genre art known as "socialist realism."[56] In its lack of these elements, common to many social movements, and in its positive attributes, Solidarity showed how deeply marked it was by the twentieth-century experience of war and revolution. In this case, unarmed peoples, face-to-face with centralized modern states, sought to avoid reproducing those states, and thus consciously labored to avoid authoritarian modes of behavior while fighting against such systems. The struggle, then, became focused upon simple integrity and human solidarity.

A painting of December 1970 drawn by a primary-school pupil and displayed at the Solidarity Congress captured this spirit. In it, helmeted shipyard workers, carrying a national flag, march. Before them in the distance, flames shoot into the sky. Step by dignified step, carrying their dead, the unarmed workers march toward the flames.[57]

# The Ideological Origins of Solidarity

SOLIDARITY reversed the Leninist logic of social movements. Instead of a "mass" infused with consciousness and organization from above by an elite, Solidarity developed from below. It was not a spontaneous apparition but rather the product of forty years of conscious but anonymous struggle in Polish factories. To excavate this history, it has been necessary to devote two chapters of this work to a narrative account of one decisive week in December 1970, another chapter to the development of forms of workers' resistance from 1931 to 1981, and another to the sociology of work in the shipyards. The chapter devoted to symbolic politics has been crucial, because the symbolic tradition not only functioned as the carrier of a myth of resistance during 1970 and 1980, but also allowed all the members of Solidarity to create a popular ideology that was an unusual synthesis of socialism, religion, and nationalism, a synthesis that is deeply informed by a response to the problems posed by the French and Russian revolutions.

Another type of evidence, one that permits statistical analysis of popular ideology, was provided by Solidarity. As a result of Solidarity's victory in 1980, several hundred sets of demands written by work forces in coastal factories during the August strikes were deposited in the Gdańsk Solidarity Archive. The following year, the team researching the history of 1970 unearthed several dozen sets of demands, often by the same factories, that had been written during the strikes in December 1970 and the state-sponsored demand-gathering campaign in 1971.[1] Written by workers themselves, this material lends itself to statistical comparison. The case for the limited political consciousness of workers and their tutelage in consciousness and action by the intellectuals therefore can be examined, and speculation can give way to facts.

To remain as true as possible to the data, the analysis began by recording every demand of every third workplace or shop. These demands were then sorted and grouped to establish repetition among the different workplaces. A coding sheet with 94 possible demands and the characteristics of each workplace was then drawn up. The characteristics that were isolated concerned the date of the demands, the branch of industry, to whom the demands were addressed (interfactory strike committee, party, government, enterprise director, or parliament), the location of the workplace (large, medium, or small town, or countryside), whether the demands were from an entire enterprise or one shop, and whether from blue-collar or white-collar workers. The final criterion concerned the size of the workplace. An enterprise of more than 1,000 workers was defined as "large," 100–1,000 as "medium," and under 100 as "small." (These broad numerical categories are necessary because of lack of access to factory data.) The demands of every workplace were then coded. Each workplace's demands and coding sheet were verified by two investigators. The results were then transferred onto computer punch cards, verified one more time, and put into computerized form. The most popular demands for each year are listed in Table 1.

This assessment focuses on three sets of demands: the demands for free trade unions independent of party, state, and enterprise management; the demands for elimination of the political and economic privileges of the state apparat; and demands for economic equality. The most systemic demands in all three years clearly were for free trade unions and for abolishing the privileges of the apparatus. The demand for free trade unions constituted the irreducibly essential core of the platform of Solidarity. It was the only non-negotiable demand of the 21 put forward by the Lenin Shipyard in August 1980. It was the one demand that guaranteed an organization that would represent Polish society. The claim of intellectuals is that the demand for free trade unions arose among workers as a result of consciousness-raising by intellectuals beginning in 1976. To question elite privileges, meanwhile, or to demand they be abolished, was to question the state's very legitimacy. This demand made visible the monopolized power in Poland and its illegitimate disposal by a self-serving elite. Both demands were incompatible with the system.

## The Demand for Free Trade Unions

The first two of the 21 demands put forward by the Lenin Shipyard in August 1980 asked for free trade unions independent of the party and management and for the guarantee of the right to strike. Both demands, of course, are irreconcilable with the theory and practice of trade unions in Soviet-style societies. In Lenin's formulation, a union is "a school of administration, a school of economic management, a school of communism." Unions should serve the party "as transmission belts from the Communist party to the masses, and the party's leadership is a guarantee of success in the work of our unions." For Lenin, "an independent trade union is a counterrevolutionary machination."[2]

In the Soviet and Polish constitutions and labor and penal codes, work is an obligation and rights are bestowed by the state. Attempts to strike or form work associations independent of the party have been opposed by

Table 1. Workers' Top Demands in 1970, 1971, and 1980

| Demand | Workplaces making the demand (%) |
|---|---|
| **1970 (N = 59)** | |
| 1. Pay raise | 68 |
| 2. Free trade unions | 61 |
| 3. No reprisals against the striking workers | 58 |
| 4. Free arrested workers | 44 |
| 5. Pay for strike | 41 |
| 6. Punish those guilty of the shootings of workers | 39 |
| 7. Full information on the December strikes in the mass media | 32 |
| 8. Publish the demands of the strike committee | 31 |
| 9. Punish those guilty for the economic crisis | 31 |
| 10. Eliminate privileges of the apparat (party, government, army, police) | 24 |
| **1971 (N = 47)** | |
| 1. Reform of pay system | 59 |
| 2. Free trade unions | 59 |
| 3. Pay raise | 56 |
| 4. Earlier retirement | 54 |
| 5. Punish those guilty of the shootings of workers | 51 |
| 6. New elections to the existing unions | 51 |
| 7. Free arrested workers | 46 |
| 8. Protective work clothing | 44 |
| 9. Eliminate privileges of the apparat (party, government, army, police) | 36 |
| 10. Organization reform of work | 36 |
| 11. Improve working conditions | 36 |
| **1980 (N = 305)** | |
| 1. Pay raise | 65 |
| 2. Raise family subsidies to the level of the apparat (party, government, army, police) | 63 |
| 3. Free Saturdays | 53 |
| 4. Free trade unions | 52 |
| 5. Reform of pay system | 51 |
| 6. More housing | 44 |
| 7. Support of the interfactory strike committee | 42 |
| 8. Improve working conditions | 40 |
| 9. Eliminate privileges of the apparat (party, government, army, police) | 39 |
| 10. Earlier retirement | 37 |

Source: 1970 Archive and 1980 Archive.

administrative, legal, police, or psychiatric measures. In the macabre judgment of the Polish joke, "Under capitalism, the unions are to protect workers from the capitalists; under socialism, they exist to protect the socialists from the workers."[3] More soberly, the joke is no more than a repetition of a martial-law editorial in the official paper of the Polish government, *Rzeczpospolita*, after the outlawing of Solidarity, which specified the role the new trade unions would play in protecting the government from the working class: "Trade unions defend the working class against the bureaucratic abuses of their own state. But on the other hand, their task is to defend the workers' state from the anarchic, instinctive, or actual defense of their rights by workers."[4]

Of the 94 statistically significant demands, 8 concerned trade unions. Among the things they called for were new elections for the existing trade unions; a change in the election procedure; the right to strike; payment for the strike; personal safety for the strikers; support for the strike committee; and free trade unions independent of party, government, and enterprise management. Of these demands, the right to strike, payment of wages to the strikers, and the safety of the strikers are complementary to the demand for free trade unions independent of the state. The demands for new elections and for a change in the election statutes seek to alter in the existing state unions and are more reformist and less systemic than the demand for free trade unions. Of the possible demands concerning unions, the demand for free unions led in each year.

In 1970, 61 percent ($N = 59$) of workplaces demanded free trade unions. Only three workplaces wanted new elections, according to the existing union statutes. In the December 1970 strike in Szczecin, 55 workplaces were entered in the register kept by the strike committee of the Warski and Repair Shipyards. Some sent no demands, thus implicitly approving the founding document, the 21 demands of the Warski and Repair Shipyards, of which the first 2 call for "the dissolution of the Central Council of Trade Unions, which has never defended the working masses" and "trade unions that will represent the working class."[5] Of 31 workplaces that sent demands to the Warski Shipyard, 27 explicitly demanded free trade unions:

> *Post Office no. 5*: "We demand independent trade unions that will really represent workers' interests";
>
> *Szczecin Truckers*: "We demand independent activity of trade unions in the defense of working people and the return of the right to strike";[6]
>
> *A Tool-and-Die Factory*: "Freeing trade unions from the party and state administration and guarantee of the right to strike";[7]
>
> *Provincial Printing Plant*: "We demand fully self-governing union organizations that will truly express the will of workers";

*An Electronics Factory*: "We demand completely self-governing trade unions that will really represent the will of workers."[8]

The use of the words "truly" and "really" is revealing. In employing them, the workers open the Orwellian theme of words that stand for the opposite of what they are supposed to mean. Other such words in the Leninist context are "union," "election," "council," "cooperative," "republic," and "democracy."

It was possible to be merely reformist on the issue of unions. The agreement signed on December 15, 1970, between the city of Gdynia and the seven-person Gdynia strike committee has as its ninth point a reform proposal for worker autonomy: "Workers will choose new officers in the trade unions."[9] But more frequently, workers sought basic political change.

On December 16, 1970, the Gdańsk Lenin Shipyard demanded that "trade unions on all levels should be made up of nonparty members," while its companion Repair Shipyard wrote on the same day, "Eliminate the interference of the party in the work of the trade union." The Gdańsk Port demanded that "trade unions should be nonparty and must support the working class."[10] Ten years later, the essential demand for unions independent of the party remained the same. The Woodworkers' Enterprise at Gdynia said simply, "We demand free trade unions,"[11] while a Słupsk factory put it this way: "Create trade unions free and independent of the party and government, and conditions for their independent activity."[12] Gdańsk construction workers called for the "creation of new, independent, uncontrolled trade unions."[13]

The first major finding to emerge from a statistical analysis is the continuity of the demand for free trade unions. The workers' devotion to this demand is so consistent that there is no evolution or turning point. In fact, its overall support is higher in 1970 (61 percent) and 1971 (59 percent) than it is in 1980 (52 percent). This paradoxical result is explained by the greater percentage of vanguard heavy industry factories in the data from 1970 and 1971.

Reform sentiments that favored working within government unions were as weak in 1970 (9 percent) as they were in 1980 (also 9 percent). Unsurprisingly, this method of reform was much more in evidence in the government-sponsored fact-gathering campaign of 1971 (51 percent), but even under these conditions, a deferential or moderate approach was statistically less evident than the demand for free trade unions. In the 1971 campaign, the same factories and shops demanded both free trade unions and reformed unions.[14] Whatever the year, the majority of workers took the issue of the party's political control over the unions as decisive.

The archival documents also contain evidence on the nature of the "free trade unions that would express the workers' will."[15] They go into such detail that they anticipate aspects of the Solidarity Union Statute, which was written by lawyers Jan Olszewski, Wiesław Chrzanowski, and Władysław Siła-Nowicki and was brought to the Gdańsk Shipyard during the August strike of 1980.[16]

In 1971, the Lenin Shipyard specified the need to abolish the holding of several positions simultaneously in the highest state, party, and union posts and, even more broadly, demanded "that union activists not be party members."[17] The 1980 statute decreed that "union posts cannot be occupied by persons who have an executive function in a workplace . . . or executive post in a party organization."[18]

Control of the union's purse was considered a crucial ingredient in keeping locals strong and avoiding domination by central union or party authorities. The Lenin Shipyard in 1971 proposed that 90 percent of union dues should remain at the disposal of the locals. A decade later, the Solidarity statute set membership dues at 1 percent of earnings and guaranteed control of revenues to the workplace locals. The locals decided what percentage to give to regional and national union bodies.[19]

As part of the state's system of multiple controls over the unions, union officers were not paid from union members' dues; that is, they were directly dependent on and beholden to the state. The Lenin Shipyard workers in 1971 addressed to this practice with brevity: "Union officials should be paid out of union dues," a phrase repeated ten years later in the union statute.[20]

The direct connection between 1970 and 1980 extended to the written word: the Lenin Shipyard in 1971 asked for "the publication of an independent newspaper of the trade unions,"[21] while the 1980 union statute simply states that "the union possesses its own press and publications."[22] The attention to detail demonstrates the extraordinary influence of the negative lessons administered on a daily basis to Polish workers by their state-controlled unions, state factory managers, and party secretaries in their factories.

The demand for free trade unions independent of party, government, and factory direction, in the context of the Leninist state, does not reflect "trade union consciousness," but rather signifies the emergence of political or systemic consciousness. In a Leninist state, the demand for a free trade union is most political. A comparison of the demands of 1970, 1971, and 1980 reveals that the heart of the Solidarity platform—the free trade union—was as present in 1970 and 1971 among Polish workers as it was in 1980. And in 1970 and 1971, workers thought and acted without benefit of clergy or intellectuals. In short, there is no evidence for the view that in 1980, a new workers' consciousness suddenly emerged because of elite influence.

## The Attack on Political and Economic Inequality

A striking feature of the three sets of demands was the focus on structured political and economic inequality. Not only were workers' perceptions of structural injustice many-faceted, but they were rooted in an egalitarianism worthy of English levellers. The workers directly addressed the issue of political privilege, as if in an ironic application of Lenin's observation that "politics cannot but have dominance over economics. To argue otherwise is to forget the ABC of Marxism!"[23] In a Leninist state, power and privilege derive from offices bestowed by the state rather than the relation to capital; in Poland the workers displayed an understanding of the realities of the system in which they lived and worked. The criticism of these power-based privileges is one of the major themes of their demands.[24]

Demands directly criticizing the privileges of the state's officials—the People's Polish Army, the police, the state security police, the government administration and party—appear in two formulations: a call for the elimination of the privileges of the apparat or a demand that family subsidies be raised to parity with the subsidies received by the apparat. In the demands themselves, a part of the apparat was frequently singled out, or a specific privilege was protested. In percentages, the evolution from 1970 to 1980 is as follows: abolish apparat privileges—1970, 24 percent; 1971, 36 percent; 1980, 39 percent; family subsidies brought to parity—1970, 9 percent; 1971, 5 percent; 1980, 63 percent. Although the content remains remarkably similar over ten years, no other demand so vividly shows the change in the workers' psychology as they evolve from an equality of scarcity to an equality of rising expectations. The first demand asks for the removal of illegitimate privileges. The second asks that the benefits of modernity be extended to the whole society.[25] In all the writings about the many things the workers supposedly learned from others, the one thing that did take on a new significance in 1980 is never mentioned. Once again, the data on worker self-definition confounds the speculation about outside influence.

Both demands are egalitarian and question illegitimate state privileges. But the first, to eliminate these privileges, remains more or less constant over the years, occupying ninth and tenth place out of 94 demands. The second—to raise everyone to the level of the apparat—rises to second place in 1980 (63 percent), just behind the demand for a pay hike (65 percent). Here the opposition found a mobilizing issue, which was included in the twelfth of the 21 Gdańsk demands in 1980: to abolish the privileges of the police, security service and the party apparat by "leveling family subsidies," and by "abolishing special supply."[26] A similar demand appeared in the 21 demands of 1970. But the workers went beyond this level of analysis and questioned the very criteria employed by the state in selecting functionaries. In other words, they were concerned with efficiency: "Introduce the principle of cadre selection on the basis of qualification, not on the basis of party membership."[27] Written in chalk on a Szczecin factory wall in December 1970 were the words, "Level the pay of members of the Central Committee of the party to the average pay of a worker."[28] The Szczecin Ship Repair Cooperative simply asked for the liquidation of all privileges of the political and regular police, the army, and the party. The Szczecin Steel Mill demanded "limiting and leveling the pay of workers of the government and party apparats to the average earnings in industry." Three more specific types of demands asked for the "elimination of lower taxes for the army, police, and party apparat,"[29] the "abolition of special low prices in the cafeterias of the police and party apparat,"[30] and a division of housing "without favoring privileged social groups."[31]

A more sweeping demand was for the reduction of the overbuilt apparat at all levels and sections—both in the party and in the government—in order to reduce the state budget.[32] In 1980, the Northern Shipyard called for the abolition of "commercial shops and special shops in city administrations, provincial party committees, commissariats of the citizens' militia, police, and army, for all working peoples should have equal access to food and other goods." The thought was echoed in 1980 by the Elblag Brewery: "Abolish the privileges of the militia, party, and army, for all working peoples should eat the same bread." Not surprisingly, the workers addressed the matter of retirement. "Bring everyone up to the level of retirement and pension pay of the army and the militia."[33] They objected to double-dipping, another privilege of the apparat, "Do not hire former workers of the army and political police who are receiving 100 percent of their pensions."[34] "We demand equal rights with the privileged (railway, militia, and army), such as years worked to retirement, pay raises, leveling of family subsidies, and health and hospital care and retirement benefits."[35]

One of the more sensational revelations during Solidarity's sixteen months was that the Polish Council of State had issued two decrees in 1972, one on pay and another on retirement benefits for high officials and their relatives. Only the bare outlines came to general attention in late 1980, but they were theoretically important because they exposed a strong tendency to pass on the benefits of state office to future generations, as if Poland were a feudal society and noble positions were handed down by blood ties and marriage contracts. Even grandchildren, parents, and collateral relatives were included, and a short term in office sufficed to qualify for such positions. For this reason, they were popularly referred to as "dynastic decrees." They may have been the reason for the expansion of ministerial-level posts in the 1970s. One workplace in 1980 attacked these secret decrees directly:

> Immediately abolish the Decree of the President of the Council of Ministers on special pensions for high dignitaries of the government, party, and trade unions, for it is contrary to elementary sentiments of equality and social justice and to the decree on universal right to retirement. Introduce equal criteria for distributing pensions and abolish extraordinary pensions given to artists, singers, musicians, journalists, publicists, and radio and television journalists.[36]

The party called on workers to sacrifice in order to build a better Poland, but worker perceptions of structural inequality were clear and accurate. On the subject of housing and housing allowance, Polish truckers in Malbork called for "a just division of housing—that is, an equal time to wait for everyone, which includes the army and the militia."[37] Słupsk printers added, "Abolish the housing grants given to the state security police and the militia."[38]

In the state-controlled economy, access to life-saving drugs is dependent on office, with 40 percent or more of basic drugs not available to the general public. Special apparat clinics and hospitals are open only to office holders and their families. The goal of egalitarian medical services was expressed in general terms. "Create conditions for obtaining drugs equal to those in the militia and army."[39] "Bring medical care up to the level of other employees—railway, militia, and army."[40]

Gdynia transport workers focused on inequalities in cultural facilities: "Scrupulously respect the bases of social justice and abolish unwritten privileges of the workers of party and government organs in their access to material and cultural goods, such as vacation and recreation. Combat the enjoyment of these privileges by right of holding high office."[41] Attention was devoted to problems surrounding inequitable access to existing facilities: "All vacation centers of the Central Committee of the Central Council of Trade Unions, of the Office of the Council of Ministers, and of other state administrations should be obliged to have available 50 percent of their vacation funds to workplaces that do not enjoy their own vacation facilities."[42]

Demands extended to the general conception of justice and law. A construction firm asked for "equality before the law without regard to office or function."[43] Gdańsk agricultural cooperatives demanded "elimination of corruption and bribery in administration and public institutions."[44]

Another factory was even more forthright: "Take measures for the public trials of those in the party and government apparats who are guilty of economic crimes."[45]

In a system rife with parasites, workers also demanded equal responsibility to work. One aspect of corruption and mismanagement in the factories was the creation of sports teams paid for out of the enterprise wage fund, in part for the amusement of the apparat, in part as a device to create bogus positions to distribute to favorites. In one enterprise, workers demanded "an examination of the financial records and the liquidation of fictitious work positions."[46] Another, "that the work positions of those who never work be eliminated." "Raise work discipline for all posts from the director to the night watchman." "Reduce the number of positions at managerial level. Resolutely discipline all those employees who do not fulfill their agreed work tasks."[47]

At points, the demands took on the quality of existential affirmations of existence and a right to dignity: "Stop ignoring the co-op workers and start treating them as partners—let the managers finally cease treating the cooperative as private property."[48] The women of a garment factory in Gdańsk wrote, "The time has finally come to knock these oriental despots off their thrones and teach them to work for the pennies they offer us working people whom they treat as black slaves, simply as nothings."[49]

The demands protesting political privilege drive to the heart of the political system. The hatred and fear of the apparat that enjoys those privileges is patent throughout. The army was targeted along with the police and the party. This does not tally with studies claiming high social prestige for the army before martial law was declared on December 13, 1981.[50] The reality is more complex. Ordinary Poles had to serve in this dependent army with its Petainist symbols of national sovereignty—national in form, Soviet in content. As a conscript army, it was full of loved ones; as a part of the state, its professional cadres participated in the system of secret privilege, not justified by the hegemonic ideology. The army consequently was hated, loved, and feared all at once.

Everyone knew that police and army officers, not to mention high state and party officials, enjoyed a different standard of living from ordinary citizens, but the state could not openly acknowledge these privileges. They lay outside the party's socialist claim of state work as service and socialism as equality. The workers attacked the socialist hegemony in its corrupt essence, where it had to hide what was plain to everyone.[51]

## Economic Equality

If the attack on political privileges represented the diagnosis of the problem and free trade unions provided the remedy, the workers placed both matters within a wider criticism of structural inequality throughout Polish society. Whereas workers in the U.S. tend to define distributive justice as equality of opportunity and merit, Polish workers defined justice as an egalitarianism in which everyone gets more or less the same because everyone has more or less the same needs. As Lech Wałesa has put it, "Everyone has just one stomach."[52] As the socialist regime threatened basic needs of food and shelter, it stimulated the most egalitarian sentiments of justice. It may be that these sentiments applied only to moments of stress and crisis, when everyone was asked to sacrifice for the common good. This was suggested by the belief in hard work and the bitter feelings against party parasites.

One of the most dramatic manifestations of this attack on inequality was the accord of the striking workers of Gdynia with the city's president, Mariański, and the City Presidium on December 15, 1970. The agreement is dominated by the issue of equality. Point 4 of the document reads, "The earnings of manual unskilled workers should be about 100 złoty per month below those of skilled workers." Point 5: "The differences between the earnings of unskilled manual workers and those with higher education should be about 200 złotys monthly" (this would include engineers and managers). Point 6: "The director of the enterprise should earn no more than 1,000 złotys more than an employee with higher education."[53]

In 1970, the average wage of an unskilled manual worker was about 2,500 złoty. If we adopt that as our base figure, then skilled workers would earn 2,600 złoty, engineers and managers would earn 2,700, and the director of the Paris Commune Shipyard, one of the largest factories in the country, with a work force of 14,000, would earn 3,700 złotys. The range of rewards in this workers' society would be less than 2 to 1, very far from the actual ratios in the U.S. or in Leninist societies.

The demand for a pay raise, which tops the lists in all years, is therefore saturated with implicit categories of justice defined as equality as well as merit. Workers do not simply ask for a raise but explain how rewards should be divided. A construction firm justified its strike "by the unjust division of the earnings of working peoples."[54] Another workplace demanded "leveling of the large differentiation in pay scales,"[55] And another, "the abolishing of the excessive differences in earning."[56] A garment factory asked for 1,000 złoty for each worker from "the cleaning lady to the very top."[57] Gdynia bus transport workers presented another way to achieve more egalitarian wage rates: "In setting wage raises, follow the principle: lower raises for the higher paid and higher raises for the lower paid."[58]

Workers and employers demanded structural changes, and they gave reasons or justifications for their demands. For the purposes of this study, justifications were divided into corporate reasons (in which workers asked for something by industrial branch, such as railway or shipbuilding) and reasons of general equality or justice as merit, such as age or qualification.

Ten percent of workplaces put forth merit justifications by reason of professional qualification, and 30 percent by reason of age. Twenty-three percent asked for corporate privileges, 8 percent asked that the least well-off be favored, and 66 percent gave arguments based on equality. Equality could mean raising or leveling, but it also included issues extending far beyond the economic realm.

## Differences by Branch of Industry

The register of the members of the strike committee of Szczecin in December 1970 confirms the breadth of the strike and the importance of the basic industries, in particular metalworking and construction. (There were 24 workplaces from heavy industry, 8 from light industry, 5 from transport, 6 from service, 11 from construction, and 1 from administration.)

By 1980, there was a sufficient number of workplaces to permit an analysis by industrial branch, by size of workplace, and to some extent by size of the town in which the workplace was located. Decisions to strike, to hold strike meetings, to speak up publicly, and to discuss and agree on demands and send them to the Lenin interfactory committee required considerable courage. To strike entailed possibly disastrous consequences that were difficult to foresee. It was a self-defining act. This is why many workplaces sent pages of workers' signatures as an integral part of their demands, like founders placing their lives and honor behind their declaration.

For this study, industry in 1980 was divided into ten branches. The breakdown of industry by workplace reveals the differential support for Solidarity: heavy industry, 55 workplaces; light industry, 56; transport, 59; service, 71; administrative, 9; education, 18; health, 12; rural, 8; construction, 30; and commerce, 10.[59] The heavy industry category was composed of large factories, some as huge as the Lenin Shipyard, at the time numbering around 16,000 workers, not counting contracting firms within its terrain, or the Paris Commune Shipyard, with 10,000 workers. Some light industry and construction workplaces were also relatively large—up to 1,000 workers. All the other categories were lilliputian by comparison, such as the staff of a vocational school, the clerks in a supermarket, a planning office in the local government, or the clerical workers of a branch of the Polish National Bank. Although there were many hundreds more white-collar workplaces, they were almost uniformly unable to summon enough political resources to send in their demands. As we shall see, those that did send in demands tended to express more economic and less systemic demands than did blue-collar workplaces. In other words, the further from the political influence of the intelligentsia, the higher the consciousness.

In 1980, 52 percent of the workplaces overall supported free trade unions, but when broken down by industry, two—heavy industry at 75 percent and construction at 67 percent—led by far. Weaker support for trade unions was expressed by teachers (33 percent), service workers (39 percent), and commercial workers (49 percent).

In general, support for free trade unions was closely related to the size of the workplace and the branch of industry: 77 percent of the large (more than 1,000 workers) supported them; 54 percent of the medium workplaces (100–1,000 workers); and 48 percent of the small workplaces (under 100 workers). In light industry, 49 percent of the workplaces supported free trade unions. Trailing far behind were white-collar employees in education, health, and services. An apparent anomaly was the 56 percent level of support for free trade unions given by workers in administration, but in addition to having some of the most economistic workplaces, such as the largely feminine clerical staff of a branch of the Polish National Bank, this category also included several planning and computer bureaus. These had demand profiles not at all like those of low-echelon workers in state administration. Here the intellectual opposition may have had an effect.

On the two demands attacking apparat privileges in 1980, 39 percent of workplaces overall were in favor of abolishing apparat privileges, and 63 percent favored family subsidies similar to those obtained by the apparat. Here again differences among branches of industry were considerable. In heavy industry, 53 percent of the workplaces supported abolishing privileges; in construction, 47 percent; in transport, 44 percent. Notably below the average were the health sector (17 percent), education (28 percent), service (32 percent), and light industry (36 percent). Support for family subsidies equal to the apparat was greatest among construction workers (87 percent), heavy industry (76 percent), transport (70 percent), and light industry (67 percent). Below the average were educators (39 percent), health sector workers (39 percent), and commercial sales (30 percent). These last three are highly feminized and badly paid sectors, in which workers suffered a double burden of work and family responsibilities aggravated by the social and economic conditions typical of socialist countries.

Internal evidence from the 1970 strikes strongly indicates that the politically active elements—those who struck, went out on the streets, elected strike committees—were almost exclusively blue-collar workers.

In contrast to their actions in 1980, white-collar employees in 1970 remained passive and often did not participate in the occupational strikes at the shipyards and other workplaces. This impression is strengthened by the 1971 demands, in which in some cases, notably at the Lenin Shipyard, it is possible to distinguish the political and economic sectors. Demands reflecting a broad political consciousness emanate from the metalworking shops—hull-welding, fitting, and engines—while the more economistic demands for pay increases are the main concerns of white-collar workers in administration. The most economistic of all were the highly feminized clerical bureau of the shipyard. Feminine work forces were the least systemic and most economistic, but their political consciousness varied not by sex but by location in industry. Women in administration were like men in their demands; women in light industry were also like men. But there were few women in heavy industry.

The demands of 1970, 1971, and 1980 are crucial evidence of the consciousness of the workers of the coast, because they were produced by workers in several hundred workplaces and were not filtered through a sociological study or journalistic reporting. In substance and style, they are almost frightening in the moonscape quality of the worker's reality they portray. In this blasted landscape, there are only the factory and the factory mates, the party and its bureaucracies, and finally, the family. In these documents, there is no history, no culture, no religion.

# Fashionable Myths and Proletarian Realities

UNARMED CIVILIANS subject to highly developed systems of domination may flee into utopian hopes and dreams or into suicidal acts of utopian radicalism. Some analysts of Polish society detect a deep current of "utopian and anarchical forms of thought among workers."[1] They emphasize the workers' lack of "geopolitical wisdom," evidenced by impossible radical demands that had to be tempered by intellectuals who possessed the necessary sophistication.[2]

Strategically, Solidarity found a middle road between political passivity and hopeless violent revolt. It is commonly believed that the special contribution of the intellectuals was not only to politicize workers but also to temper their desires and restrain their impulses towards violence or hopeless demands such as abolition of the ruling role of the party. Thus, Adam Michnik has written, the peaceful progress of the 1980 strikes was due to KOR, while the entire Gdańsk agreement and Solidarity itself were "possible thanks to the functioning of a political strategy perfected in the KOR epoch."[3]

The demands in all three strike years contradict this thesis. In 1970 and 1971, there were no intellectuals on the scene to moderate demands. In 1980, the strikes and the demands they generated occurred too rapidly and were too decentralized for intellectuals to have moderated them. Although systemic and political, the demands from 1970 to 1980 place much more emphasis on the Solidarity program for a free trade union and generally follow the middle line between passivity and radicalism. What has been thought to be a strategic breakthrough by KOR or the church turns out to have been present in 1970. Moreover, the moderation was the product not of an elite strategic breakthrough but of popular experience.

For an explanation of this political creativity, it seems more fruitful to focus on the collective historical experience of the Polish people. In addition to the historical memory of the Polish uprisings of 1831, 1863, and 1944, there is also the bloc experience of the sudden, violent, and failed Hungarian Revolution of 1956, the failed party-directed Czech reform of 1968, and, of course, the Polish memory of 1956, 1968, 1970, and 1976.

Given the movement character of Solidarity, this kind of collective learning through historical experience, discussed more fully in Chapter Five, seems to explain the movement's self-discipline more adequately than does the concept of a strategy formulated by intellectuals and imparted to workers.

Strong evidence against the thesis of utopian radicalism is also provided by the almost total lack of mention of the U.S.S.R. in workers' demands, as if by collective wisdom this was a taboo not worth attacking. Instead, the subject of imperial relations is approached indirectly, with demands for the elimination of foreign aid to socialist countries and a review of the conditions of foreign trade, either generally or specifically with the Soviets. The U.S.S.R. is mentioned sarcastically on only two other occasions, with the Lenin Shipyard's question in 1971, "Why do our leaders fly to Moscow whenever there is crisis?" and again with this request: "Let us have Saturdays free from work as in the most progressive country—the U.S.S.R."[4]

## Workers' Authoritarianism

In the face of daily and dehumanizing injustice, the dominated may not necessarily react with democratic and humane impulses. The division of labor, power, and distribution can create demands for harsh vengeance against those who seem to succeed without thrift and honest work. The oppressed population may select scapegoats for its condition. As has happened in several Communist countries, the rulers may propose the scapegoats. In Poland, elements within the party, the church, the opposition, and Solidarity proposed the "fool's alternative" of "nativistic populistic scapegoating" at various times during the rise of Solidarity.[5] The party told its soldiers that they were fighting Germans on the coast in 1970. From 1976 on, the Polish police ran a campaign against KOR, whose members were claimed to be Jews and Communists, or at least Jews with a Communist past. Other nationalities were brought in according to need. Jan Rulewski was supposed to be a German or a German war criminal (he was born in 1944). Jacek Kuroń, who could not be proved to be a Jew, became a Ukrainian. The significant point is that "populist scapegoating" was an alternative that lost out in Poland's case but might come to the fore in breakdowns of other Leninist regimes.

The elitist thesis strongly suggests that workers, with their various incapacities and limited political horizons, will be susceptible to this alternative. To what extent, then, is the thesis of "workers' authoritarianism," directly sustained by Professor Staniszkis, supported by the evidence?[6] As measures of authoritarianism, two issues seem relevant indicators: anti-Semitism and the demand to punish "social parasites."

Both issues are visible in Poland. Polish society in the interwar period was deeply influenced by anti-Semitic parties. The historic Christian basis of anti-Semitism was augmented in Poland by widespread beliefs in the Jewish origin of Bolshevism. After World War II, anti-Semitism was stimulated first by the highly visible presence of Communists of Jewish origin in the highest reaches of the state and then by three state-sponsored anti-Semitic campaigns—in 1956, 1968, and 1976-85. Although the state failed to mobilize anyone but its own apparats, the attitude of the Polish population toward these campaigns is unclear. The demands of 1970, 1971, and 1980 do offer some evidence: While the demands are full of less-than-flattering references to the party, the police, and the army (a particularly cutting one in 1970 asks that the police be restrained from robbing and looting in the city of Gdańsk), not the slightest hint of anti-Semitism appears. On the contrary, several factories in 1970 and three in 1971 demanded that the victims of the state's anti-Semitic campaign of 1968 be released.

As for "social parasites," or layabouts, the sheer disorganization of daily life under central planning creates a highly visible social stratum with no discernible means of support. Like the Jews, the supposed social parasites have been a recurring target of Polish mass-media campaigns. The linking of the two in an authoritarian syndrome is illustrated by articles in 1968 in *Prawo i Życie* (Law and Life), one of the most active anti-Semitic papers of the regime, which spoke against both Zionists and parasites who don't want to do honest work and insult the working class. Despite these mass-media incentives, no workplaces demanded that "social parasites" be forced to work in 1970 and 1971. In 1980, 9 workplaces, or 3 percent of those making demands, asked that "something be done about social parasites." Three workplaces (1 percent) demanded that "social parasites" be placed in forced-labor camps. On the other hand, complaints about the parasitic behavior of the party and its bureaucracies are numerous.

A minimum conclusion is that organized Polish workers refused to accept the scapegoats proffered by the Leninist state. The absence of support for the state's mass-media campaigns and the evidence of the demands seriously undermine the thesis of working-class authoritarianism.

## A Regional or National Origin of Solidarity

Although the demands clearly show the fundamental plank of Solidarity—for free trade unions—to be as strong among coastal workers in 1970 and 1971 as in 1980, a question remains: If demands were available from other regions of Poland, might they not show that Solidarity was the result of a national evolution of workers and society?

Two types of evidence support the hypothesis that popular attitudes embedded in the experience of 1970 were specific to workers of the coast. First, when assertions from the Baltic Coast are compared with demands from Lublin, another region of Poland, there is a considerable difference in the level of political consciousness.[7] The strongest demands in Lublin in 1980 generally only attain the level of the weaker workplaces on the coast in 1970–71 and 1980. Lublin workers demanded pay raises, guarantees for the strikers, and egalitarian aid for the less well-off through the raising of family subsidies to the level of the apparat. They also attacked "commercial" food prices and the sale of domestic products in foreign-currency stores. But even the strongest factories rarely called for free trade unions independent of the party, choosing instead to ask for new elections to the state's trade unions. The workers also avoided criticism of the political privileges of the state apparat, except for the demand for family subsidies like the apparat's (which on the coast was also often voiced by the weakest factories).[8]

These results are significant because Lublin's two universities and its propitious mix of intellectuals and workers later made it one of the strongest regions of Solidarity. It was a region well within the reach of KOR's influence, a region in which *Robotnik* and other opposition journals were presumed to have found a certain audience in the factories. Yet the pattern of the July 1980 demands shows the propagandizing efforts of KOR to have had little or no effect—if those efforts are understood as energizing. The workers most available to influence by intellectuals were among the least politically advanced.

When the organizational forms utilized by workers against the party are examined for differences, a second type of evidence supporting Solidarity's link with the coastal region emerges. The implications are wider than simply the regional origin and development of Solidarity. What organizational forms are connected to these varying ideological assertions by Polish workers? That is to say, what organizational forms would be adequate to realize them?

According to oral history prevalent in Poland, which has found its way into academic literature, Jacek Kuroń of KOR explained to the workers that they should cease burning committees (of the party) and begin to build their own committees (their own trade union structures).[9] But in the struggles of December 1970, Polish workers desperately searched for an organization and program capable of addressing this strategic problem. A rapid evolution ensued. Workers first gathered to protest before various enterprise administrations along the Baltic Coast. Protests escalated in stages to marches on government and party buildings at Gdańsk, Gdynia, Elbląg, and Szczecin; to occupational strikes based on one enterprise; to interfactory strike committees in Gdynia and Szczecin uniting many factories; and even, in one instance, to a conspirational political group.[10] In this rapid series of political forms, the coastal workers created the inter-factory strike committee uniting all factories and other workplaces against the central state. In its quick rise ten years later, Solidarity rested on the creative organizational lessons learned in 1970 on the coast. Here again, the role of KOR was not causal.

In fact, the effects of the coast's history and local lessons are rarely clearer than in the history of protest in the 1970s and in July and August 1980 under First Secretary Gierek. After December 1970, coastal work-ers knew they had to stay in their factories in order to protest. Street marches or assaults on party buildings lost their appeal as long as there was no chance for successful overthrow of the state. Such marches were clearly hopeless, and additionally offered the state too inviting a target for distortion of the strikers' aims. By comparison, during the 1976 workers' protests, angry workers from noncoastal areas of Poland did leave their factories. In Radom and Płock, they attacked the party headquarters. In Ursus, they blocked and tore up the international railway line. Though strikes rippled across Poland from July 1, 1980, no interfactory strike committee was formed on the 1970 coastal model until August 16 in the Lenin Shipyard. The closest approach to such a strike committee was made by Lublin. There, strikes eventually became a general strike; work-ers elected strike committees, wrote demands, and negotiated with man-agement and government, but they did not create a union of striking fac-tories. Like the rest of the Polish factories, they negotiated with the state through individual factory committees. In light of such evidence, it is dif-ficult to resist the conclusion that there was an important difference among regions. It seems that the MKS—the interfactory strike commit-tee—stood in a direct relationship to the workers' strongly held demand for free trade unions on the Baltic Coast. This is one of the major conclu-sions of this study—that the regional foundation of Solidarity was un-known in the rest of the country for the ten years leading up to August 1980.

A major current of interpretation of the place of Polish workers in the history of postwar Poland has claimed that there was an evolution from economic to political concerns by workers in the decade preceding the rise of Solidarity.[11] A usual corollary position represented by Kołakow-ski, Pelczynski, Lipski, Touraine, Garton Ash, and many others is that this evolution was accomplished thanks to the consciousness-raising activities of the intellectual opposition, or of the church, or of both.[12] As Lenin claimed, the limited consciousness and organization of the "masses" could only be overcome by injection of superior consciousness by elites. A third line of interpretation represented by Michnik, Smolar, and Staniszkis is that the workers remained essentially unchanged at a level of low consciousness but formed an explosive force that was successfully channeled by intellectual leaders and advisors.[13] As in Trotsky's famous metaphor of the Russian Revolution, the workers were the exploding steam, and intellectuals possessing consciousness were the engine chamber, shaping and directing the steam.[14]

The evidence generated in the written demands of 1970, 1971, and 1980 overwhelmingly contradicts these suppositions. The demands of 1970–71 were as political and systemic in their criticism of the Leninist system as the demands of 1980. In general, they offer no support to interpretations that detect strong sentiments of utopian radicalism or authoritarianism in workers. Before the founding of KOR or the social activation of the Catholic Church, the demands clearly set forth the program of Solidarity: free trade unions independent of party, government, and factory management. Although they were not the treatises of political philosophers, the workers' concerns extended beyond wage and working conditions within the factory to the Leninist state. The demands were also not simply anti-state, or destructive in their aim, but proposed an alternative that included Solidarity's strategic breakthrough: the demand for a free trade union and a nonviolent way to achieve it through the sit-down strike and the interfactory strike committee.

## Workers and Intellectuals

In the eyes of sundry analysts cited at the outset, the workers seem to be child-brutes handicapped by inadequate concepts, language, and symbol-making capacity. Some analysts hold that this condition of the workers is irredeemable; others that "workers' consciousness" can be raised only through the organizational and educational efforts of the intellectuals. This understanding is deeply rooted in Polish history. In Poland, the very word for worker, *robotnik,* carries heavy cultural baggage. Its meaning is connected to the late abolition of serfdom in Eastern Europe. The continued low status of manual work in a society dominated by aristocratic values give a special resonance to the word "worker," which is derived from the Old Slavonic *rab*, meaning "bereft of father," or "deprived of free status," i.e., a slave.[15] (In this context, it is helpful to remember that the word "intelligentsia" means "people of reason.") A common slang term derived from the root word *rab* is the word *robol*, which is used in a derogatory way by white-collar Poles to refer to workers. The word carries a complex meaning: lazy, incompetent, drunken, interested only in one's earnings. An article by the Polish writer Ryszard Kapuściński expands upon the Polish understanding of *robol*:

> The *robol* doesn't discuss—he fulfills the plan. . . . The *robol* cares only about one thing—how much he is going to earn. When he leaves the factory, he smug-

gles out stolen parts and tools in his pocket. If not for the management, the *robols* would steal the whole factory. They play cards in the train on the way to work the next morning. When they arrive at the factory they immediately get in line for the factory's clinic to obtain a doctor's exemption from work.[16]

Those familiar with the literature on North American slavery will notice many shared characteristics between the images of the Polish *robol* and the black slave.[17] But those who believe in these images fail to see how the actions of the *robol* and the slave, including their work, are a protest against their condition.

After the Polish August, Kapuściński felt the cultural revision in the Polish view of workers would be permanent: "The workers on the coast once and for all did away with the stereotype of the *robol* that prevails in official offices and elite salons."[18] In view of the subsequent development of Polish and Western literature on Solidarity, it is apparent that Kapuściński's optimism was premature.

In everyday speech, use of the word *cham* ("ham") as a term of abuse for someone with coarse, brutal manners, is also revealing. It refers to the belief common in eighteenth-century Poland as in the rest of Europe that different estates had different racial genealogies. The *szlachta* gentry were children of Japhet, the common people descendants of Ham, and the Jews the children of Shem. Similarly in the American South, slavery was justi-fied by whites on the same basis: whites were the children of Japhet, blacks, the forever cursed progeny of Ham. As Polish sociologist Józef Chałasiński bitterly concluded, "All this does not belong to science or learning but to the mythology of the Polish intelligentsia."[19]

In the whispered propaganda against Lech Wałesa, which was propa-gated by his opponents in both Solidarity and the party, elements of these images of workers played an important role. Within Solidarity it was confined to the attempt to put an intellectual loyal to KOR in the leader-ship. From the state, a demonstration of the workers' incompetence was the main political aim of interviews conducted in *Polityka* with the Szcze-cin and Gdańsk Solidarity leaders in 1980. To show the incompetence of workers to society at large was to demonstrate the party's legitimacy. An important part of the party's shaping of the perception and self-percep-tion of workers was the claim that they were only interested in economic issues. As brutes, they cared only about immediate, material things. That is, they were incompetent as citizens in the political and civic sense of the word and therefore were legitimately ruled by the party.[20]

Compare what the state's media had to say about the workers' de-mands in 1970 and 1971. Colonel Marian Nowiński, writing in the daily newspaper of the Polish army, *Żolnierz Wolności* (Soldier of Freedom), stated, "The workers demanded primarily a pay raise. They wanted to talk about that with competent people. Unfortunately, there was no one to talk to them."[21] A journalist from *Polityka* wrote, "There was really only one demand: for competent engineering, economic, and administrative professionalism in the exercise of power whether in a city or a factory."[22] Their accounts do not differ significantly from the version presented by the Polish opposition or that of Western academic scholars. The Polish state, the Polish intellectual opposition, and Western academic scholarship were united in their image of the worker. The party's version of events was successful in Poland and the West because it spoke to this image.

## The Intellectuals

These images are of great theoretical interest because of what they suggest about the ideologies of those who hold them. In the nineteenth century, when the Polish nobility was in decline and the bourgeoisie was mostly German, Austrian, or Jewish, the intellectuals became the representatives of Polish nationalism. Issuing to a large extent out of landless nobility, they entered the free professions and there infused the status of intellectual with enormous political and social connotations. They turned education into a permanent asset where a diploma was like a knightly title—a symbol of dignity.

For Aleksander Gella, "They [the intelligentsia] are a culturally homogeneous social stratum of educated people united by charismatic feeling and a certain set of values" that have an "above-class character [sic]." This stratum has a "dominating influence on the other strata."[23] Their knightly values—such as courage and fidelity—contributed much to KOR and Solidarity. But these values, along with the moral component they brought to the status of a person of learning, frequently have a double-edged quality. A group's sense of its own charismatic responsibility for an entire society can also carry with it condescension or contempt toward other groups. More precisely, whatever its virtues, this is an authentic domination ideology.

If the gentry inheritance continues to be a significant element in the interaction of intellectuals with other classes and strata, a second element appears to be the historical incorporation of the intellectuals into modern bureaucratic politics. As Joseph Rothschild writes,

> In interwar Poland, the intelligentsia then not only mastered the state apparatus but effectively controlled all political parties, no matter how contrasting their programs. It was thus a sociological rather than an organizational entity. Not deliberately dictatorial, the intelligentsia simply took for granted its supposedly unique qualification for public affairs. Not until the mid-1930s did the peasants and workers challenge and repudiate this political and psychological

domination on the part of the intelligentsia over the state and over their own movements.[24]

A third element is the Leninist legacy, which sharpened the Polish intellectuals' sense of their "unique qualification for public affairs" and their "political and psychological domination."

> The Marxist-Leninist Party called the intellectuals into the ranks of the "conscious minority," which according to the theory of dialectical materialism should guide the masses to the fulfillment of their historical task. For this party calling and mythology, the road was paved by past mythologies, which framed the successive self-definitions of the intellectuals: those of a philosopher counselling the king in the style of the Enlightenment, of the romantic prophet reaching for spiritual leadership by divine inspiration or the authority of history, of the teacher of the masses in the positivist mood—of the apostle of science and progress. . . . The intellectual class has a 200-year-long history, during which its self-image went through many changes; what did not change was its belief in its own superiority.[25]

The historiography of Solidarity presented here suggests a significant seepage of Leninist categories into the Polish intelligentsia even as they turned against the Leninist party in the name of democracy. In an ironic way that he perhaps did not have in mind, the ideological history of the intellectuals engaged in Solidarity fulfills Arthur Koestler's prediction that Communism would end in a battle of Communists against ex-Communists.

Intellectuals in Poland and analysts in the West were mistaken in their understanding of Solidarity because Polish elites acted as cultural gatekeepers for Western knowledge of Solidarity and Polish society. The gatekeepers informed Western observers that the gatekeepers themselves were the source of Solidarity. This is understandable enough. Outside of Poland, the idea of an intelligentsia-generated movement resonated within elitist traditions imbedded in Western politics. On the right, there is a rejection of broad participatory politics, which, if it does not necessarily end in Fascism or Communism, is seen as leading to the "populist" excesses of the 1960s. In the West, too, competing elites are taken to be guardians of democratic politics against the impulses of the uninformed and unreliable "masses." On the left, hopes for a transition to socialism have been disappointed by *embourgeoisement* of the working class and have been accompanied by an unwillingness to confront the tyrannical reality of Leninist regimes acting in the name of socialism. Both left and right now look for the motor of social change in the knowledge elites, i.e., the intellectuals.[26] So deeply entrenched are these elitist ideas that they suffuse social perceptions of historical causality—on the left and on the right. Consequently, elite explanations of Solidarity seemed intuitively correct to foreign elites. As Sheldon Wolin had put it many years earlier: Lenin's analysis was not simply "a quirk of revolutionary theory; . . . it was symptomatic of a broad tendency in twentieth-century thought."[27]

Significant in their own right as part of the political trajectory of the West and as a redefinition of the meaning of democracy, these theoretical ways of looking at politics blinded interpretation to important aspects of the origin and nature of Solidarity. Understanding lagged far behind reality.

## Conclusion

In the days when it was still fashionable to believe in the working class as a motor of history, James Thurber wrote that the intellectuals are divided into two parts: those who tell the workers that they should have a revolution, and those who tell the workers that they have had a revolution. The structure of the argument and evidence presented here inevitably lead to a certain disproportion in the view of Solidarity that it is now time to correct. The argument presented here does not aim at glorification of workers, as hinted by Thurber. This is a book about the origins of Solidarity, which are overwhelmingly working-class. But Solidarity was a broad front for all Polish citizens; it was a strategic alliance of intellectuals, white-collar workers, blue-collar workers, and farmers that rested in large part on breakthroughs achieved on the Baltic Coast by workers. There would not have been a Solidarity without the intellectuals, but the Solidarity they joined was built on the framework developed by workers. In other words, the roots of Solidarity were in the Baltic working class, and the intellectuals made a necessary but not causal or creative contribution.

The achievements of KOR and other groups in the intellectual opposition have not been questioned here. What has been questioned is the understanding of these events by Polish intellectuals and Western analysts. It does need to be said that that understanding, based as it is on a powerful domination ideology, inevitably shaped political actions. By so radically demeaning the contribution of the Polish people to Solidarity, that elite understanding has also demeaned the intellectual opposition that it was meant to exalt. As the account presented here has tried to demonstrate, this elite thesis is not only demeaning—it is historically invalid.

Before the Russian Revolution, Lenin advanced two theses: that most people, including workers, could not imagine general remedies to the injustices they suffered, and that politicized intellectuals could help them by imparting superior consciousness and organization. Marx himself had written, "Just as philosophy finds its *material* weapons in the proletariat, so the proletariat finds its *intellectual* weapons in philosophy. And once the lightning of thought has penetrated deeply into this virgin soil of the people, the Germans will emancipate themselves and become men."[28]

The workers of the coast did not bear out Lenin's pessimism. They criticized the state's principles of political reliability and control and proposed in their place new criteria of competence and economic equality. In place of hierarchical command structure, they advocated the widest possible democratic associations. As for the state apparat's privileges, the workers proposed to abolish them. If their demands were not "revolutionary" in the sense that they called for a violent overthrow of the political and social system, they were nonetheless incompatible with the prevailing order. Tantalizingly, they seemed to take the state's official ideology—its cant about democracy, equality, and workers' management—seriously. In this sense, they did show the influence of party ideology. Structural changes underlay these developments.

As the state expanded in Eastern Europe and other socialist countries, the meaning of words such as "industrial workers" or "trade unions" changed. In the West, the term "trade union" acquired a meaning within the context of the development of economic, civil, political, collective, and social rights striven for and partially achieved over centuries in a related but often contradictory sequence.[29] These rights were won against elites entrenched in state structures that were very weak by contemporary standards. The rise of the modern Leninist state, combining control of the political, economic, and social realms, negated the sequence of rights.[30] Consequently, the meaning of a free trade union became quite different in the modern context of "really existing socialism." Within that context, a free trade union becomes an organically revolutionary organization in the struggle for economic, religious, political, and national rights. It comes into direct collision with the modern state. That state's political controls are so direct and so undisguised that they force a critique of state power within the workplace. As Max Weber suggested, the state is "transparent"—that is, "members of . . . subordinate groups are able to perceive an immediate connection between their personal situation and the overall structure of power and privilege."[31] How might workers in the Paris Commune or Lenin Shipyard make such connections in their daily work? Not only are the shipyards part of the state's central plan—the consequence of which workers suffer every month as they wait idly for parts, materials, or organizing ability—but the workers must then "storm" to fulfill the plan at the very end of each month. The lesson regularly driven home is as simple as it is stark: any other system would be more rational, more efficient. After 1970, the shipyards were included in Gierek's co-optive system of direct consultations between "leading factories" and the Central Committee in Warsaw. This centralization further increased the transparent responsibility of the state for conditions of daily life and work. Beyond this, the connection of political power to daily conditions became patently clear to the most remote worker because of the presence of the state's hierarchical command structures within the shipyards—the industrial and political police, the cadre and employment section, the government trade unions, and the party organizations.

Even the most elementary matters within the shipyards thus became subject to the state. The lowest foremen were within the nomenklatura, and their nomination had to be cleared by the party. Moreover, the system raised the already politicized horizons of the shipyard workers beyond the ministers and Central Committee in Warsaw. A considerable portion of their production was for the Soviet Union and was based (as every worker was convinced) on unequal contracts highly disadvantageous to Poland. There were even Soviet contract-fulfillment supervisors in the shipyards. In sum, all social and work conditions and the most narrow questions led to Warsaw and often even to Moscow.

In all these ways, the monolithic state-employer became transparent to its worker-employees, both as an institution and as an ideology. Its hegemonic ideology conferred a prima facie validity upon the counterclaims of its socialist workers.

Workers' demands and the organizations that workers developed to struggle for these demands illustrate the pedagogic influence of the Leninist state and stand in a dialectical relationship to it: instead of the nomenklatura and privilege, equality; instead of hierarchical pillars of control, the utmost in decentralized democracy. Indeed, the workers proposed safeguards for these new democratic forms that were so far-reaching that they astounded many observers. It was as if the Leninist state that had created a working class now discovered its recalcitrant and unruly students had absorbed its lessons, only in reverse. The demands and the organization generated by workers were so connected to the Leninist state's control of political and social life that they suggest a clear answer to the question of whether the Solidarity crisis was specific to Poland—whether they arose out of a unique national history and culture and were confined to it or were part of a general crisis of Leninist states. The Leninist state is common to the bloc. And if there was a tutor's rule in this schoolmaster state, the language, structure, and concerns of the workers' demands, as well as the form of workers' organizations generated to realize them, emphatically suggested that the teacher was not the Polish Catholic Church or opposition intellectuals, but the Leninist state. The state generated its opponent.[32]

This interpretation of the pedagogic role of the state can be stated even more precisely. The formation of workers' strike committees and the writing of demands were deliberately stimulated by state officials as a stratagem to get workers off the streets in 1970. The committees immediately escaped from party control and took on a life of their own. The recovery of the lost tradition of the sit-down strike was facilitated by the party and military's blockades of the Lenin and Warski shipyards, which let workers in to work but didn't let them out. The development of a territorial strike of all state employees against the state in the shape of the interfactory strike committee owes even more to the state opponent. The logic of a conflict against a single state employer demanded that workers create horizontal forms of association to counter the vertical lines of command and communication controlled by the party.

As we have seen, the prevalent explanation of the origins of Solidarity is that the movement emerged from the educative efforts of the opposition intellectuals beginning in 1976. This, of course, amounts to something approximating a classic Leninist interpretation of Solidarity and has consequences for an understanding not only of Solidarity's origins, but of its very nature. As this study has tried to document, the prevailing view is inappropriate. The facts suggest that the intellectuals in KOR and other groups played an important but relatively separate role in their own sphere.

The evidence and conclusions presented in this study directly contradict the dominant trend of understanding of postwar Polish history and of Solidarity. The near unanimity of this understanding, the remarkable way in which it has been sustained as assertion without being tested by the standards of scientific investigation, suggest that it may be a ruling paradigm controlling categories of thought and ways of seeing. If this happened with Solidarity, which was one of the most intensely scrutinized recent political events in Eastern Europe, then it may be that other significant nonelite phenomena are escaping serious investigation.

One of the shortcomings in Marx's revolutionary theory was the failure of its prediction (until Solidarity) that the industrial workers would act as the leading force in a social movement or revolution. Even in the Russian Revolution (granting that the basic revolutionary force was in the nationalities and peasantry, contrary to official Soviet scholarship), the Bolsheviks were most successful in organizing artisan-like workers in small, technologically backward factories, and were least successful among workers in the largest and most advanced factories.[33]

This democratic movement, based as firmly as it was among the industrial workers and with many workers as leaders, stood in a Marxist tradition—even as Solidarity fundamentally threatened the theory and practice of the Leninist state. In other respects, the movement examined here was very un-Marxist. As shown most particularly in the chapter on sacred politics, its ideology was a complex synthesis of socialism, nationalism, and religion, the last two of which Marx had hoped to eliminate from history. In their concern for building democratic political institutions and political life, Polish workers also addressed an area Marx had barely noticed.

If the conflict with the Leninist state played a crucial role in the creation of the Polish workers' movement, this may mean that working classes in other socialist countries will also come to play autonomous and explosive roles in the future. The possibility that this may occur is increased by the structural technological dilemma facing the Soviet Union and many socialist states. They have been successfully industrialized to the level of the second industrial revolution, with its appropriate technological level based in big steel and chemicals and a huge working class. As many other countries have entered the third industrial revolution, socialist economies have been unable to change their pattern of growth from extensive to intensive use of labor, materials, and technology. Now they stand before the necessity of such a transition, which is forced by their falling growth rates and their difficulties in meeting Western technological competition, which is crucial for military security. Gomułka's and Gierek's attempts to force such a transition in the Polish economy had disastrous political consequences, because they aroused Polish workers threatened by redoubled economic exploitation and unemployment. All attempts at a transition to an intensive economy by socialist states, such as that attempted by Gomułka or that underway by Gorbachev, have to face not only the difficult restructuring of an anachronistic industrial structure, but also a class of insecure party functionaries and a dying class of workers threatened by the reforms.

So far, Solidarity has been almost the only movement in socialist countries to have this endogenous working-class-generated character. The structural crisis drive attempts at reform and creates openings for resistance, but people create their own political meaning in their specific situations. As a working-class-created movement, Solidarity in this strict sense may turn out to be the exception rather than the rule. But the broader lessons of the Solidarity example go much farther than that.

The strategic breakthroughs made by workers of the Baltic in 1970 opened the way to Solidarity in 1980. Nine years of resistance to General Jaruzelski's attempt to reform the system ultimately failed leading to the elections in 1989. The Soviets faced a choice between direct Soviet military occupation of Poland or a political compromise drawing Solidarity into the political system. The Soviet leaders miscalculated the viability of reform communists like themselves in East Europe, but their miscalculation was forced by Solidarity and it led to the union's electoral victory in 1989 and the rapid collapse of neo-Stalinists and reformers in the rest of East Central Europe. In this broadest sense the workers of the Baltic Coast opened a prison door that all the peoples of the East have come crowding through.

CHAPTER ONE

1. KOR (Committee for the Defense of Workers) was founded by Polish intellectuals to defend workers persecuted for protests against price rises in June 1976. After one year of activity, with most of its aims achieved, KOR redefined its aims and changed its name to Committee for the Defense of Society—hence the acronym KSS-KOR. In succeeding years, KOR was the most active group within a broad front of social activity that developed in Poland before Solidarity. In addition to publishing free of censorship, KOR developed such activities as the Intervention Bureau, which monitored civil and human rights. It served as a patron and protector of numerous activities, such as independent trade and peasant unions. There were other groups, such as Young Poland, that played an important role in the pre-Solidarity ferment in Gdańsk, but KOR was the most active and the best known. The formal number of members varied but never exceeded twenty-four. The term "members" was used more loosely to refer to those active in KOR activities. It was also used in a colloquial way to refer to the inner circle of KOR activists surrounding Jacek Kuroń and Adam Michnik. KOR was formally dissolved by its members at the Solidarity Congress in Fall 1981. For a history of KOR, see Jan Józef Lipski, *KOR* (Berkeley: University of California Press, 1985.)

2. Leszek Kołakowski, "The Intelligentsia," in *Poland: The Genesis of a Revolution*, ed. Abraham Brumberg (New York: Random House, 1983), p. 65. A similar statement is made by the Oxford political philosopher and historian of postwar Poland, Z. A. Pelczynski, in "Solidarity and the 'Rebirth of Civil Society' in Poland, 1976–81," in *Civil Society and the State*, ed. John H. Keane (London and New York: Verso, 1988), pp. 361–80, esp. 361–63, 378.

3. Mieczysław F. Rakowski, "Czasy nadziei i rozczarowań" (Time of hope and disillusion), *Polityka* 32 (August 10, 1985). Similarly, according to former Party First Secretary Stanisław Kania, "The demand for free trade unions originated not among workers but among the anti-socialist adventurers, a year and a half, two years ago, in Kuroń's group." "Teleconference with Provincial First Secretaries, August 27, 1980," in *Sierpień 1980 roku w Szczecinie* (Szczecin: Socjalistyczny Związek Studentów, 1981), p. 130. Józef Cardinal Glemp, primate of Poland, describes a Solidarity quite similar to the entity discerned by the Polish party, one infiltrated and manipulated by different Marxist groups, including Trotskyists. As a result, Glemp stated, the worker movement "lost its bearings in defense of the workers." It suffered a leader, Wałęsa, who was "independent within the pure union line" but was "manipulated" by others to such an extent he had "lost control" (interview in *O Estado de São Paolo*, March 2, 1983). It is necessary to note that "Trotskyist" is usually a codeword for "Jewish" in Eastern Europe; a similarly extreme ecclesiastical interpretation is supplied by Father Michal Paradowski. In his article "Stulecie śmierci Karola Marksa" (On the 100-Year Anniversary of the Death of Karl Marx), in *Duszpasterz Polski Zagranicą*

(Rome) 34, 2 (April-May-June 1983), he concludes, "The Trotskyists through KOR, the Committee for the Defense of Workers, strove to exploit Solidarity and manipulate this healthy Christian movement for their own nefarious aims." The author further holds that the Trotskyists and their agents in Poland, KOR, and the Michnik family are financed by Jewish Wall Street financiers. The same thesis was advanced by a professor of the Catholic University of Lublin, Father Piotr Taras, at the Polish Institute of Sciences in New York, April 15, 1983 (*Kultura* [Paris] 7 [1983]: 61–62). In an ideological convergence, Vadim Trubnikow in *Krach Operatsii Polonia* (Moscow: P. Novosti, 1984) analyzes the activities of Jacek Kuroń, Adam Michnik, Bronisław Geremek, and Karol Modzelewski in Solidarity as a conspiracy of the Pentagon together with the Trostkyist-Zionist Organization KOR.

4. Alain Touraine, François Dubet, Michel Wieviorka, and Jan Strzelecki, *Solidarity: The Analysis of a Social Movement, Poland 1980–1981* (Cambridge: Cambridge University Press, 1983), p. 36.

5. Władysław Majkowski, *People's Poland* (Westport, Conn. and London: Greenwood Press, 1985), p. 153.

6. David S. Mason, *Public Opinion and Political Change in Poland, 1980–1982* (Cambridge and London: Cambridge University Press, 1985), p. 50.

7. Jonathan Schell, "Introduction," in Adam Michnik, *Essays from Prison* (Berkeley: University of California Press, 1985), p. xxii; Adam Przeworski, "The Man of Iron and Men of Power in Poland," *Political Science* 15, 1 (Winter 1982):17.

Jacek Kuroń was born in 1934 in Lwów in a socialist family. He was an activist in the Communist youth movement in the forties, and became a member of the Polish United Workers' Party (PZPR) in 1953. He was expelled the same year. A student from 1954 at Warsaw University, he was the founder of a troop of Red Scouts in 1956. He reentered the party and became a national executive board member of Polish scouts. In 1961, he was removed from his post in the scouting movement. The Red Scout troop, which included Seweryn Blumsztajn and Adam Michnik, was dissolved by the Warsaw Party Committee. In 1964, Kuroń was the co-author with Karol Modzelewski of "Open Letter to the Party." In 1965, he was sentenced to three-and-a-half years in prison. In March 1968, he was again arrested and sentenced. In 1976, he was a founding member and leader of the Committee for the Defense of Workers (KOR), and editor of *Information Bulletin* and *Robotnik*. He was very active in July and August 1980 until his arrest on August 21. He was an advisor to Gdańsk Solidarity from September 2, 1980, and to national Solidarity from September 17. He was again arrested and interned December 1981. Since Fall 1989, he has been deputy to Parliament and minister of labor and social welfare. He is the author of an autobiography, *Wiara: Wina* (London: Aneks, 1989).

8. Adam Bromke, *Poland: The Protracted Crisis* (Oakville, Ontario: Mosaic Press, 1983), p. 170.

9. Jean-Yves Potel, *The Promise of Solidarity* (New York: Praeger, 1982), p. 122.

10. Timothy Garton Ash, *The Polish Revolution: Solidarity* (New York: Vintage, 1985), pp. 24–25, 43.

11. Lipski, *KOR*, p. 424.

12. Jadwiga Staniszkis, *Poland's Self-Limiting Revolution*, ed. Jan T. Gross (Princeton: Princeton University Press, 1984), pp. 51–52, 122.

13. Aleksander Smolar, "Contestation Intellectuelle et Mouvement Populaire," in *Solidarité Résiste et Signe* (Paris: Nouvelle Cité, 1984), pp. 147–48.

14. *Izvestiia* (Moscow), April 6, 1985.

15. J. M. Montias, "Observations on Strikes, Riots and Other Disturbances," in *Blue-Collar Workers in Eastern Europe*, ed. Jan F. Triska and Charles Gati (London: Allen and Unwin, 1981), p. 184.

16. Adam Michnik, "KOR i Solidarność," *Zeszyty Historyczne* (Paris), no. 64 (1985): 70, 75, 85, 86, 90. See also "A Time of Hope" and "Letter from the Gdańsk Prison, 1985," in *Letters from Prison*, p. 105 and pp. 78–79.

17. George Kolankiewicz, "Poland, 1980: The Working Class under 'Anomic Socialism,' " in *Blue-Collar Workers in Eastern Europe*, ed. Triska and Gati, p. 136.

18. De Weydenthal, "The Worker's Dilemma of Polish Politics: A Case Study," *East European Quarterly* 13, 1 (1977):95, 105. The debate between exogenous and endogenous theories of worker radicalism has a long history. In addition to Lenin, other notable exogenous explanations are advanced by Selig Perlman, *A Theory of the Labor Movement* (New York: A. M. Kelley, 1949), and Barrington Moore, Jr., *Injustice: The Social Bases of Obedience and Revolt* (White Plains, N.Y.: M. E. Sharpe, 1978). For endogenous theories, that workers can generate revolutionary consciousness on their own, in addition to Marx, see E. P. Thompson, *The Making of the English Working Class* (New York: Pantheon, 1964). For the convenient classification endogenous/exogenous, see Victoria E. Bonnell, *Roots of Rebellion: Workers' Politics and Organizations in St. Petersburg and Moscow, 1900–1914* (Berkeley: University of California Press, 1983), p. 7.

19. Sidney Tarrow, *Struggle, Politics and Reform: Collective Action, Social Movements and Cycles of Protest*, Western Societies Program, Occasional Paper no. 21 (Ithaca, N.Y.: Center for International Studies, Cornell University, 1989), pp. 18–19.

20. George L. Mosse, *The Culture of Western Europe: The Nineteenth and Twentieth Centuries* (Chicago: Rand McNally, 1961), p. 4.

21. The professional Polish historian Jerzy Holzer is a notable exception. He carefully notes the lack of solid evidence on crucial points, and for that reason limits himself to a political history based on central documents, which, he notes, means he has to exclude the social movement from his consideration. Jerzy Holzer, *Solidarność, 1980–1981* (Paris: Instytut Literacki, 1984), p. 8. Although Solidarity was, if anything, a social movement, his refusal to step beyond his evidence puts Holzer far ahead of most of the others in this field.

22. Jan Malanowski, *Polscy robotnicy* (Warsaw: Książka i Wiedza, 1981), p. 18.

23. Historical material was gathered by Joanna Wojciechowicz and Antoni Węga for the exposition prepared for the unveiling of the Gdańsk monument to the fallen shipyard workers. Joanna Wojciechowicz was succeeded by Janusz Krupski, Wiesława Kwiatkowska, Ewa Dering, Aleksander Klemp, Jan Stępek,

and Krzysztof Żórawski. Their efforts preserved a vital part of Poland's postwar history.

24. The general elitist understanding of the place of workers in postwar Polish history is documented in this chapter, above. As for the 1970 crisis specifically, a high point in understanding was reached soon after with the publication of the transcript of the 9½-hour meeting with Gierek in the 1971 Warski Shipyard in *Rewolta szczecińska i jej znaczenie*, ed. Ewa Wacowska (Paris: Instytut Literacki, 1971). In the same year, Kazimierz Zamorski did an exhaustive study of the regime press during the crisis, which appeared as "Kronika Wydarzeń," in *Poznań 1956–Grudzień 1970*, ed. Ewa Wacowska (Paris: Instytut Literacki, 1971). The special issue of the journal of the Polish United Workers' Party *Nowe Drogi* (1971) devoted to the February 1971 plenum also provided insights, particularly on the economic and elite crisis. Z. A. Pelczynski contributed an analysis of "The Downfall of Gomułka," *Canadian Slavonic Papers* 15, 1–2 (1973): 1–22, which has not been superseded. All these works showed the effects of the regime's successful effort to suppress knowledge of the workers' attempts at organization and the formulation of a program through the writing of demands. Bolesław Sulik's "Robotnicy," in *Kultura* (Paris) 10 (October 1976):65–77, was based on interviews of the January 1971 strike leaders in Szczecin and contained much valuable information, but in crucial ways it confirmed the dominant thrust of interpretation. Sulik did not have access to the December 1970 strike leaders and did not give that strike as much emphasis as it deserved. In 1980 and 1981, much new material was published in the Solidarity and official press concerning 1970. It tended to focus on the dramatic events in the streets and contained little evidence of workers' organizational or ideological strivings. In 1981, Mieczysław F. Rakowski published *Przesilenie grudniowe* (Warsaw: Państwowy Instytut Wydawniczy, 1981), which essentially was a summary of the official story. In 1983, the pseudonymous Zygmunt Korybutowicz published *Grudzień 1970* (Paris: Instytut Literacki, 1983), which remains the definitive critical study of the crisis from the open sources available through 1981. Korybutowicz was able to analyze critically the official materials and the accounts published in the Solidarity and opposition press, but he did not have access to workers' demands or to the other work of the Gdańsk 1970 historical team. He was forced to remain at the level of the published sources and did not have a full account of the developments in ideology and organization among workers.

Fitting within the elite interpretation, the workers in 1970 were seen as having carried out resistance that was violent, but limited in its consciousness, organization, and aims. So David Lane, a British sociologist, wrote that "the chief trust of the manual workers' grievances was economic, not political, and was for an immediate improvement in conditions" ("The Role of Social Groups, in *Social Groups in Polish Society*, ed. David Lane and George Kolankiewicz [New York: Columbia University Press, 1983], p. 313). Zygmunt Korybutowicz, in his book on the events of 1970, wrote that the "workers did not put forward demands that the intellectuals could relate to: their demands were above all economic and particular" (*Grudzień 1970* [1983], p. 142).

According to Polish sociologist Jadwiga Staniszkis, workers were characterized by "limited semantic competence, reification of the power structure, the mentality characterized by ahistoricism, political moralism, one-dimensionality, and status orientation." "The evolution of forms of working-class protest . . . was an evolution from a populist form based on one enterprise (December 1970)." Workers demands in 1970 suffered from "excessive modesty of claims." Professor Staniszkis also asserted that workers' demands in the 1970s were entirely economic: "Because they have difficulty articulating their demands, the workers artificially reduced all their claims (including noneconomic ones) to the concrete language of wage demands" (Staniszkis, *Poland's Self-Limiting Revolution*, pp. 146, 38, 41, 40, 122). Also conforming to the elite thesis are Jakub Karpiński, *Countdown* (New York: Karz Cohl, 1982), pp. 157–65; Stanisław Starski, *Class Struggle in Classless Poland* (Boston: South End Press, 1982), pp. 41–43; and Krzyszof Pomian, *Wymiary Polskiego Konfliktu 1956–1981* (London: Aneks, 1985), pp. 94–98.

In February 1983, the author published a short account entitled "La longue marche de la classe ouvriére polonaise" in *Le Monde Diplomatique*, in which the thesis was that the rediscovery of the sit-in strike, the formation of interfactory strike committees, and the formulation of the demand for free trade unions made 1970 a breakthrough year, preparing Poland for the rise of Solidarity. This was followed by an article titled "Solidarité et les luttes ouvrières en Pologne 1970–1980," in *Actes de la Recherche en Sciences Sociales* (Paris) 61 (March 1986), and by a shorter English version, "Worker Roots of Solidarity," *Problems of Communism* 35 (July–August 1986). This article, which is basically Chapter Seven of this study, included a summary account of the origins of the sit-down strike and the interfactory strike committee in 1970, and was essentially an analysis of workers demands from 1970, 1971, and 1980.

Valuable articles were published by social scientists concerning Szczecin. Teresa J. Makowska and Lucjan Adamczuk wrote an analysis of the conflict of workers and party in December 1970 and January 1981, "Robotnicy w dwu sytuacjach konfliktowych," *Studia Socjologiczne* 4, 9 (1983):53–72. Adamczuk followed this with an article called "La révolte des années 70 à Szczecin: les enseignements de l'histoire," *Économie et Humanisme* 278 (July-August 1984): 8–20. Andrzej Głowacki did a book-length study, *Kryzys polityczny 1970 roku w świetle wydarzeń na Wybrzeżu Szczecińskim* (Szczecin: Szczecińskie Towarzystwo Naukowe, 1985). Also see Głowacki's "Wydarzenia grudnia 1970 r.-stycznia 1971 r. w Szczecinie," *Zapiski Historyczne* (Toruń) 46, 4(1981): 127–54; also published in *Vacat* 11–12 (November-December 1983): 58–73. These works benefitted from Głowacki's intimate knowledge of Szczecin, including the Szczecin party headquarters, where he had been an employee. They are informative on the inside details of the workers' strike and actions within the party, but they avoid police and military questions.

The aftermath of Solidarity also brought the publication of three books of interviews. Jerzy Surdykowski's *Notatki gdańskie* (London: Aneks, 1982) is based on life histories of workers in Gdańsk and Gdynia. *Szczecin: Grudzień-Sierpień-Grudzień* (London: Aneks, 1986) is a book of interviews by Małgorzata Szejnert and Tomasz Zalewski dealing with Szczecin and is of considerable historical interest. Finally, in 1986, a large proportion of the work of the Gdańsk 1970 historical research team was published in *Grudzień 1970* (Paris: Éditions Spotkania, 1986). A part relating to Gdynia was published by Wiesława Kwiatkowska in *Grudzień 1970 w Gdyni*, Archiwum Solidarności, vol. 11, Relacje i Opracowania (Warsaw: Wydawnictwo Pokolenie, 1986).

25. C. Wright Mills, "Power, Politics and People," in *Collected Essays of C. Wright Mills*, ed. I. L. Horowitz (New York: Oxford University Press, 1960), p. 256, as cited by Seymour Martin Lipset, "Industrial Proletariat in Comparative Perspective," in *Blue-Collar Workers in Eastern Europe*, ed. Triska and Gati, p. 1.

26. Guillermo O'Donnell, Philippe C. Schmitter, and Laurence Whitehead, *Transitions from Authoritarian Regimes* (Baltimore: The Johns Hopkins University Press, 1986); a critique appears in Edward Friedman, "Modernization and Democratization in Leninist States: The Case of China," *Studies in Comparative Communism* 22, 2–3 (Summer-Autumn 1989):251–64 and Carlos A. Forment, "Socio-Historical Models of Spanish-American Democratization: A Review and a Reformulation," Harvard University, Sociology Department, Center for Research on Politics and Social Organization, Working Papers Series, October 1988.

27. Barrington Moore, Jr., *Social Origins of Dictatorship and Democracy* (Boston: Beacon Press, 1966).

28. Andrew Kirby, "State, Local State, Context and Spatiality: A Reappraisal of State Theory," in *The Elusive State*, ed. James A. Caporaso (Newbury Park and London: Sage Publications, 1989), p. 208.

CHAPTER TWO

1. The statistics on industry are from Z. A. Pelczynski, chs. 12–17 in *The History of Poland since 1863*, ed. R. F. Leslie (Cambridge: Cambridge University Press, 1983), pp. 401–3, 446–50.

2. "Letter of Gomułka to the Central Committee, March 27, 1971," in Jakub Andrzejewski, ed., *Gomułka i inni: Dokumenty z Archiwum KC 1948–1982* (Warsaw: Krąg, 1986), pp. 198–99.

3. Pelczynski, "The Downfall of Gomułka," pp. 19–21. Gomułka was severely criticized by numerous speakers at the February 1971 Eighth Plenum for undercutting shipbuilding and aircraft. On coming to power, Gierek let it be known that he would reverse these plans. At the Szczecin Provincial Party Conference on November 17, 1971, he said that ships came after coal as an important export and that "we have rejected anachronistic ideas of limiting the development of the shipbuilding industry" (*Trybuna Ludu*, November 18, 1971). The same newspaper had announced a new long-range investment plan for the aeronautics industry on August 28.

4. Henryk Król, "Rozwój intensywny a zatrudńienie," *Trybuna Ludu*, February 15, 1971, and Antoni Rajkiewicz, "Węzłowe problemy polityki zatrudnienia," *Ekonomista* no. 2 (1971), cited by Jan De Weydenthal in "The Worker's Dilemma of Polish Politics," p. 116.

5. This summary is drawn from sources containing the party's production campaign addressed to work forces in 1968–70 in Gdańsk and Szczecin. These are the provincial party newspapers *Głos Szczeciński* and *Głos Wybrzeża*. For a

frank discussion by a government economist, see Bronisław Fick, in the newspaper *Życie Gospodarcze*, February 7, 1971.

6. Bert Klandermans, "The Formation and Mobilization of Consensus," in *From Structure to Action: Comparing Social Movement Research across Cultures*, ed. Bert Klandermans, Hanspeter Kriesi, and Sidney Tarrow (Greenwich, Conn.: JAI, 1988), pp. 173–96, as cited by Sidney Tarrow in *Struggle, Politics and Reform*, p. 15.

Also see the interview with Zbigniew Szczypiński, an industrial sociologist in the Lenin Shipyard. In June–July 1970, he prepared a report that he says showed clearly that "we were sitting on a barrel of gunpowder." There was "an alarming state of tension and anger among the work force." "Grudzień 70," special issue, reprint from no. 5, Biuletyn NZS UJ (n.p., n.d.), p. 17.

7. Edward Jarecki, *Stocznia Gdańska im. Lenina* (Warsaw: Książka i Wiedza, 1985), p. 65; the quote appears in several interviews with shipyard workers. See the speech of Jerzy Pieńkowski, first secretary of the Lenin Shipyard, at the Eighth Plenum, published in *Nowe Drogi* (special issue, 1971), pp. 198–200.

8. Quoted by Edmund Szczęśniak in "Dusza rogata," *Czas* (Gdańsk) 42 (October 19, 1980).

9. For estimates of food budgets, see George Kolankiewicz, "The Polish Industrial Manual Working Class," in Lane and Kolankicwicz, *Social Groups in Polish Society* Table 13, p. 120.

10. Stefan Jędrychowski, "Mój pogląd na źródła kryzysów w Polsce Ludowej," *Zdanie* (April 1982): 17–21.

11. The Politburo letter to primary party organizations is printed in the article "Renesans Gomułki: Był 'satrapą'?" by Władysław Machejek, *Życie Literackie*, June 20, 1982.

12. Interview with Zbigniew Szczypiński, industrial sociologist of the Lenin Shipyard, in "Grudzień 70" (special issue), pp. 17–18.

13. Roman Zambrowski, "Dziennik," *Krytyka* 6 (1980), entry for December 16, 1970. Born in 1909, Zambrowski was one of the leading Polish Stalinists. He was passed over to succeed Bierut apparently because Khrushchev objected to his Jewish origins. He then became a leader of the Puławy faction and a major target of the Partisan and Silesian factions. He was forced out of the Politburo and Secretariat in 1963 and had lost his seat in the Central Committee by 1964.

14. In his comments to the provincial party secretaries on December 22, Karkoszka said that he had "proposed an earlier reading of the letter . . . but the Central Committee decided meetings and reading of the letter would take place on Saturday." "Notatki ze spotkania z sekretarzami KW," a report to the party secretaries by secretaries Jundziłł and Karkoszka, December 22, 1970; hereafter cited as the "Jundziłł Report."

The Jundziłł Report is one of six kinds of materials compiled by the 1970 historical commission of the Gdańsk Solidarity region, which are described in preliminary detail in Chapter One. More precisely, this 1970 archive consists of the following kinds of materials: diaries written during the strikes of 1970–71 by participants; internal party documents generated during the 1970–71 strike period, including the Jundziłł Report; official leaflets and proclamations issued by the government during the strikes; interviews of participants in the 1970–71 strikes conducted in 1980–81 by the Gdańsk historical commission; internal documents generated by workers during the 1970–71 strikes, including factory and shop demands; and "The Central Committee Report," an important and confidential party report of a summary investigation of the strike period, probably printed in 1981.

In addition to these six categories of archival material bearing on the 1970–71 strike, there is a second body of evidence concerned with the Polish August of 1980. Foremost among this material is the strike archive of the Gdańsk Interfactory Strike Committee, headquartered in the Lenin Shipyard. Additionally, there is a holding of miscellaneous audio recordings of Gdańsk Solidarity and national Solidarity. These tapes extend to several hundred hours of recordings. I have deposited this material in the Houghton Library at Harvard, where it is designated "Solidarity 1970" and "Solidarity 1980." Starting with this footnote, the account that follows is essentially based on materials previously described as the "Archive." Interviews and other materials from this archive are cited individually, such as, for example, "Henryk Jagielski, W–4, Gdansk Lenin Shipyard." The material is not catalogued in Houghton Library beyond the broad categories of "Solidarity 1970" and "Solidarity 1980."

15. Barbara Seidler, "Gdańsk-Gdynia Grudzień-Luty," *Życie Literackie*, February 21, 1971.

16. Jundziłł Report (1970).

17. Adam Sarad, P-1, Gdańsk Lenin Shipyard.

18. Roman Detlaff, Gdańsk ZNTK.

19. Bronisław Duda, S-4, Gdańsk Lenin Shipyard.

20. Henryk Jagielski, W-4, Gdańsk Lenin Shipyard.

21. "Kalendarium kryzysów w PRL w latach 1953–1980," *Zeszyty Historyczne* (Paris) 38, 66 (1983): 152. (hereafter cited as the "Kubiak Report.") The Kubiak Commission was constituted by the Party Central Committee during the Solidarity crisis with the task of determining the causes of cyclical crisis in Poland. The report by this commission is thus a confidential party account of political crises in postwar Poland. It is one of several internal documents that escaped from party control in the Solidarity period. Although not without significant omissions and distortions, this report is the fullest account available of official actions during the December crisis. The first part of the report is reprinted in *Zeszyty Historyczne* 65 (1982).

22. Anna Walentynowicz, Gdańsk Lenin Shipyard.

23. Stanisław Michel, Miastoprojekt (Gdańsk).

24. Henryk Jagielski, interview. The W-4 workers fit out a ship with its complementary systems, heat, electricity, and other equipment, after the basic hull and decks are ready.

25. Bronisław Duda, Interview.

26. "Grudniowe dni 1970 roku," an anonymous account in the Gdańsk 1970 archive, 10 pages.

27. Bronisław Duda, interview.

28. Adam Sarad, interview.

29. "Grudniowe dni."

30. Mirosław Marciniak, S-5, Gdańsk Lenin Shipyard.
31. Anna Walentynowicz, interview.
32. Henryk Jagielski, interview.
33. Anonymous "Grudzień" manuscript, cited in Zygmunt Korybutowicz, *Grudzień 1970* (1983), p. 44. Also see Henryk Jagielski, interview.
34. Bronisław Duda, interview.
35. Henryk Jagielski, interview.
36. Ibid.
37. Ibid.
38. Ibid.
39. Ibid.
40. Korybutowicz, *Grudzień 1970* (1983), p. 44.
41. Henryk Jagielski, interview.
42. Ryszard Ostrowski, Gdańsk Lenin Shipyard, interview.
43. Anna Walentynowicz, interview. "Obraz wydarzeń," *Głos Wybrzeża*, December 28, 1970.
44. Edward Kwasigroch and Henryk Jagielski, Lenin Shipyard, interviews.
45. Henryk Jagielski, interview.
46. Edward Kwasigroch, interview.
47. Ibid.
48. Jundziłł Report (1970).
49. Zambrowski, "Dziennik," pp. 47–48.
50. Edward Kwasigroch, interview.
51. *Trybuna Ludu*, December 15–17, 1970. In *Przesilenie grudniowe* (p. 29), Mieczysław Rakowski describes the contrast between the formal plenum and the conversations in the anterooms as rumors of the protests in Gdańsk spread.
52. Kubiak Report, p. 153. With all its omissions, this is the most accurate official source, but also useful are the Central Committee Report (1981), the Jundziłł Report (1970), the discussion and reports in the Central Committee's Eighth Plenum as found in *Nowe Drogi* (special issue, 1971), and the Rakowski book *Przesilenie grudniowe*. It is instructive to observe the immobilizing capacity of "democratic centralism." The major party officials from Gdańsk were in Warsaw when the Lenin Shipyard marched out. In their absence, the party on the coast did nothing until the Gdańsk first secretary, accompanied by Politburo member Kociołek and Police General Słabczyk, arrived early in the afternoon.
53. Antoni Tomaszewski, Gdańsk Lenin Shipyard, interview.
54. Kubiak Report, p. 155.
55. Włodzimierz Ostrowski, Gdańsk Lenin Shipyard, interview.
56. Antoni Tomaszewski, interview.
57. Henryk Jagielski, interview.
58. Kubiak Report, p. 155.
59. Gerard Nowak, Gdańsk Repair Shipyard, interview.
60. Ibid.
61. Jundziłł Report; Kubiak Report, p. 155, estimates the marching crowd at 200 persons.
62. Anonymous account titled 14.12.1970.
63. Stanisław Michel, interview.

64. Emil Białkowski, "Dziennik, Grudzień 1970 r."
65. Włodzimierz Ostrowski, interview.
66. Stanisław Michel, interview.
67. Edward Nowicki, Gdańsk Lenin Shipyard, interview.
68. Henryk Jagielski, interview.
69. Anna Walentynowicz, interview; Kubiak Report, p. 155.
70. Henryk Jagielski, interview.
71. Ibid.
72. "Obraz wydarzeń," *Głos Wybrzeża*, December 28, 1970.
73. Kubiak Report, p. 155. The first Warsaw official to go to Gdańsk, Vice Premier and Politburo member Kociołek, had arrived at 1 P.M. Although Kliszko and Loga-Sowiński were better known, the obscure General Korczyński was in fact one of the policemen most intimately involved in the establishment of Communist power in Poland. He was born in 1915, in a Warsaw worker's family; his real name was Stefan Kilanowicz. As a young worker he joined Communist youth groups, and in 1937 he left Poland as a volunteer in a Polish international brigade in Spain. The French interned him in 1939, but with the aid of the French Communist party, he escaped and clandestinely worked in the Polish section of the French party. In July 1942, he returned to Poland to command a partisan unit in Lublin Province under Mieczysław Moczar, whom he succeeded in 1944. In the postwar period, Korczyński organized Communist police in Warsaw, Lublin, and Gdańsk and was deputy chief of one of the largest security operations against partisans—Operation Vistula. On Gomułka's fall in 1949, Korczyński was arrested, tried, and sentenced to death for the murder of Jewish partisans during World War II. Although his arrest was connected with the anti-Gomułka campaign, the charges were probably true. In any event, the sentence was not carried out. In 1956, he was released and appointed general in charge of Army counterintelligence. In 1956, he was appointed vice minister of defense and given command of internal troops. Because of his connections to General Moczar, he was frequently identified as a member of the partisan faction, but others describe him as blindly loyal to Gomułka. Korczyński's obituary was published in *Wojskowy Przegląd Historyczny* 16, 4 (1971):354–65.
74. Emil Białkowski, "Dziennik, Grudzień 1970r."
75. Ibid. This is the only account of this attempt by the party to mount a counterdemonstration.
76. "Obraz wydarzeń," *Głos Wybrzeża*, December 28, 1970; Kubiak Report, p. 165.
77. Bronisław Duda, interview.
78. Edward Nowicki, interview; Henryk Jagielski, interview; Kubiak Report, p. 156; Stanisław Michel, interview.
79. Kubiak Report, p. 156.
80. Ibid.
81. Zenon Kliszko, in *Nowe Drogi* (special issue, 1971), p. 192.
82. Anonymous lawyer's account, 1970 Archive.
83. "Obraz wydarzeń," *Głos Wybrzeża*, December 28, 1970.
84. Edward Nowicki, interview.
85. "Obraz wydarzeń," *Głos Wybrzeża*, December 28, 1970.
86. Stanisław Michel, interview.

87. Ibid.

88. Ibid.

89. Kubiak Report, p. 158. The Kubiak Report is the fullest available account of the decision, but also see the Central Committee Report (1981), p. 5; Rakowski's *Przesilenie grudniowe*, pp. 160–61; and Gomułka's letter to the First Secretary of the PZPR, February 6, 1971, in Andrzejewski, *Gomułka i inni: Dokumenty*, pp. 188–90. "The use of arms was a necessity. But it was not I who first proposed sending the army into Gdańsk. Before the meeting Cyrankiewicz informed me that he had ordered Comrade Jaruzelski to send a division stationed in Elbląg to Gdańsk as Kociołek had demanded. It was also at Comrade Cyrankiewicz's suggestion, which I regard as correct, that the army division stationed in Koszalin was moved into Gdańsk. In my presence, Comrade Cyrankiewicz telephoned Comrade Jaruzelski concerning this" (Andrzejewski, *Gomułka i inni: Dokumenty*, p. 189). These two divisions were part of the Pomeranian Military District, commanded by General Józef Kamiński and his political officer, General Józef Baryła.

90. "Obraz wydarzeń," *Głos Wybrzeża*, December 28, 1970; Kubiak Report, pp. 158–59.

91. Roman Detlaff, interview.

92. Ibid.

93. Ibid.

94. Henryk Jagielski, interview. Jagielski's report that the security troops had been told that they were fighting Germans is the first of numerous accounts. One of the senior surgeons in the Gdańsk Provincial Hospital was told by troops that they had come "to pacify the German revanchists." In another such incident a student discovered a friend riding in a tank. "He'd just been mustered in and hadn't even completed his basic training and made his oath of service. The disturbances were explained as a rebellion of the Gdańsk Germans" (H. Matuszewski, interview).

95. Anonymous surgeon of the Gdańsk Provincial Hospital, 1970 Archive.

96. Anonymous doctor of the Gdańsk Provincial Hospital, 1970 Archive.

97. Gomułka, in Andrzejewski, *Gomułka i inni: Dokumenty*, p. 188.

98. Ibid.

99. In *Robotnik* (Warsaw) 70–71 (December 12, 1980). This account is confirmed by the interview with Roman Detlaff. The militiamen were taken to the Lenin Shipyard and were released unharmed; Bronisław Duda, interview.

100. Roman Detlaff, interview.

101. Romuald Micoch, Gdańsk longshoreman, interview.

102. Anonymous account in *Robotnik* 71–72 (December 12, 1980). Kubiak Report, p. 145.

103. Kubiak Report, p. 145. Of many accounts, see the interview with Bogdan Lis in Jerzy Surdykowski, *Notatki gdańskie*, pp. 163–74; and "Obraz Wydarzeń," *Głos Wybrzeża*, December 28, 1970; Kubiak Report, p. 61.

104. Romuald Micoch, interview.

105. *Nowe Drogi* (special issue, 1971), pp. 191–93. Kliszko's point is confirmed by workers' accounts. For example, see interviews with Bronisław Duda and Adam Sarad.

106. Jerzy Pieńkowski, *Nowe Drogi* (special issue, 1971), pp. 198–200; Bron-

isław Duda, interview; Edward Nowicki, interview; and Shipbuilding Association Telex 3897/70 in "Opis przebiegu wydarzeń w Stoczni im. Komuny Paryskiej w gdyni w dniach od 14 do 21 Grudnia 1970 r." ("A Description of the Occurrences in the Commune of Paris Shipyard in Gdynia from the 14th to the 21st of December 1970," with the handwritten notation, "noted during the events by order of the Director Michał Tymiński"), 15 pp. (1970), hereafter, cited as "Paris Commune Log."

107. Bronisław Duda, interview.

108. Edward Nowicki, interview; Lech Wałęsa, *Kontakt* (Paris) 11 (November 1983).

109. Paris Commune Log; Tadeusz Jaroszyński, Shop E, Paris Commune Shipyard interview; Ryszard Śwista, worker at Unimor, interview in *Grudzień 1970* (1986), pp. 312–15.

110. Hugon Malinowski, Gdynia Party First Secretary, interview.

111. Andrzej Niecki, worker in W-l, Paris Commune Shipyard, in *Grudzień 1970* (1986), pp. 323–32.

112. Tadeusz Jaroszyński, interview; Edmund Hulsz, Dalmor worker, interview.

113. Hugon Malinowski, interview. According to Malinowski, "The rumor that I left the building hidden in the bottom of a car is a vulgar lie."

114. Hugon Malinowski, interview. Ludwik Janczyszyn was born in 1923 in eastern Poland, presently Ukrainian S.S.R. He enlisted in the Kościuszko Division in 1944, served as a political officer, and transferred to the Navy in 1946. In 1947, he "fought the anticommunist bands." In 1950–52 and 1955–57, he attended Soviet military schools. He was rear admiral and chief of staff of the Polish Navy from 1959 to 1969; in 1960 he was appointed vice admiral and made commander-in-chief of the Polish Navy. He was a member of the Military Council of National Salvation from 1981 to 1983. He retired in 1986. He was a sergeant in the Soviet Armed Forces before he joined the Kościuszko Division as a second lieutenant. At least until 1950, when he was a lieutenant colonel in the Soviet Army, he held simultaneous rank in both armies and was a Soviet citizen. The source for his double status is M. Sadykiewicz, presently at Rand, a 1957 graduate of the Soviet General Staff Academy, in his unpublished manuscript, "Siły Zbrojne PRL," cited in "Poland," by Teresa Rakowska-Harmstone, in *Warsaw Pact: The Question of Cohesion*, phase 2, vol. 2, *Poland, German Democratic Republic, and Romania*, ed. Teresa Rakowska-Harmstone, Christopher D. Jones, and Ivan Sylvain (Ottawa: DND, 1984), pp. 229, 269.

115. Tadeusz Jaroszyński, interview.

116. Ibid.

117. Mieczysław Mierzejewski, hullworker, Paris Commune Shipyard, interview.

118. Jan Mariański, interview. Edward Hulsz and Tadeusz Jaroszyński described Mariański as "trembling and pale with fright."

119. Jan Mariański, interview.

120. Edward Hulsz, interview.

121. Zbigniew Grabowicz, engineer of the Paris Commune Shipyard, as cited in Wiesława Kwiatkowska, *Grudzień 1970 w Gdyni*, p. 35.

122. The agreement is found in *Grudzień 1970* (1986), pp. 219–20.

123. Edward Hulsz, interview.

124. Jan Mariański, interview.

125. The information in Korybutowicz, *Grudzień* (1983), p. 58, that Mariański was interned and his career ended for signing the agreement is in error. As is evident from his own interview, Mariański played a much more ambiguous role. In January 1971, Mariański was a serious candidate to be party first secretary in Gdynia. He was subsequently the deputy *wojewoda* or prefect in Gdańsk, and in 1973 he was a deputy to the Parliament.

126. Ryszard Śwista, Unimor worker, interview in *Grudzień 1970* (1986), p. 314; Kubiak Report, p. 300; Stanisław Słodkowski, interview in *Grudzień 1970* (1986), p. 300. The original strike leader, Edmund Hulsz, surprisingly was nowhere to be found when strikers gathered to elect a city-wide committee—a fact that strongly suggests he had been visited and threatened by security police. He was subsequently forced into exile and later testified in Rome before an international commission on human rights.

127. Jan Mariański, interview; the appeal of the strike committee announcing an occupation strike in the city written on the night of December 15 can be found in *Grudzień 1970* (1986), pp. 221–22; Tadeusz Rosiak, Gdynia port director, interview.

128. *Wieczór Wybrzeża*, December 16, 1970.

129. Ibid.

130. From the transcript of the executive meeting, as cited by Provincial Secretary Karkoszka at the Eighth Plenum, *Nowe Drogi* (special issue, 1971), p. 83.

131. Hugon Malinowski, interview.

132. Kubiak Report, p. 161; Central Committee Report (1981).

133. Stanisław Słodkowski, interview, in *Grudzień 1970* (1986), p. 300.

134. Lech Wałęsa, *Un Chemin d'Espoir* (Paris: Fayard, 1987), p. 93.

135. Ibid.

136. Jan Pydyn in an article by Krystyna Jagiełło, "Koniec wielkiego strachu," in *Tygodnik Solidarność* 19 (August 7, 1981). Włodzimierz Ostrowski, Gdańsk Lenin Shipyard, interview.

137. "Obraz wydarzeń," *Głos Wybrzeża*, December 28, 1970; Kubiak Report, p. 162.

138. The Lenin Shipyard First Secretary Jerzy Pieńkowski at the Eighth Plenum in February 1971. This detail was censored from the special issue of *Nowe Drogi* (February 1971); Rakowski, *Przesilenie grudniowe*, p. 150.

139. The location and the date became the focus of symbolic opposition to the regime on the coast for the next ten years. See a discussion of this aspect of worker's resistance in Chapter Seven.

140. Several eyewitness accounts, including Czesław Siwka, employee in charge of the PA system in the Lenin Shipyard, *Grudzień 1970* (1986), p. 183.

141. A handwritten list of the members of the Strike Council, 1970 Archive. One member of the strike committee went on to become leader of the resurgent Lenin Shipyard in August 1980. Lech Wałęsa was born in 1943 in Central Poland to a peasant family. He completed vocational school, served in the Polish army, and in 1967 started work as an electrician in the Gdańsk Lenin Shipyard. He

participated in protests against the government in March 1968. In December 1970, he served in both strike committees. In 1976, he participated in the June strike and was fired. In 1978 he joined the Free Trade Unions of the Baltic. He was the leader of the August strike in the Gdańsk Lenin Shipyard and subsequently was chairman of National Solidarity and chairman of the Gdańsk region. Reelected in fall 1981, he was interned in December 1981. He is a winner of the Nobel Peace Prize and the author of *Un Chemin d'Espoir*.

142. 1970 Archive.

143. Paris Commune Log.

144. Michał Tymiński, interview.

145. Ibid.

146. Ibid.

147. Ibid.; W. Porzycki (in December 1970), first secretary of the Paris Commune Shipyard; from January 1971, First Secretary of Gdynia, interview.

148. Michał Tymiński, interview; W. Porzycki, interview.

149. Andrzej Niecki, Paris Commune worker, interview in *Grudzień 1970* (1986), pp. 326–27. Also see Admiral Ludwik Janczyszyn, interview.

150. Michał Tymiński, interview; Władysław Porzycki, interview; Paris Commune Log; Kubiak Report, p. 164.

151. W. Porzycki, interview; Zdzisław Ślesarów, interview; Paris Commune Log; Michał Tymiński, interview.

152. Michał Tymiński, interview.

153. *Głos Wybrzeża*, December 17, 1970. The personal corruption of Kociołek has been described by Gomułka's personal interpreter Erwin Weit, in the book *Eyewitness* (London: Andre Deutsch, 1973), pp. 29–30.

154. *Głos Wybrzeża*, December 17, 1970.

155. Michał Tymiński, interview; Hugon Malinowski, interview; Jan Mariański, interview. All three saw Kociołek that night.

156. Central Committee Report (1981).

157. *Czas* (Gdańsk) 43 (December 7, 1980).

158. Antoni Węga, *Biuletyn Informacyjny Solidarność* (Gdańsk) 27 (December 11, 1980); Wiesława Kwiatkowska, *Grudzień 1970 w Gdyni*, p. 12.

159. W. Porzycki, interview.

160. Lech Wałęsa, *Un Chemin d'Espoir*, pp. 95–96.

161. Anna Walentynowicz, interview.

162. Bronisław Duda, interview.

163. Hugon Malinowski, interview; Jan Mariański, interview.

164. Edmund Pepliński, interview.

165. Adam Gotner, interview.

166. Mrs. Jurkowska, interview.

167. "Wywiad z lekarzem na temat wypadków grudniowych, 1970 r.," n.d.

168. Henryka Halmann, interview.

169. Paris Commune Shipyard, Gdynia, "Treść komunikatów nadawanych przez rozgłośnie ... [illegible] w rejonie wiaduktu i stacji kolei elektrycznej Gdynia-Stocznia w dniu 17 grudnia 1970 r. w godzinach od 5:50 do godz. 16:00" ("Announcements made over the loudspeakers in the vicinity of the viaduct and the Gdynia Shipyard station of the electric railway line on the 17th of December

1970 from 5:50 A.M. to 4:00 P.M.) Internal evidence indicates that they were recorded by the shipyard management.

170. Ibid.

171. Ibid.

172. Ibid.

173. Jacek Węglarz, interview.

174. W. Kodzik, interview.

175. Zdzisław Ślesarów, interview.

176. Adam Gotner, interview.

177. Franciszek Kaszubowski, interview. Apparently military units throughout Poland were given the German cover story: "When my son Marian arrived on leave from the army after the New Year, he said that his unit had slept in full readiness for several days. They were told that the Hitlerites want to take over the coast. How low those scoundrels can sink. This is how they lie and degrade the nation. The 'workers'' government and party did not hesitate to use militia, helicopters, armored cars, and tanks against this working class which they supposedly represent. It was all in the name of the 'defense of the interests of the working class' which are supposedly 'threatened' by brawlers and 'anti-socialists' " (Paweł Pranga, "Wspomnienia o wypadkach grudniowych 1970 r."). See also Adam Gotner, interview.

178. Mr. Lubarczewski, interview.

179. Edward Stobiński, interview.

180. Recorded tape (5½ hours) of militia radio communications on December 17 in Gdynia, 1970 Archive; Kubiak Report, p. 168.

181. Mr. Lubarczewski, interview.

182. Mieczysław Mierszejewski, interview.

183. Marianna Ruczyńska, interview.

184. Hubert Kaczkan, interview; these details about the flowers and the cross are confirmed by Naval Lt. Commander Kazimierz Kunert, M.D., letter in 1970 Archive.

185. "Decree on Public Order, no. 2, of the Presidium of the Provincial National Council in Gdańsk," December 17, 1970, in *Głos Wybrzeża*, December 18, 1970. The official count of the dead in Gdynia on December 17 was seventeen.

186. Requiem Mass for the dead, with notes on the sermon preached by Fr. R. Tadrowski. Archive of the Parish of the Sacred Heart of Jesus, Gdynia, entry for December 21, 1970 (1970 Archive).

187. Ibid.

188. Ibid.

189. Ibid.

## CHAPTER THREE

1. Jerzy Zimowski, Szczecin district prosecutor, interview.

2. Diary of Józef Piłasiewicz, director of the Social Bureau, Szczecin Port.

3. Ibid.

4. Interview with a noncommissioned officer of the Citizen's Militia—Central Station, Szczecin; hereafter cited as "Militia Sergeant Interview."

5. Grzegorz Durski, Warski Shipyard worker, interview.

6. The meeting was reported in *Kurier Szczeciński*, December 17, 1970. Walaszek's working assumptions are reported by Andrzej Głowacki, then a party worker in the party headquarters, on the basis of interviews with party secretaries: "Wydarzenia grudnia 1970 r.-stycznia 1971, r. w Szczecinie," *Vacat* 11–12 (November-December 1983): 58. *Vacat* was an underground journal published free of censorship.

7. Lucjan Adamczuk, interview. Born in rural eastern Poland, Adamczuk worked as a welder in Warski while completing lyceum and evening courses in sociology. Active as a party reformer, in 1970 he began work as an industrial sociologist. He was not a significant player in the December strike, but he was an advisor in the succeeding January 1971 strike, in which he played a major role in the deradicalization of the demands. According to the strike's leader, E. Bałuka, at one point Adamczuk attempted to unilaterally call off the strike and was never forgiven for it by the strike committee. He then left the shipyard for further studies at the Higher Party School of the Central Committee. In the 1970s he worked in the Central Statistical Office. By 1980, he was a sociologist at the Polish Academy of Sciences. He turned in his party card in December 1981. Adamczuk is the author of an unpublished dissertation on the Szczecin strikes for the Central Committee's school. He also is the author of articles entitled "La révolte des années 70 à Szczecin: les enseignements de l'histoire," *Économie et Humanisme* 278 (July-August 1984): 8–20; and with Teresa J. Makowska, "Robotnicy w dwu sytuacjach konfliktowych," *Studia Socjologiczne* 4, 9 (1983):53–72.

8. Lucjan Adamczuk, interview.

9. Ibid.

10. Antoni Kij, Warski Shipyard worker, interview.

11. Ibid.

12. Głowacki, "Wydarzenia grudnia," p. 56. Based on conversations with Walaszek and Provincial Party division directors. Antoni Walaszek, the first secretary of Szczecin, a client of Edward Gierek, had been first secretary since 1960. Even in the postwar Communist apparat, he was a legend for his ignorance and high-handedness, a kind of living Gogolian inspector general. Stories about him—some true, some apocryphal—circulated among the political elites in Poland throughout the 1960s. For example, when party and state officials started to upgrade their professional qualifications, Walaszek is said to have registered in Poznań's university. He never set foot on the university grounds, but every month or so called the rector to ask, "Do I have my doctorate yet?" Whether this is true for Walaszek is impossible to confirm, but after the fall of Gierek, investigative reporters went to the Mining and Metallurgical Academy in Kraków to try to find the engineering master's theses of several prominent political leaders, including Gierek, Politburo member M. Grudzień, and former minister of the interior Franciszek Szlachcic. They were unable to locate any such documents. The article about the scandal was entitled "Express Master's Diplomas!" All this confirmed the general sense of the leaders' incompetence and corruption.

13. "Relacja z grudnia 1970 Roku," a 27 page interview with leaders of the Warski 1970 strike, Józef Kasprzycki, Mieczysław Dopierała, Józef Fischbein, and Kazimierz Szmurło; hereafter cited as "Relacja z grudnia."

14. Ibid.

15. Marian Jaszczuk, interview, in Małgorzata Szejnert and Tomasz Zalewski, *Szczecin*, p. 37; Antoni Kij, interview.
16. Antoni Kij, interview.
17. Ibid.
18. Ibid.
19. Henryk Szorc, Szczecin Repair Shipyard worker, Gryfia, interview.
20. Ibid.
21. Ibid.
22. Ibid.
23. Antoni Kij, interview.
24. Cited in Szejnert and Zalewski, *Szczecin*, pp. 37, 38. The source of this account is Andrzej Zieliński, a graduate of Poznań Law School, who was a junior officer and legal counsel for the 12th Division. Zieliński was in the staff headquarters of the division when the exchange took place. The source for the number of troops in the party headquarters when it took fire is General Jaruzelski (Wacowska, *Rewolta Szczecińska*, p. 136).
25. Henryk Poświatowski, Szczecin Repair Shipyard, Gryfia, interview.
26. Militia Sergeant Interview.
27. Dr. Zieliński, interview. Rakowski, in *Przesilenie Grudniowe*, p. 44, estimates the crowd at 15,000 in front of the party headquarters. The Kubiak Report, p. 172, estimates a crowd of 10,000 in front of the Provincial Militia Headquarters. Both omit the presence of army troops.
28. Józef Kasprzycki, in "Relacja z grudnia."
29. Andrzej Zieliński, in Szejnert and Zalewski, *Szczecin*, p. 40. The scene in the besieged militia headquarters was pungently described by a militia sergeant. The party secretaries, Walaszek and Lenart, were in the midst of the militiamen whose respect they manifestly did not enjoy. "We mocked and cursed Walaszek. 'You bastard; you didn't even know we existed until today and here you are crying at our doorstep.' Colonel Urantówka was beside himself with panic. He and Walaszek yelled and screamed. 'We're all done for.'" The account continues: "Our bosses were continually on the telephones to Warsaw. . . . Also in the building and armed with machine guns were soldiers, practically on every floor and in every window. The army also shot. Most of the shots were in the air with tracer bullets, but I suspect the more zealous just shot straight into the crowd. As soon as it was completely dark, provincial First Secretary Walaszek, who was at the station, escaped in an armored car to divisional headquarters" (Militia Sergeant Interview).
30. Kubiak Report, pp. 172–73.
31. Andrzej Ostapiuk, in Szejnert and Zalewski, *Szczecin*, pp. 47–48. In June 1976, the modus operandi of the police was the same: "These were not individual abuses. The chief method of torture inside police headquarters involved the so-called path of health, in which the detainee was forced to run the gauntlet, passing through a long row of policemen, each of whom would strike the victim. This was a collective action, conducted probably on the orders, and certainly with the knowledge, of superiors." Jan Józef Lipski, *KOR*, p. 34.
32. *Trybuna Ludu*, June 29, 1956.
33. *Trybuna Ludu*, December 18, 1970.
34. Ibid.

35. Ibid.

36. The structure established in 1970 presaged the form of martial law instituted on December 13, 1981. A government communiqué in 1970 read: "Port workers of Gdańsk! In view of your refusal to return to work, the Committee for National Defense (KOK) was forced to assume command over the Ministry of Ports. Effective at 7:00 A.M. today, all workers of the Gdańsk Port are militarized by virtue of the complete militarization of the Gdańsk Port as an entity vital to the national economy. The militarization does not require any further announcements or individual notification. As a military economic unit, the port is subject to all regulations and punishments of military service. Refusal to work is a violation of these regulations and incurs appropriate punishments and sanctions." The communiqué was signed: "The Gdańsk Port Authority, A Militarized Economic Detachment, B. Bujwid, Director." 1970 Archive.

In 1981, the same committee organized the entire martial-law operation, setting up the Military Council of National Salvation (WRON) as its front organization. As a public legitimation of these measures, state propagandists prepared articles justifying martial law. In 1970, they claimed that "Bonn revisionists inspired the disturbances on the coast." Only seven days before, Gomułka had carried out his greatest foreign-policy success in a peace treaty with West Germany. Rakowski, *Przesilenie Grudniowe*, pp. 36–37.

37. District Prosecutor Jerzy Zimowski, interview.

38. Tuczapski's partner, Brigadier General Matejewski, with General Szlachcic, who was already in Gdańsk, had prepared, according to an unconfirmed report, the extreme scenario of the party's anti-Semitic campaign in 1968—namely show trials of prominent Jewish "wreckers" to be followed by expulsion of Jews from certain districts and towns and their concentration in camps (Michael Checinski, *Communism, Nationalism, Anti-Semitism* [New York: Karz, Kohl, 1982], p. 221). When his party patron, M. Moczar, lost the power struggle with Gierek in 1971, Matejewski was tried and condemned as the leader of a smuggling ring. In December 1970, no top political leader accompanied the generals to Szczecin. Also see Zieliński, in Szejnert and Zalewski *Szczecin*, p. 43.

39. Stanisław Wądołowski, as cited in Szejnert and Zalewski, *Szczecin*, p. 42. Born in 1938 in the Białystok province in a farmer's family, Wądołowski worked as a welder from 1956. He was elected to the strike committee in his shop in 1970. From 1970 to 1980, he was the chairman of his shop union council. In August 1980, he served on the Presidium of the Szczecin Interfactory Strike Committee and subsequently was vice chairman of Szczecin Solidarity and member of Solidarity's national commission. In Fall 1981, he was elected vice chairman of national Solidarity. In December 1981, he was arrested and interned.

40. Józef Kasprzycki, in "Relacja z Grudnia."

41. Ibid.

42. Lucjan Adamczuk, interview.

43. Franciszek Wilanowski, in *Morze i Ziemia* (Szczecin) 2 (1981): 14.

44. Stanisław Wądołowski, "Nigdy nie będę szedł bezbronny z rękami do góry," *Tygodnik Solidarność* 21 (August 21, 1981); Eugene Muszyński, party first secretary of the Warski Shipyard, interview; Edward Cochola, Warski welder, interview.

45. Stanisław Wądołowski, "Nigdy nie będę szedł. . . . "
46. Mieczysław Dopierała, in "Relacja z grudnia"; "Dzień Drugi," *Jedność* 17 (December 17, 1980).
47. Józef Kasprzycki, in "Relacja z grudnia."
48. Mieczysław Dopierała, in "Relacja z grudnia."
49. Józef Kasprzycki, in "Relacja z grudnia."
50. Józef Fischbein and Mieczysław Dopierala, in "Relacja z grudnia."
51. It is probable that the young woman was Ewa Zielińska, one of two women on the strike presidium. The other was Jola Jakimowicz.
52. Stanisław Klamecki, Szczecin Repair Shipyard, Gryfia, interview.
53. As cited in Stewart Steven, *The Poles* (New York: Macmillan, 1982), p. 176. In analyzing KOR's appeals to workers and Polish society in August 1980, Jerzy Holzer writes that "this creates the impression that KOR did not expect that political demands would be put forward by the strikers. This impression confirms information about the current views of KOR activists who believed that the acceptance of creation of independent trade unions by the state was practically out of the question" (Jerzy Holzer, *Solidarność,* p. 97).
54. The demands are reprinted in Ewa Wacowska, *Rewolta Szczecińska,* pp. 196–97.
55. Adam Michnik, "Hope and Danger," *Letters From Prison,* p. 111.
56. Ewa Wacowska, *Rewolta Szczecińska,* pp. 196–97.
57. Ibid.
58. Ibid.
59. Ibid.
60. Andrzej Głowacki, *Kryzys polityczny,* p. 65.
61. Leaflet in 1970 Archive.
62. Kubiak Report, p. 174.
63. Ibid. See, for example, the accounts in Szejnert and Zalewski, *Szczecin*; and *Jedność* 17 (December 17, 1980).
64. Militia Sergeant Interview; army and police personnel were ordered to evacuate their families as rumors of mob vengeance against police and army families in Gdańsk circulated. Soldiers were kept locked in their barracks and prohibited even from listening to official radio or television broadcasts: Henryk Górnicki, 2nd Regiment, Fighter Squadron "Kraków."
65. Militia Sergeant Interview.
66. Józef Piłasiewicz, diary notation for January 11, 1971.
67. Głowacki, *Kryzys polityczny,* p. 171.
68. Józef Kasprzycki, in "Relacja z grudnia."
69. Krzysztof Żórawski, member of the Gdańsk 1970 Historical Commission, interview by the author.
70. Józef Kasprzycki, in "Relacja z grudnia."
71. As printed in *Głos Szczeciński,* December 19, 1970.
72. Rakowski, *Przesilenie grudniowe,* p. 53. Also Kubiak Report, p. 174.
73. Col. R. Kukliński, "Wojna z narodem widziana od środka," *Kultura* (Paris) 4 (1987): 14.
74. *Nowe Drogi* (special issue, February 1971), p. 45. Also see the reports of regional secretaries at the Eighth Plenum: for example, the situation in the Ursus

Tractor Plant (p. 152) or in Wrocław factories (pp. 300–302). For evidence based on local newspapers and radio broadcasts, see the chronicle of events by Kazimierz Zamorski, published in Wacowska, *Poznań 1956—Grudzień 1970*; also published in an English version as Radio Free Europe Research, Poland 16 (June 15, 1971).

75. The general facts have been known. The quotations and details are from Gomułka's letter to the Central Committee, March 27, 1971, in Andrzejewski, *Gomułka i inni: Dokumenty*, pp. 221–23.

76. The best study of Gomułka's fall remains Z. A. Pelczynski's "The Downfall of Gomułka."

77. Józef Kasprzycki, in "Relacja z grudnia."

78. For the appeals, see *Grudzień 1970* (1986), pp. 435–36.

79. Ibid.

80. This account is based on the Protocol and Agreement that resulted from the negotiations, and on interviews with Dopierała, Fischbein, and Kasprzycki in "Relacja z grudnia." The Protocol and Agreement are reprinted in *Grudzień 1970* (1986), pp. 442–46.

81. *Kurier Szczeciński*, December 20, 1970.

82. *Trybuna Ludu*, December 20, 1970.

83. Szczecin Building Enterprise (South), 1970 Archive.

84. *Grudzień 1970* (1986), pp. 442–46; also see "Relacja z grudnia."

85. *Grudzień 1970* (1986), pp. 442–46.

86. Ibid.

87. Ibid.

88. Ibid.

89. Ibid.

90. Serafin, quoted in Szejnert and Zalewski, *Szczecin*, p. 55.

91. *Trybuna Ludu*, December 21, 1970.

92. From the written record of announcements over the PA system during the strike in the 1970 Archive, and *Grudzień 1970* (1986), pp. 432–33.

93. See the accounts of Fischbein and Kasprzycki in "Relacja z grudnia," the communiqué over the PA system of the co-optation (1970 Archive), and Bałuka's account in *Grudzień 1970* (1986), p. 502. The other new leaders, Bogdan Szymaniak, Klaudiusz Wózniak, and Eugeniusz Szerkus, were also included in the strike committee. Szerkus was a leader of Warski Solidarity in 1980–81. This episode is the most murky in the history of the strike. Both leadership groups were very hostile toward each other and minimized each other's achievements while exaggerating their own intransigence towards the party.

Edmund Bałuka was very different from Dopierała, Fischbein, and Kasprzycki. Forty years old in 1970, he had tried to escape to the West in 1956 and had been imprisoned for a year. He had worked as a seaman before coming to the shipyard, where he had risen to the post of work-task distributor. In August 1970, he supported 35 workers in his shop in a two-hour strike for a pay raise and new work norms. Sent to a new post, he was strike security commander on the Vulcan slip during the first part of the strike. He was the leader of the January 1971 Warski strike and led the worker negotiations with Gierek.

94. Emil Wysoczański, interview.

95. Józef Piłasiewicz, diary.

96. 1970 Archive.

97. Edmund Bałuka, quoted in *Grudzień 1970* (1986), p. 302.

98. Franciszek Wilanowski, in *Morze i Ziemia* 2 (1981): 22.

99. The political maturity of the work force was demonstrated by the popularity of the demand for free trade unions, which came from 60 percent of the shops and factories participating in the December mobilization. Despite the constraints implied by party supervision, the demand-gathering campaign in January produced the same demand for free trade unions from 59 percent of the shops and factories. The demand was in first place among the workers' priorities, marginally ahead of the demand for a rise in salaries. For a fuller discussion of this subject, see Chapter Eight.

100. A worker delegate gave a full account to Gierek and Jaruzelski; see Ewa Wacowska, *Rewolta Szczecińska*, p. 85.

101. Gdańsk Party Secretary Zenon Jundziłł at a meeting of the Gdynia Party Executive, January 23, 1971; 1970 Archive.

102. Edmund Bałuka, interview.

103. For a photograph of the propaganda effort, see *Głos Szczeciński*, January 20, 1971.

104. Edmund Bałuka, interview.

105. Rogowski eventually published a novel about the 1970 strikes in Szczecin: *Biały Punkt* (Szczecin: Krajowa Agencja Wydawnicza, 1986).

106. The Szczecin encounter between the workers and Gierek, Jaroszewicz, Szlachcic, and Jaruzelski was taped. The entire transcript with extensive notes by Ewa Wacowska, was published as *Rewolta Szczecińska i jej znaczenie*; useful English-language excerpts appeared in the *New Left Review* 72 (March-April 1972). See also *Głos Wybrzeża*, January 26, 1971; Paweł Pranga, Gdynia longshoreman, "Notes on the Meeting with Gierek," gives a worker's view of the meeting with Gierek, Jaroszewicz, and Szlachcic in Gdańsk on January 25.

107. Gierek, in Wacowska, *Rewolta Szczecińska*, p. 40.

108. Ryszard Wasik, mechanic, Defenders of Peace Textile Plant, Łódź, interview. This summary of the internal dynamics of the Łódź strikes rests on the interviews with Wojciech Lityński, Marchlewski Textile Plant; Ryszard Kłyś, Ortal Factory (in 1971, Defenders of Peace Textile Plant); Mr. Matuszyński, Defenders of Peace Textile Plant; Czesława Augustyniak, Marchlewski Textile Plant.

109. On the morning of February 15, there were 32 factories with 20,000 workers on strike; Kubiak Report, pp. 179–80.

110. Frances Fox Piven and Richard A. Cloward, *Poor People's Movements: Why They Succeed, How They Fail* (New York: Vintage, 1979).

111. Czesława Augustyniak, interview. The interview does not specify which verses were sung.

112. Ibid.

CHAPTER FOUR

1. Jerzy Giedroyć, "Rozmowa z Jerzym Giedroyciem sprzed dwunastu lat," *Aneks* (London) 44 (1986): 48.

2. *Słowo Powszechne*, November 5, 1956, cited in Bogdan Szajkowski, *Next to God . . . Poland* (New York: St. Martin's Press, 1983), p. 17.

3. Joint Communiqué of the Government and the Episcopate, December 7, 1956, cited in Szajkowski, *Next to God . . . Poland*, p. 18.

4. Szajkowski, *Next to God . . . Poland*, p. 20.

5. *Trybuna Ludu*, December 21 and 24, 1970.

6. Quoted in Szajkowski, *Next to God . . . Poland*, p. 30.

7. 1970 Archive, Church folder; Szajkowski, *Next to God . . . Poland*, pp. 32–33.

8. January 27, 1971, 123rd Conference of the Episcopate (copy in the 1970 Archive).

9. Stefan Cardinal Wyszyński, letter to Fr. Hilary Jastak, February 15, 1971, from the Archive of the Parish of the Sacred Heart of Jesus, Gdynia (1970 Archive).

10. Cited in Zygmunt Korybutowicz, *Grudzień 1970* (1983), pp. 112–13.

11. American political scientist Andrzej Korboński supports his citation of the phrase in the following manner: "The author first heard this phrase repeated time and time again at the 4th of July cocktail party at the residence of the U.S. Ambassador in Warsaw" (Andrzej Korboński, "Poland: Changed Relationship between the Polish United Workers' Party and the Polish People's Army," in *Security Implications of Nationalism in Eastern Europe*, ed. Jeffrey Simon and Trond Gilberg [Boulder, Colo. and London: Westview Press, 1986], pp. 266–68, 274 n. 18). State Department analyst Dale R. Herspring supports the phrase with the following footnote: "The statement has been related to me by several recent travelers to Poland" (Dale R. Herspring, "The Polish Military and the Policy Process," in *Background to Crisis: Policy and Politics in Gierek's Poland*, ed. Maurice D. Simon and Roger E. Kanet [Boulder, Colo.: Westview Press, 1981], pp. 228, 237 n. 16). Paul C. Latawski supports the phrase with the following footnote: "Jaruzelski's alleged statement has been widely repeated in the Western Press. For example John Darnton, 'Once Again, to whom and what is the Army Loyal,' *The New York Times*, February 1, 1981" (Paul C. Latawski, "The Polish Military and Politics," in *Polish Politics: Edge of the Abyss*, ed. Jack Bielasiak and Maurice D. Simon [New York: Praeger, 1984], pp. 275, 289 n. 33).

12. Wacowska, *Rewolta Szczecińska*, p. 142. The role of other commanders such as Admiral Janczyszyn and Generals Szlachcic, Tuczapski, Baryła, Chocha, and Kamiński, was also kept secret.

13. See, for example, A. Ross Johnson, Robert W. Dean, Alexander Alexiev, *East European Military Establishments: The Warsaw Pact Northern Tier* (Santa Monica, Calif.: Rand, 1980), p. 60; State Department analyst Dale Herspring, "The Polish Military and the Policy Process," p. 228; Andrzej Korboński, "The Dilemmas of Civil-Military Relations in Contemporary Poland, 1945–1981," *Armed Forces and Society* (Fall 1981): 12; Andrzej Korboński and Sarah M. Terry, "The Military as a Political Actor in Poland," in *Soldiers, Peasants, and Bureaucrats*, ed. Roman Kołkowicz and Andrzej Korboński (London: Allen and Unwin, 1982), p. 169; former State Department political officer Nicholas G. Andrews, *Poland 1980–81* (Fort Lesley J. McNair, Washington, D.C.: National Defense University Press, 1985), p. 115; Larry Watts, "Civil Military Relations in Eastern Europe: Some Reflections on the Polish Case," *Nordic Journal of Soviet and East European Affairs* 2, 4 (1985):10; Ivan Volgyes, "Military Politics of the Warsaw Pact Armies," in *Civil-Military Relations*, ed. Morris Janowitz (Beverly

Hills, Calif. and London: Sage Publications, 1981), p. 196; Latawski, "The Polish Military and Politics," pp. 275–76; David S. Mason, *Public Opinion and Political Change in Poland, 1980–82* (Cambridge and London: Cambridge University Press, 1985), p. 206; George Sanford, *Military Rule in Poland* (London and Sydney: Croom Helm, 1986), p. 65; Robin Alison Remington, "Foreword," in Jerzy J. Wiatr, *The Soldier and the Nation: The Role of the Military in Polish Politics* (Boulder, Colo. and London: Westview Press, 1988), pp. xiii–xiv; Wiatr, *The Soldier and the Nation*, pp. 118–29. In Remington's Foreword it is noted that Jerzy Wiatr is an "insider" "who worked as a civilian sociologist at the Military Political College in the 1950s" (p. xii). On all decisive points, Professor Wiatr cites Western sources and seems to be unaware of the existence of the original and widely available Polish sources that have been cited in this study and that contradict his thesis of "Corporate Military Professionalism." See note 15 below.

14. See Jan De Weydenthal, "Martial Law and the Reliability of the Polish Military," in *The Warsaw Pact and the Issue of Reliability*, ed. Daniel W. Nelson (Boulder, Colo. and London: Westview Press, 1984), pp. 225–49; Teresa Rakowska-Harmstone, "Poland"; Andrew A. Michta, *Red Eagle: The Army in Polish Politics, 1944–1988* (Stanford, Calif.: Hoover Institution Press, 1990), pp. 67–72.

15. The essential facts about 1970, as detailed earlier, were available in 1971 from a special issue of *Nowe Drogi* (February 1971) and the Zamorski chronology ("Kronika Wydarzeń"). The precise numerical details of military troops deployed has been established by the testimony of a General Staff officer, Col. Ryszard J. Kukliński, in "Wojna z narodem widziana od środka," *Kultura* (Paris) (April 1987): 14.

During the Solidarity crisis in 1980, various secret party documents escaped into public view. The letter from Gomułka to Gierek and the Central Committee after his dismissal, the Central Committee Report, and the Kubiak Report all show that Wojciech Jaruzelski and other military commanders followed the orders they received from Gomułka. This fact, of course, does not preclude their support for or participation in the maneuvering to bring Gomułka down.

See Gomułka's letter to Gierek, February 6, 1971, and the letter to the Central Committee, March 27, 1971, published in Andrzejewski, *Gomułka i inni: Dokumenty*, pp. 185–232. In this matter (sending "regular divisions to Gdańsk"), "Comrade Cyrankiewicz in my presence telephoned Comrade Jaruzelski" (p. 189). At 9 A.M., December 15, 1970, at a meeting of the party and state leadership that included Jaruzelski, Gomułka proposed martial law and a police curfew in Gdańsk (Kubiak Report, p. 158). The Kubiak report contains no mention of the two divisions sent in to Gdańsk and Gdynia.

16. *Nowe Drogi* (special issue, 1971), Eighth Plenum, p. 217.

17. General Jaruzelski in an interview by Eric Bourne, *Christian Science Monitor*, April 11, 1984.

18. Perhaps the most heartfelt sentence uttered by Admiral Janczyszyn in his 1981 interview was his final comment, "Never again will Polish soldiers allow their tanks and their weapons to be taken away from them" (1970 Archive).

19. Kuklinski, "Wojna z narodem," p. 22.

20. In 1970, trainees from the Słupsk police noncommissioned officers' school were used both in the tri-cities and in Szczecin. Some special police units arrived in

Szczecin from southern Poland on Friday, December 19, too late to be used. This can be contrasted with their performance in Radom in 1976. The disturbances there began with the start of the morning shift, when workers marched on the provincial party headquarters. Between 1:00 and 3:00 P.M., the building was pillaged and set on fire. Specialized detachments began arriving at the Radom airport at noon. By 5:00 P.M., they had entered into action, carrying out indiscriminate arrests and beating anyone found in the streets. Although more efficient in this respect, their behavior on the streets and in the prisons was remarkably similar to that of the "amateurs" six years before, with the same gauntlets of baton-swinging police and automatic brutality shown toward anyone they encountered.

21. Bolesław Sulik, "Robotnicy," pp. 65–67.

22. Wałęsa, *Un Chemin d'Espoir*, p. 116.

23. Michael Bernhard, "The Strikes of June 1976 in Poland," *Eastern European Politics and Societies* 1, 3 (Fall 1987):363–92.

24. For a detailed account of government policy, see Keith John Lepak, *Prelude to Solidarity* (New York: Columbia University Press, 1988).

25. See the documentation of this assertion in Chapter One.

26. Editorial note in Adam Michnik, *Letters from Prison*, p. 134.

27. The best account of this phase is Jan Józef Lipski's *KOR*.

CHAPTER FIVE

1. Jerzy Holzer, *Solidarność*, pp. 113, 129.

2. Touraine et al., *Solidarity*, p. 36.

3. Ibid., pp. 37–38. It should be noted that Touraine and his fellow authors did not conduct research into these assertions.

4. *From Max Weber*, ed. Hans Gerth and C. Wright Mills (New York: Harcourt Brace Jovanovich, 1986), p. 35.

5. E. J. Hobsbawm, *Primitive Rebels* (Manchester: Manchester University Press, 1959).

6. Robert Michels, *Political Parties: A Sociological Study of the Oligarchical Tendencies of Modern Democracies* (New York: The Free Press, 1962).

7. Piven and Cloward, *Poor People's Movements*.

8. See Maria Ciechocińska, *Położenie klasy robotniczej w Polsce 1929–1939* (Warsaw: Książka i Wiedza, 1965), pp. 145–46, citing T. Nułkowski (T. Daniszewski), *Proletariat polski w ogniu walk strajkowych* (Moscow, 1936), p. 28.

9. On the history of the sit-down strike, see Sidney Fine, *Sit-Down: The General Motors Strike of 1936–37* (Ann Arbor: University of Michigan Press, 1969), pp. 122–28; Irving Bernstein, *Turbulent Years: A History of the American Workers, 1933–1941* (Boston: Houghton Mifflin, 1971), pp. 572–634; Daniel Nelson, "Origins of the Sit-Down Era: Worker Militancy and Innovation in the Rubber Industry, 1934–1938," *Labor History* 23 (Spring 1982); David Brody, "The Expansion of the American Labor Movement: Institutional Sources of Stimulus and Restraint," in *Institutions in Modern America*, ed. Stephen E. Ambrose (Baltimore: The Johns Hopkins University Press, 1967).

10. J. Malara and L. Rey review forms of popular resistance in their *La Pologne d'une occupation à l'autre* (Paris: Éditions du Fuseau, 1952), pp. 213–26, 270–79. For an account of how some of these forms evolved, see Charles F. Sabel

NOTES TO CHAPTER FIVE

and David Stark, "Planning Politics and Shop-Floor Power: Hidden Forms of Bargaining in Soviet-Imposed State Socialist Systems," *Politics and Society* 11, 4 (1982):439–76.

11. Jaime Reynolds in "Communists, Socialists and Workers: Poland 1944–48," *Soviet Studies* 30, 4 (October 1978):516–39. According to Reynolds, "To the list Poznań 1956, Szczecin 1970, Radom 1976, we should add Łódź 1947" (p. 528). On the Dąbrowa strikes, see Malara and Rey, *La Pologne*, pp. 275–76.

12. Jarosław Maciejewski and Zofia Trojanowicz, eds. *Poznański Czerwiec 1956* (Poznań: Wydawnictwo Poznańskie, 1981), pp. 23–24.

13. Stanisław Matyja, "Działaliśmy jawnie i głośno," in Maciejewski and Trojanowicz, *Poznański Czerwiec*, pp. 231–33. I am indebted to Professor Lawrence Goodwyn for the general account of the destruction of the councils.

14. During the 1960s the government press in Poland headlined general strikes in France, Italy, and England, possibly alerting workers to the utility of such organizational weapons.

15. "Relacja z grudnia."

16. Sidney Tarrow, *Struggle, Politics and Reform*, p. 32.

17. See Chapter Eight for an analysis of worker's demands.

18. Michael Bernhard, "The Strikes of June 1976 in Poland," pp. 364, 387; Peter Green, "The Third Round in Poland," *New Left Review* 101–2 (1977).

19. The Agreement is conveniently presented in A. Kemp-Welch's *The Birth of Solidarity* (London: Macmillan, 1983), pp. 168–79. "The Interfactory Strike Committee as the Founding Committee of these unions, has a free choice over which form of a single union or association to adopt on the coast" (p. 169).

20. *Trybuna Ludu*, September 15, 1980. The Szczecin agreement, signed in August 1980, is an illustration of the importance of careful negotiation with the Polish Communist Party. In this agreement, the strike committee and its advisors made several ill-advised concessions. There, the right to strike was not guaranteed. The safety of those who had struck was guaranteed on paper, as it had been in 1956 and 1970–71, but everyone knew it had not been respected. Although the agreement was signed by the Szczecin interfactory strike committee, after the strike that body ceased to exist, and all that remained were individual factory committees, just as in 1971.

Two little-known documents were also integral to the agreement: a "Legal Opinion of the Experts Commission on the Question of New Trade Unions," which was kept under lock and key in the safe of the Warski management, and "Propositions Concerning the Ending of the Strike," signed by the Strike Committee Presidium and the Government Commission on August 29. The "Legal Opinion . . .," as Point 3, had the sentence: "Unity on the basis of free choice is the fundamental basis of the union movement in the Polish People's Republic." This would suggest that the principle of union uniformity rather than pluralism was to prevail. This seems to be confirmed by Point 4: "It is agreed that the registration of trade unions by the Central Council of Trade Unions has a constitutive character in accordance with Article 9, Decree on Trade Unions." This point was repeated in the "Propositions. . . ." In short, the Szczecin strikers had signed an agreement to join the government central union. The Central Council of Trade Unions would remain as overseer of the new unions, deciding whether they could exist, at what levels, with what structure, and even when to dissolve them if they acted contrary to socialist principles. In summary, the Szczecin agreement was a legal and political catastrophe.

The Szczecin strike leadership signed this agreement a day before the Gdańsk Accords, thereby weakening the Gdańsk strike and creating cause for future resentment. The Szczecin agreement is reproduced in *Protokoły Porozumień, Gdańsk, Szczecin, Jastrzębie* (Warsaw: Krajowa Agencja Wydawnicza, 1981). The "Legal Opinion" and the "Propositions Concerning the Ending of the Strike" are reprinted in *Sierpień 1980 roku w Szczecinie* (Szczecin: Socjalistyczny Związek Studentów Polskich, n.d.), pp. 166–71; see the article by Tadeusz Kowalik, "Experts and the Working Group," in Kemp-Welch, *Birth of Solidarity*, pp. 143–67. It should be noted that the Szczecin strikers were advised by several prominent Polish intellectuals.

21. Max Weber, as cited in Jack A. Goldstone, ed., *Revolutions* (New York: Harcourt Brace Jovanovich, 1986), p. 35.

22. Lech Wałęsa, *Un Chemin d'Espoir*, p. 250.

23. Karol Modzelewski was born in 1937 in Moscow. He was the adopted son of Polish Minister of Foreign Affairs Zygmunt Modzelewski. From 1954 to 1959, he was a student at Warsaw University. He was active politically in October 1956 as a member of the Revolutionary Youth Union. In 1957, he joined the Polish United Workers Party (PZPR). In 1964, he and Jacek Kuroń wrote the *Open Letter to the Party*, an analysis of the party's bureaucratic degeneration. Expelled from the PZPR in 1965, he was arrested and sentenced. In March 1968, he was arrested and sentenced on the charge of organizing an illegal association. In the 1970s he completed a doctorate in medieval economic history. In August 1980, he was an organizer of the independent trade union in Wrocław. In September he was elected a member of the Presidium of Solidarity of Lower Silesia. He was press spokesman for the National Consultative Commission, and he resigned in March 1981 after the Bydgoszcz crisis. Elected to the Union National Commission in fall 1981, he was arrested and interned under martial law. In 1989, he was elected to the Polish Senate.

24. Wałęsa, *Un Chemin d'Espoir*, p. 292. For more evidence of the effort to oust Wałęsa, see Lech Bądkowski's "The Man of What?" in *The Book of Lech Wałęsa* (New York: Simon and Schuster, 1982), pp. 120–21.

25. The full transcript is found in "Powstanie KKP (Posiedzenie Delegacji MKZ-17 IX 1980 w Gdańsku)" (the creation of the National Coordinating Commission of Solidarity, September 17, 1980), *Krytyka* 18 (1984):87–127; hereafter cited as "Powstanie KKP."

26. Wałęsa, *Un Chemin d'Espoir*, p. 297.

27. Ibid.

28. "Powstanie KKP," p. 95.

29. This account is based on the meeting transcript ("Powstanie KKP") and on the author's interviews with Krzysztof Wyszkowski, a founder of the Free Trade Unions of the Baltic (March 1982), and Jolanta Strzelecka, journalist for the Solidarity weekly *Tygodnik Solidarność* (February 1982), both of whom were present at this meeting.

30. "Powstanie KKP," p. 96.

31. Ibid., p. 93.

32. Ibid., p. 94.

33. Ibid., p. 110.

34. Jan Olszewski was born in 1930 to a Warsaw socialist family. In 1944, he fought in the Warsaw Uprising. He completed legal studies in 1953 and was immediately banned from professional activity by the Ministry of Justice. He was on the editorial board of the revisionist *Po Prostu* in 1956–57. From 1959, he worked as a lawyer specializing in political cases. He defended Kuroń and Modzelewski in 1964 and 1968 and workers in 1976. He was co-author of the founding appeal of KOR as well as the Report of Human Rights in Poland to the Madrid Conference on Human Rights in Europe. He also was co-author of the August Gdańsk Union Statute.

35. "Powstanie KKP," p. 115.

36. Ibid.

37. Olszewski also added that the unions should not in any way recall the government's central unions. "It cannot be a centrally administered union" (ibid., p. 116).

38. Ibid.

39. Ibid., p. 120. Modzelewski also pointed out that the Gdańsk regional statute would be inappropriate for the national union he favored.

40. Ibid., pp. 122–24.

41. After the meeting, Wiesław Chrzanowski, Bronisław Geremek, Tadeusz Mazowiecki, Andrzej Wielowieyski, and Andrzej Kaczyński revised the Gdańsk regional statute.

42. Krzysztof Wyszkowski, interview by the author, March 1982.

43. See the final report of the National Consulting Commission in *Tygodnik Solidarność* 24 (September 11, 1981): 7–10.

44. Ernest Skalski, "Punkt zapalny," *Tygodnik Solidarność* 25 (September 18, 1981).

45. Jan Józef Lipski, *KOR*, pp. 339–40, 492–500.

46. For a summary discussion of how intellectuals have misread the dynamics that produced Solidarity, see the Introduction and Chapter Eight.

47. For documentation of how the leadership was caught by surprise by a new wave of strikes that eventually led to Solidarity's legalization, see *The New York Times*, May 3, 4, 5, 7, 8, 11, 1988. According to Wałęsa, "We didn't think these spontaneous things would happen. But we promised we would always be with the people. I had to come" (*The New York Times*, May 6, 1988, p. A10).

48. L. P. Gerlach and V. H. Hine, *People, Power, Change: Movements of Social Transformation* (Indianapolis: Bobbs-Merrill, 1970), p. 33.

49. Ibid., p. 34.

CHAPTER SIX

1. No sociological evidence was available for another objective characteristic that merits investigation: workers' participation in religion.

2. Bauman is cited in George Gömöri, "The Cultural Intelligentsia: The Writers," in *Social Groups in Polish Society*, ed. David Lane and George Kolankiewicz (New York: Columbia University Press, 1973), p. 177; see also Charles Tilly,

"Collective Violence in European Perspective," in *A History of Violence in America*, vol. 2, ed. Ted Robert Gurr (Newbury Park, Calif. and London: Sage Publications, 1989).

3. Trotsky, *1905* (New York: Pathfinder Press, 1972), p. 291.

4. See the discussion of the effects of different peasant experiences on labor movements in Spain in Dick Geary, *European Labor Protest 1848–1939* (London: Croom Helm, 1981), pp. 179–80.

5. Eugenia Brzosko, *Problemy zatrudnienia w przemyśle województwa szczecińskiego* (Poznań: UAM, 1971), p. 42. It appears that Gdynia and its Paris Commune Shipyard may have been exceptions. Situated on prewar Polish territory, the city drew migrants from among the Kaszubs, a heavily Germanized West Slavic group. See Wieslawa Kwiatkowska, *Grudzień 1970 w Gdyni*, p. 7.

6. *Głos Szczeciński*, May 1, 1969.

7. From an internal Lenin shipyard study report, "Przyszli stoczniowcy o sobie" (n.d., but after 1977). According to Georges Mink, in advanced industries such as metalworking, more than 50 percent of workers had worker fathers by the 1960s: "La classe ouvrière en Pologne," in *Structures sociales en Europe de l'ést*, no. 2, *Transformation de la classe ouvrière*, coordinated by Georges Mink, *Notes et études documentaires*, no. 4511–4512, La Documentation Française, (May 10, 1979): 95.

8. Fikus and Urban, "Szczecin," *Polityka* 6 (February 6, 1971).

9. Gomułka, in his letter to First Secretary Gierek published in Andrzejewski, *Gomułka i inni: Dokumenty*. The shipyards were to some extent an employment of last resort in which people with criminal records could find work. See, for example, the comments of Solidarity leader Bogdan Lis on the hull workers, in Jerzy Surdykowski, *Notatki gdańskie*, p. 169.

10. "Płynność kadr w Stoczni," November 29, 1974. One detail in the study of the shipyard trades school is revealing: one-half of those studying for the undesirable job of hull worker were from other provinces. The Three Cities pupils were concentrated in more desirable slots, such as electrician (from Lenin Shipyard report "Przyszli stoczniowcy o sobie").

11. Wałęsa, *Un Chemin d'Espoir*, p. 64.

12. *Czas* (Gdańsk), July 20, 1980.

13. Fine, *Sit-Down*, pp. 102, 119.

14. Mink, "La classe ouvrière en Pologne," p. 93.

15. *Głos Szczeciński*, May 1, 1969.

16. "Large-scale industry concentrates in one place—a crowd of people unknown to one another. Competition divides their interests. But the maintenance of wages, this common interest which they have against their boss, unites them in a common thought of resistance—combination." Karl Marx, "The Poverty of Philosophy," in *Karl Marx, Selected Writings*, ed. David McLellen (Oxford: Oxford University Press, 1977), p. 214.

17. *Głos Szczeciński*, January 2, 1970.

18. *Głos Szczeciński*, May 1, 1969.

19. An internal Lenin Shipyard report, "Praca i życie załogi Stoczni Gdańskiej w Świetle jej oceny i opinii," Pracownia Socjologii Pracy Stoczni Gdańskiej im. Lenin, June-July 1972.

20. Fikus and Urban, "Szczecin."

21. "Praca i życie załogi."

22. "Płynność kadr w Stoczni."

23. But peasant-workers were one of the groups most likely to join Solidarity (20 percent of the membership) in 1980; see Jacek Kurczewski, "Solidarność od wewnątrz" (August 1981), p. 8 (an unpublished report in the author's possession).

24. Thus, according to statistics compiled by Georges Mink, the percentages of industrial manual workers in the active population in the countries of Eastern Europe at the beginning of the 1970s were: Bulgaria, 50 percent; Hungary, 58 percent; Poland, 42 percent; GDR, 57 percent; Romania, 45 percent; Czechoslovakia, 63 percent. Introduction to "La classe ouvrière en Pologne," p. 3.

25. From 1950 to 1969, the U.S.S.R. bought 78.8 percent of all Polish ships sold abroad. Other socialist countries accounted for 7.6 percent. *Radio Free Europe Research: East Europe* (Poland) 12 (September 4, 1970): 5. On problems of the industry, see Jerzy Surdykowski, "Przemysł okrętowy," *Perspektywy* (September 10, 1970).

26. This statement is based on conversations with Lenin Shipyard workers in August 1981. Even the shipyard orientation guide spoke of the unequal contracts. Also see Michael Checinski, "Poland's Military Burden," *Problems of Communism* 36 (May-June 1983):42, citing Bogusław Lesiewicz, "Friends are tested in need," *Życie Partii* (Warsaw) 21 (December 8, 1982): 16. There is strong evidence contradicting this belief. According to Franklyn Holzman, in 1980 the Soviets paid the Poles 150 percent over world prices for fishing trawlers, while they sold petroleum to Poland at 50 percent of the world rate: Holzman, *The Soviet Economy* (New York: Foreign Policy Association, 1982), p. 41. But that the shipyard workers believed their country was exploited, whether true or not, is politically decisive.

27. Stanisław Smoleński, "Przemysł okrętowy," *Życie Gospodarcze*, July 29, 1969.

28. "Płynność kadr w Stoczni."

29. Lech Wałęsa, *Un Chemin d'Espoir*, p. 67; "Płynność kadr w Stoczni."

30. "Płynność kadr w Stoczni."

31. This observation is based on the author's several months in Gdańsk and a two-week sociological stage in the Lenin Shipyard in August 1981.

32. "Płynność kadr w Stoczni."

33. A delegate from W-1 at the meeting with Gierek in the Warski Shipyard, January 24, 1971: Wacowska, *Rewolta Szczecińska*, p. 81.

34. "Praca i życie załogi."

35. Ibid.

36. See the remarks of Lech Wałęsa on the elemental solidarity of the shipyard workers against their superiors, *Un Chemin d'Espoir*, p. 73.

37. Józef Tabin in Krystyna Jagiełło, "Koniec wielkiego strachu."

38. Wacowska, *Rewolta Szczecińska*, p. 77.

39. Andrzej Głowacki, *Kryzys polityczny*, p. 14.

40. *Nowe Drogi* (special issue, 1971), p. 192.

41. Edward Jarecki, *Stocznia Gdańska im. Lenina*, p. 127.

42. Ibid., p. 33.

43. At the Eighth Plenum of the Central Committee of the PZPR, October 19–21, 1956, *Nowe Drogi* 10 (1956): 39, cited in Jarecki, *Stocznia Gdańska im. Lenina*, p. 58.

44. Jarecki, *Stocznia Gdańska im Lenina*, p. 53.

45. Ibid., p. 59.

46. Ibid., p. 75.


CHAPTER SEVEN

1. The 1970 Archive contains a folder of poetry, songs, and jokes that circulated on the coast in the 1970s.

2. Brogowski, *Wydarzenia: Dokumenty z historii* Solidarności (Gdańsk: Galeria GN, 1981). The photographs are by P. Borkowski. They were shown in a December 1980 exposition in Gdansk and published in the exposition's catalog.

3. Thomas Nipperday, "Nationalidee und Nationaldenkmal in Deutschland im 19. Jahrhundert," *Historische Zeitschrift* 206, 3 (1968):529–85; reprinted in Thomas Nipperday, *Gesellschaft, Kultur, Theorie* (Gottingen, 1976), as cited in Peter Paret and Beth Irwin Lewis, "Art, Society and Politics in Wilhelmine Germany," *Journal of Modern History* 57, 4 (December 1985):697.

4. Murray Edelman, *The Symbolic Uses of Politics* (Urbana: University of Illinois Press, 1967), p. 20.

5. Steven Lukes, "Political Ritual and Social Theory," in *Essays in Social Theory* (New York: Columbia University Press, 1977), pp. 68–69, 72, and passim.

6. "I suggest, in short, that we should go beyond the somewhat simplistic idea of political ritual expressing-producing value integration seen as the essence of social integration (which is the banal but widely applied aspect of Durkheim's theory) and take up instead the fertile idea that ritual has a cognitive dimension . . . though placing it . . . within a class structural, conflictual and pluralistic model of society" (Lukes, "Political Ritual," in *Essays in Social Theory*, p. 68).

7. Arnold Van Gennep, *The Rites of Passage* (Chicago: University of Chicago Press, 1960); Victor Turner, *Dramas, Fields and Metaphors* (Ithaca, N.Y.: Cornell University Press, 1974).

8. Lukes, "Political Ritual," in *Essays in Social Theory*, p. 69.

9. Turner, *Dramas, Fields and Metaphors*, p. 110.

10. For a wonderfully textured account of the European Revolutionary tradition that employs these categories, see James Billington's *Fire in the Minds of Men* (New York: Basic Books, 1980).

11. For accounts of Polish political religion, see Andrzej Walicki, *Philosophy and Romantic Nationalism* (New York: Oxford University Press, 1982); Ewa Morawska, "Civil Religion vs. State Power in Poland," *Society* (May-June 1984); H. G. Schenk, *The Mind of the European Romantics* (New York: Doubleday, 1969); Maria Janion and Maria Żmigrodzka, *Romantyzm i Historia* (Warsaw: Państwowy Instytut Wydawniczy, 1978); Donald Pirie, "The Agony in the Garden: Polish Romanticism," in *Romanticism in National Context*, ed. Roy Porter

and Mikuláš Teich (Cambridge and New York: Cambridge University Press, 1988); Patrick Michel, *La societé retrouvée* (Paris: Fayard, 1988).

12. For accounts of contemporary Polish symbolism that emphasize the continuities with the nineteenth-century tradition, see Elizabeth Kaczyńska, "Les symboles traditionnels dans le mouvement ouvrier d'aujourd'hui en Pologne," p. 14, presented at "La cultura operaia nella industria lizzaia," Convegno Internazionale, May 1982, Torino; Maria Janion, "On the Difference between a Worker and a 'Representative of the Working Class,'" in Bądowski, *The Book of Lech Wałęsa*; and Rudolf Jankowsky, "History and Tradition in Contemporary Poland," *East European Quarterly* 19, 3 (September 1985):349–+62. If symbols are unchanging essences, they would seem to have little analytic interest. The point of this analysis is that a closer look reveals considerable continuity and change. Much of what looks like continuity is changed by its new context. To quote Turner, *Dramas, Fields and Metaphors*, p. 55, "Since I regard cultural symbols including ritual symbols as originating in and sustaining processes involving temporal changes in social relations and not as timeless entities, I have tried to treat the crucial properties of ritual symbols as being involved in these dynamic developments."

13. The estimate is by Witold Pilecki, in the Polish underground publication, *Polityka Polska* (n.p., 1983), pp. 2–3.

14. Author's observations in Summer and Fall 1981. In the U.S.S.R., a parallel rumor held that food shortages were caused by the Soviet state's aid to the lazy, striking Poles: author's conversations with Soviet citizens in 1981. Also see Richard Cobb's essay on "Dearth, Famine and the Common People," in *The Police and the People* (London: Oxford University Press, 1970), pp. 246–317, esp. p. 278. By taking control of everything, the Leninist state created material and cultural conditions amazingly similar to those in prerevolutionary France.

15. See Peter Leinhardt, "The Interpretation of Rumour," in *Studies in Social Anthropology: Essays in Memory of E. E. Evans-Pritchard*, ed. J.H.M. Beattie and R. G. Leinhardt (Oxford: Clarendon Press, 1975), pp. 105–31.

16. Victor Turner, *The Ritual Process* (Ithaca: Cornell University Press, 1977), p. 95.

17. When he arrived in Barcelona in 1936, George Orwell wrote how "waiters and shopwalkers looked you in the face and treated you as an equal. Servile and even ceremonial forms of speech had temporarily disappeared. Nobody said *Señor* or *Don* or even *Usted;* everyone called everyone else 'Comrade' and 'Thou' and said *Salud* instead of *Buenos Dias*." George Orwell, *Homage to Catalonia*, in *The Orwell Reader* (New York: Harcourt Brace, 1956), p. 168. On universal *tutoiement* at certain stages of the French Revolution, see A. Aulard, "Le tutoiement pendant la révolution," *Études et leçons sur la révolution française*, 3rd series, vol. 28, 1 (1914); and Serge Bianchi's *La Révolution Culturelle de l'an II Élites et peuple (1789–1799)* (Paris: Aubier Montaigne, 1982), p. 144.

On the other hand, when the Polish Communists tried to institute *tutoiement* and the universal use of "Comrade" in place of *Pan* and *Pani* in the Stalinist period, it was fiercely resisted. In that context, it meant being a man or woman undifferentiated from the mass and subordinate to the state rather than being equal. For a late example of workers' resistance of the term, when the Gdańsk first secretary addressed striking workers with the title "Comrades" in 1976, the Lenin Shipyard workers replied, "We are not comrades: comrades—that is you, the bureaucracy's people." "Relacja robotników gdańskich," *Aneks* 12 (1976):31–32, as cited in Michael Bernhard, "The Strikes of June 1976 in Poland," p. 382.

18. Victor Turner, "Religious Celebrations," in Victor and Edith Turner, *Celebration* (Washington, D.C.: Smithsonian Institution Press, 1982), p. 205.

19. Florian Znaniecki, *The Method of Sociology* (New York: Farrar and Rinehart, 1936), ch. 3, cited in Turner, *Dramas, Fields and Metaphors*, p. 45.

20. Turner, *The Ritual Process*, p. 166.

21. Turner, *Dramas, Fields and Metaphors*, p. 177.

22. Turner, *The Ritual Process*, p. 167.

23. Turner, *Dramas, Fields and Metaphors*, p. 14.

24. Józef Przybylski, "Wspomnienia," *Kontakt* (Paris) 1, 21 (January 1984):32.

25. J. Gayda, "August 1980 as I Saw It,' *Sisyphus*, Polish Academy of Sciences, Institute of Philosophy and Sociology, vol. 3 (1982):251.

26. "Powstanie KKP."

27. Interview with Jerzy Janiszewski in *Tygodnik Solidarność* 1 (April 5, 1981).

28. Wałęsa's oath is printed in *Informator Solidarność*, the Repair Shipyard—Nauta (Gdynia), November 25, 1980; Marian Zalecki's *Theology of a Marian Shrine, Our Lady of Częstochowa* (Dayton, Ohio: University of Dayton Press, 1976), very usefully sets out the Polish national Marian cult. See also Patrick Michel, *La societé retrouvée*. For a comparison with another Marian nation, Mexico (the Mexican peasant revolutionary Emiliano Zapata, like Wałęsa, wore an image of Mary, Our Lady of Guadalupe, on his breast, and she was the symbol of the revolutionaries in the war of independence), see Jacques Lafaye, *Quetzalcoatl et Guadalupe: La formation de la conscience nationale au Mexique* (Paris: Gallimard, 1974), and Eric R. Wolf, "The Virgin of Guadalupe: A Mexican National Symbol," *Journal of American Folklore* 71, 279 (January-March 1958):34–39.

29. Hannah Arendt, *On Revolution* (New York: Viking Press, 1963), p. 252.

30. Claude Lévi-Strauss, *Structural Anthropology*, trans. Claire Jacobson and Brooke G. Schoepf (New York: Basic Books, 1963), p. 292. This derives from the famous sentence of Durkheim, "Les Dieux ne sont que l'expression symbolique de la societé."

31. For a discussion of boundaries in the French Revolution, see Mona Ozouf, "La Révolution Française et la perception de l'espace national: fédérations, fédéralisme, et stéréotypes régionaux," in *L'École de la France* (Paris: Gallimard, 1984), pp. 27–54.

32. We can also contrast the spatial arrangement of the First Solidarity Congress in fall 1981 with the Ninth Extraordinary Congress of the Polish Party in summer of the same year. The Congress of Solidarity, held in the Oliva Sports

Stadium, had a horizontal arrangement. The 800 or so delegates were arranged by regions, each of which had its own microphone. All were on the same level. There was an elevated podium, but it was occupied by record-keepers and meeting co-ordinators.

Like Leninist party conferences the world over, the Congress of the Communist party held in the Great Hall of Congresses of the Palace of Culture in Warsaw had a pyramidal structure. Delegates were placed below the tribunal of notables. The spatial arrangements adequately mirrored the flow of homage and information to the top of the pyramid and the flow of orders from the top of the pyramid to the base.

33. For analogous points on style in language and dress, see François Gendron's analysis of the Muscadins during the French Thermidor: "Derrière les pièces de tissus, c'était les valeurs republicaines et toute l'idéologie de la liberté quon remettait en cause." *La Jeunesse Dorée* (Sillery, Québec: Presses de l'université de Québec, 1979), p. 126; also see Richard Cobb on the beret as a symbol in occupied France, in *French and Germans, Germans and French* (Hanover and London: New England Universities Press, 1983), pp. 170–77.

34. Bohdan Pietruszak's account appears in Jacek Susul's article in *Tygodnik Powszechny* (Kraków), December 14, 1980. Also see a one-page information sheet produced by the monument committee (1980) Archive, and Pietruszak's interview in "Grudzień 70," special issue, reprint from no. 5, Biuletyn NSZ, UJ, n.p., n.d. (Hoover Institution Archive), pp. 43–47.

35. Timothy Garton Ash, *The Polish Revolution: Solidarity*, p. 102.

36. The poem was written in 1950 and published in 1953 in the book *Światło Dzienne* (Daylight). The translation is by Michael J. Mikos and appears in *The Polish Review* 16, 2 (1981); reprinted by permission of *The Polish Review*. The poem ends with the advice to the tyrant: "A winter dawn would be better for you and a rope and branch bent under the burden."

37. From conversations the week of the dedications and the Commune of Paris Solidarity bulletin, *Biuletyn Informacyjny Solidarność przy Stoczni im. Komuny Paryskiej w Gdyni* 5 (September 27, 1980).

38. Translation by Count Potocki of Montalk in *Forefathers*, by Adam Mickiewicz (London: The Polish Cultural Foundation, 1968), p. 125.

39. The author was present at the dedication. An excellent account of the ceremony by Father Stanisław Musiał appears in *Tygodnik Powszechny* (Kraków), July 5, 1981.

40. On creation of leaders in order to discipline and control societies, see Murray Edelman, "The Construction and Uses of Political Leaders," in *Constructing the Political Spectacle* (Chicago and London: University of Chicago Press, 1988), pp. 37–65.

41. Turner, *The Ritual Process*, p. 110.

42. The Rzeszów Solidarity Journal, *Wryj* 1 (November 1981).

43. Carlos Franqui, *Family Portrait with Fidel* (New York: Random House, 1984), pp. 13, 21, 33.

44. Seymour Drescher, David Sabean, and Allan Sharlin, "George Mosse and Political Symbolism," in *Political Symbolism in Modern Europe*, ed. Seymour

Drescher, David Sabean, and Allan Sharlin (New Brunswick, N.J. and London: Transaction Books, 1982), p. 3.

45. The translation is found in "Solidarity: A Documentary History," *World Affairs* 145, 1 (Summer 1982):20.

46. *The Marx-Engels Reader*, ed. Robert C. Tucker (New York: Norton, 1972), p. 362. During the August 1980 strike, the last sentence "working men of all countries, unite," was changed to "workers of all factories unite." A joke in the strike newspaper had Marx addressing the workers in 1980, "Workers of the World, Forgive Me!" (*Strajkowy Biuletyn Informacyjny Solidarność* 10 [August 20, 1980]). On the unexpected appearance of the chains on the arms of the worker monument, see Tomasz Zieliński's article in *Jedność* (Szczecin), July 24 1981.

47. For a history of May Day, see Maurice Dommanget, *Histoire du Premier Mai* (Paris: Éditions de la tête des feuilles, 1972). For the German situation, George L. Mosse, *The Nationalization of the Masses* (New York: Howard Fertig, 1975), pp. 167–71.

48. Author's interviews. The declaration is reported in *Solidarność* (Gdańsk) 13/43 (April 23, 1981).

49. Author's conversations in Kraków, May 1982.

50. Lukes, "Political Ritual and Social Theory," in *Essays in Social Theory*, p. 68.

51. For an account of the confusion induced across the entire spectrum of left and right in the West, see Timothy Garton Ash's chapter "Under Western Eyes," in *The Polish Revolution: Solidarity* pp. 305–42.

52. According to James H. Billington, Solidarity was "an unexpected improvisation forged out of old materials, a classic case of Hegelian Aufhebung." "It was the peculiar genius of the Solidarity movement to incorporate all three of these modern secular ideas—liberty, fraternity and equality into its lifeblood. It sought at once to restore some of Poland's lost liberties, to recover a sense of shared dignity and purpose and to fulfill the betrayed egalitarian promise of the socialist ideal." Introduction in Steve W. Reiquam, ed., *Solidarity and Poland* (Washington, D.C.: Wilson Center Press, 1988), p. 2.

53. The distinction between critical and mythical thinking is fundamental to Ernst Cassirer's *The Philosophy of Symbolic Forms*, trans. Ralph Manheim, 3 vols. (New Haven: Yale University Press, 1953, 1955, 1957).

54. Norman Davies, *God's Playground* (New York: Columbia University Press, 1982), 2:193.

55. David Gross, "Myth and Symbolism in Georges Sorel," in *Political Symbolism in Modern Europe*, pp. 100–117. "It was especially important for myths to identify enemies so that an unbridgeable gulf could be established between two sides, as happened between Christians and pagans in the late Roman era" (p. 109).

56. On the common inclination to sentimental genre art by Communism and National Socialism, see Martin Damus, *Sozialistischer Realismus und Kunst im Nationalsozialismus* (Frankfurt am Main: Fischer Taschenbuch Verlag, 1981); *Affiches et Imageries Russes 1914–21* (catalogue), with an introduction by Marc

Ferro and an essay by Wladimir Berelovitch, "Huit années de tourmente en images" (Paris: Musée des deux guerres mondiales et B.D.I.C., 1982). Borys Stepanovich, Butnyk-Siversk'yi, *Sovetskii plakat epokhi grazhdanskoi voiny* (Moscow: Izdatelstvo vsesoiuznoi knizhnoi palaty, 1960); Berthold Hinz, *Art in the Third Reich* (New York: Pantheon, 1979).

57. A photograph of this painting is in the author's possession.

CHAPTER EIGHT

1. As noted earlier, these materials are deposited in the Houghton Library, Harvard University, where they are cataloged under two broad categories, 1970 Archive and 1980 Archive. The demands of most of the factories that took part in the December 1970 Szczecin strike are not in these archives, and information and citations based on them are drawn from the author's notes made in October 1981 in Szczecin.

2. From the article, "Bourgeois Myths about the Interrelations of the CPSU and the Trade Unions," *Voprosy Istorii KPSS* 11 (1972), quoted in Joseph Godson, "The Role of the Trade Unions," in *The Soviet Worker*, ed. Leonard Schapiro and Joseph Godson (New York: St. Martin's Press, 1981), p. 107. Before Solidarity, the statute of the Communist party, the Polish United Workers Party (PZPR), stated that "the party directs the correct political line of the trade unions," and the trade union statute stated that the "trade unions carry out the correct line of the PZPR in the interests of the working class and the Polish nation." Also see Lenin's "Left-Wing Communism—An Infantile Disorder," for a bald statement of the subordination of trade unions to the party and a denunciation of such "counter-revolutionary machinations as independent trade unions" (*The Lenin Anthology*, ed. Robert C. Tucker [New York: Norton, 1975], pp. 572–73).

3. A joke current in Warsaw in January 1982, author's observation.

4. *Rzeczpospolita,* February 23, 1982.

5. The Warsaw Shipyard demands are reprinted in Wacowska, *Poznań 1956–Grudzień 1970,* pp. 217–18. Some factories expressed an interesting resolve with respect to state power. The Szczecin Construction Enterprise (South) sent no demands but wrote to the Warski Shipyard, "We send you brotherly workers' greetings. We support your demands. We inform you that we recognize you as the workers' *władza* [state or power] and will faithfully carry out your orders." In 1980, the Gdańsk Northern Shipyard declared, "If the political police begin repressive action, the work-team will take appropriate action in defense of the interests of the working class."

6. ZTSL Number 11, 1970.

7. ZPS Urządzeń, 1970.

8. SELFA, Szczecin, 1970.

9. Protocol of the Agreement, 1970.

10. Region 2 of the Gdańsk port, 1970.

11. Wood Industry Enterprise, Gdynia, 1980.

12. PZPS ALKA Słupsk, 1980.

13. Rejon Budynków, Gdańsk, 1980.

14. Other examples of formulations that were classified as demands to reform the existing unions are: "trade unions closer to working people," Gazy Techniczne, Szczecin, 1970; "that trade unions be separated from the strong influence of the party," ZPR DANA, Szczecin, 1970.

15. SELFA (Garment Workers), Szczecin, 1970.

16. The statute written during the strike for the Gdańsk region was later modified for the national union Solidarity after the meeting of 17 regions on September 17, 1980. After the Solidarity Congress, September-October 1981, further amendments, notably providing for a permanent executive resident in Gdańsk, were made. The citations are from the pre-Congress statute as published in the collection of texts, *Protokoły porozumień, Gdańsk, Szczecin, Jastrzębie, Statut NSZZ Solidraność.*

17. Lenin Shipyard, 1971.

18. Statute, article 9, pt. 6.

19. This varies from 15 percent to 40 percent in regions such as Leszno, Płock, Radom, and Rzeszów. Most frequently it was in the area of 20–30 percent. Unpublished report by Jacek Kurczewski, "Solidarność od wewnątrz," p. 15.

20. Lenin Shipyard, 1971.

21. Ibid.

22. Statute, article 35, point 3.

23. Cited by Alex Nove in *An Economic History of the U.S.S.R.* (Harmondsworth and New York: Penguin, 1969), p. 7.

24. For a valuable brief introduction to the scholarly literature on the nature of such a society, see Seymour Martin Lipset's review in "Industrial Proletariat," pp. 20–24. The recent tendency to extend Jan Machajski's prophetic analysis that "the triumph of socialists would bring about a society controlled by the educated classes who would exploit the underprivileged strata" ignores the extent to which the Leninist state represses and manipulates intellectuals and intellectual activity (Lipset, "Industrial Proletariat," p. 21). See George Konrad and Ivan Szelenyi, *The Intellectuals on the Road to Class Power* (New York: Harcourt Brace Jovanovich, 1979); Jan Machajski, "On the Expropriation of the Capitalists," in *The Making of Society*, ed. V. F. Calverton (New York: Modern Library, 1937), pp. 427–36. For a study of privilege in the socialist system, see Merwyn Matthews, *Privilege in the Soviet Union: A Study of Elite Life-Styles* (London and Boston: Allen and Unwin, 1978).

25. Only in one case, in 1980, does a workplace demand family subsidies like the apparat but then specifies, "If we can't have it, the apparat should not have it either." The Gdańsk Construction Enterprise.

26. *Protokoły porozumień*, p. 6.

27. Ibid.

28. A photograph of this inscription is in the possession of the author.

29. The Szczecin Fertilizer Plant, 1970.

30. The Warski Shipyard, the Szczecin Repair Shipyard, and the Szczecin Steel Works, 1970.

31. The Warski and Repair Shipyards, 1970.

32. Post Office no. 5, Szczecin, 1970.

33. Gdańsk Industrial Construction Firm (Kwidzyń Branch), 1980.
34. Naval Shipyard, Gdańsk, 1980.
35. Printing Cooperative, Słupsk, 1980.
36. Film Distribution Enterprise, Gdańsk, 1980. The decrees were published in *Dziennik Ustaw* 42 (October 7, 1972). See also the discussion of these decrees by the jurist Andrzej Stelmachowski in *Kurier Polski*, January 3, 1981, excerpts from which were reprinted in *Solidarność Białystok* 14 (March 3, 1981). For an overview of the inequality issue in English, see also Jacek Bielasiak, "Inequalities and the Politicization of the Polish Working Class," in *Communism and the Politics of Inequalities*, ed. Daniel N. Nelson (Lexington, Mass.: Lexington Books, 1983), pp. 221–47.
37. Malbork Trucking Enterprise, 1980.
38. Printing Works Cooperative, Słupsk, 1980.
39. PZPS "Alka," Słupsk, 1980.
40. Printing Works Cooperative, Słupsk, 1980.
41. Hartwig International Transport, Gdynia, 1980.
42. Film Distribution, Gdańsk, 1980.
43. Słupsk Construction Firm, 1980.
44. Central Union of Agricultural Cooperatives, Gdańsk, 1980.
45. Słupsk Logging Machines Factory, 1980.
46. Gdańsk Travel Production Enterprise, 1980.
47. Bydgoszcz Construction Firm "East," 1980.
48. Gardening Cooperative, Elbląg, 1980.
49. Cooperative "Jedność," Gdańsk, 1980.
50. For example, in the account based on government and Solidarity polls found in David S. Mason, "Solidarity, the Regime and the Public," *Soviet Studies* 35 (1983):545–53.
51. I owe this formulation to Professor James Scott of Yale University.
52. This saying is received wisdom among Polish workers, and numerous sociological studies confirm its importance. Wałęsa recalls Gracchus Babeuf: "Let there be no other difference between people than that of age or sex. Since all have the same needs and the same faculties, let them henceforth have the same education and the same diet. They are content with the same sun and the same air for all; why should not the same portion of the same quality of nourishment not suffice for each of them?" "Manifeste des égaux" (1976), in *Les precurseurs français du socialisme de Condorcet à Proudhon*, ed. M. Leroy (Paris, 1948), pp. 67–68, translation by Steven Lukes, *Essays in Social Theory*, p. 213.

For a study of egalitarian attitudes among industrial workers, see Bogusław Błachnicki, "Równość ekonomiczna w świadomości pracowników przemysłu," *Studia Socjologiczne* 4 (1977):135–53. For American attitudes about justice as merit, see Robert Lane, *Political Ideology* (New York: Free Press, 1973). For an introduction to the abundant literature on egalitarianism in postwar Poland, see H. Malewska-Peyre, "Les Recherches sur les Modes de Pensée Égalitaire," *Sociologie du Travail* 3 (1983):333–46, and H. Flakierski, "Solidarity and Egalitarianism," *Canadian Slavonic Papers* 25, 3 (September 1983):380–91.
53. 1970 Archive; *Grudzień 1970* (1986), p. 220.
55. PSTBR no. 2, Elbląg, 1980.

55. Provincial Computing Center, Gdańsk, 1980.
56. ZDS i Cent. Starogard, Gdańsk, 1980.
57. Zakłady Przemysłu Pasmanteryjnego "Pasani," Gdańsk, 1980.
58. Gdynia Bus Service, 1980.
59. The figure does not total to 305 because several workplaces were counted in two categories, such as truckers for the Medical Academy, who had demands characteristic of both the truckers and the health branch.

CHAPTER NINE

1. Staniszkis, *Poland's Self-Limiting Revolution*, p. 50.
2. Smolar, "Contestation Intellectuelle," p. 148.
3. Michnik, "KOR i Solidarność," p. 75.
4. A Gdańsk Lenin Shipyard worker also made the following suggestion in 1971: "Change the name of the Lenin Shipyard, for it is an insult to Lenin and the ideology he stands for" (1970 Archive).
5. Edward Friedman, "Modernization and Democratization," pp. 260–62. For the church scapegoating, see articles, interviews, and speeches by Józef Cardinal Glemp, primate of Poland, Father Michał Paradowski and Father Piotr Taras, professor at the Catholic University of Lublin, as cited in Chapter One, note 3. For the party scapegoating, see Tadeusz Szafar, "Anti-Semitism: A Trusty Weapon," in Brumberg, *Poland*, pp. 109–22.
6. Staniszkis, *Poland's Self-Limiting Revolution*, pp. 51–52, 59, 122. Professor Staniszkis does not provide evidence for this view.
7. The Lublin demands were extensively excerpted in the excellent Solidarity regional journal *Miesiące* 1 (1981). The entire first issue is devoted to the July 1980 strikes. Since the demands were not complete, a computer-based analysis was not possible.
8. But the Fabryka Samochodów Ciężarowych FSC—a truck factory—asked for "freeing the activities of trade unions from the state administration and party apparat, permitting the printing in the press of everything which bears on economic and political life." *Miesiące* 1 (1981): 23.
9. "Stop burning committees, start building them" is a line spoken by the composite character representing Jacek Kuroń and Bogdan Borusewicz in Wajda's film, "Man of Iron." Due to censorship, Jacek Kuroń was not named in the film. For an American political scientist's statement of this claim, see Adam Przeworski, "Man of Iron and Men of Power," p. 17.
10. On January 14, 1971, the members of the interfactory strike committee of Gdynia, who had been released from prison, were arrested because they found a "revolutionary workers' party" that would seek to take power from the Polish Communist party. The founding of the revolutionary party was discovered by the Gdańsk 1970 historical research team. A copy of the act of indictment is in the 1970 Archive. "Postanowienie o umorzeniu dochodzenia w sprawie przeciwko Stanisławowi Słodkowskiemu i innym podejrzanym o udział w okresie 11–13 stycznia 1971 r. w związku, którego istnienie, ustrój i cel miały pozostać tajemnicą wobec organów państwowych," April 3, 1971.
11. Alex Pravda, "The Workers," in Brumberg, *Poland*, pp. 68–91.

12. Leszek Kołakowski, "The Intelligentsia," in Brumberg, *Poland*; Pelczynski, "Solidarity and the 'Rebirth of Civil Society'"; Garton Ash, *The Polish Revolution: Solidarity*; Lipski, *KOR*; Touraine et al., *Solidarity*.

13. Representative of this view are Staniszkis, *Poland's Self-Limiting Revolution*; Smolar, "Contestation Intellectuelle"; and Michnik, "KOR i Solidarność."

14. "Only on the basis of a study of political processes in the masses themselves can we understand the role of parties and leaders . . . without a guiding organization, the energy of the masses would dissipate like steam not enclosed in a piston-box. But nevertheless what moves things is not the piston or the box, but the steam." Leon Trotsky, *The History of the Russian Revolution* (Ann Arbor: University of Michigan Press, 1960), p. 19.

15. Bonnell, *Roots of Rebellion*, p. 48, citing Max Vasmer, *Russisches etymologisches Wörterbuch* (Heidelberg: C. Winter, 1953–58), "Rabochii." Also see Aleksander Bruckner, *Słownik Etymologiczny Języka Polskiego* (Warsaw: Wiedza Powszechna, 1957), p. 459.

16. Ryszard Kapuściński, in *Kultura* (Warsaw) 37 (September 14, 1980).

17. See, for example, Eugene D. Genovese's *Roll Jordan, Roll* (New York: Vintage, 1974), pp. 285–324, in particular his chapters "Time and Work Rhythms," "A Lazy People," and "The Black Work Ethic."

18. Kapuściński, in *Kultura* (Warsaw) 37 (September 14, 1980). This is also the claim of Zygmunt Bauman, citing Andrzej Kijowski, in "Intellectuals in East-Central Europe: Continuity and Change," *Eastern European Politics and Society* 1, 2 (Spring 1987): 184–85; and Andrzej Kijowski, "Co się zmieni to . . .," *Arka* 1–9 (Kraków, 1983–84): 131–42.

19. Józef Chałasiński, *Społeczna genealogia inteligencji polskiej* (Warsaw: Czytelnik, 1946), p. 19.

20. *Polityka* 42 and 44 (1980). These were the first extended interviews of the union's leaders to appear in the Polish mass media.

21. *Żolnierz Wolności*, February 3, 1971.

22. *Polityka*, April 24, 1971.

23. Aleksander Gella, "The Life and Death of the Old Polish Intelligentsia," *Slavic Review* 30, 1 (March 1971):1–27. On this point also see George Gömöri, "The Cultural Intelligentsia."

24. Joseph Rothschild, *East Central Europe between the Two World Wars* (Seattle: University of Washington Press, 1974), p. 28.

25. Andrzej Kijowski, "Co się zmieni to . . .," pp. 131–42, as cited in Bauman, "Intellectuals in East-Central Europe," p. 184.

26. See as representative of a large literature, Alain Touraine, *The Post-Industrial Society* (New York: Random House, 1971), p. 51; A. W. Gouldner, *The Future of Intellectuals and the Rise of the New Class* (New York: Seabury, 1979), p. 83; George Konrad and Ivan Szelenyi, *The Intellectuals on the Road to Class Power* (New York: Harcourt Brace Jovanovich, 1979).

27. Sheldon S. Wolin, *Politics and Vision* (Boston: Little, Brown and Company, 1960), p. 406.

28. Marx, "Critique of Hegel's Philosophy of Right," in *The Marx-Engels Reader*, ed. Robert C. Tucker (New York: Norton, 1972), p. 23. In this statement, Marx is at his most Leninist.

29. T. H. Marshall, *Citizenship and Social Class* (Cambridge: Cambridge University Press, 1950).

30. Weber applied his theory of bureaucratization to Russia. "By a sociological analysis of classes and parties in Russia, Weber—among other trains of thought—indicated that once the Czar fell, after a European war and the extreme left came to power in another revolution (he is writing during the first revolution in 1905), an unheard-of bureaucratization of the entire social structure of Russia might well result." From the Introduction by H. H. Gerth and C. Wright Mills to *From Max Weber*, p. 37.

31. Frank Parkin, *Class Inequality and Political Order* (New York: Praeger, 1971), p. 161, citing Gerth and Mills, *From Max Weber*, p. 184. I base this observation on conversations with Lenin shipyard and Paris Commune shipyards workers.

32. Note the observation by Barrington Moore in his conclusion to *Injustice*: "Nor does the fact that factory workers so far have shown little inclination, and perhaps even little capacity, for generating wide-ranging answers for the problems that plague humanity mean that answers or important contributions to the answers can never come from that quarter. Educational levels are rising along with exposure to other currents in modern culture. Workers may become a conservative force similar to nineteenth-century peasants in Western Europe, anxiously clinging to the limited gains they have achieved at great cost, and fearful of forces in the modern world that threaten them. As long as capitalism works tolerably well, that could be the predominant trend. But there is no guarantee that capitalism will continue to work that way. In response to new and severe strains, equipped with a wider cultural horizon, industrial workers could generate a surge of popular inventiveness culminating in a wholly new diagnosis and remedy for social ills" (p. 479).

33. Victoria E. Bonnell, *Roots of Rebellion*, pp. 10, 444–46.

# B I B L I O G R A P H Y

1970 ARCHIVE, SOLIDARITY COLLECTION, HOUGHTON LIBRARY, HARVARD UNIVERSITY, CAMBRIDGE, MASSACHUSETTS

Before Solidarity, members of the democratic opposition, in particular Bogdan Borusewicz and the group Young Poland, collected testimony concerning the 1970 and 1971 strikes. In the Fall of 1980, groups led by Joanna Wojciechowicz and Antoni Wręga of Gdańsk Solidarity collected more materials and gathered testimony and interviews. In early 1981, Gdańsk Solidarity formed a group to investigate 1970. This group, which was helped by many other persons, consisted of Ewa Dering, Aleksander Klemp, Janusz Krupski, Wiesława Kwiatkowska, Jan Andrzej Stępek, and Krzysztof Żórawski. In addition to gathering historical materials, this team also carried out the great bulk of the interviews found in the archive. Interviews were taped and then transcribed. Due to the losses suffered under martial law, when part of the archive was seized by the political police, it is not always possible to know when an interview was carried out. Much of this material was published in *Grudzień 1970* (1986) and Wiesława Kwiatkowska, *Grudzień 1970 w Gdyni* (1986). A significant part now is available only in the Houghton Library, Harvard University, Cambridge, Massachusetts, particularly interviews with local party and industrial managers in the city of Gdynia. A small but important portion of the archives consists of diaries and letters written during the events. Only the transcripts of interviews are available, and the archive is not classified beyond the broad category of "1970 Archive."

*Interviews, Diaries, Testimonies, Letters*

Adamczuk, Lucjan. Warski Shipyard. n.d.

Anonymous account, labelled 14.12.1970.

Augustyniak, Czesława. Marchlewski Textile Plant, Łódź. N.d.

Balewski, H. Technical Gases, Gdańsk-Oliwa. A letter to the Gdańsk branch of the Polish Sociological Association. January 5, 1981.

Bałuka, Edmund, Warski Shipyard. N.d.

Barthold, Stefan, Szczecin Port. N.d.

Białkowski, Emil. "*Dziennik* Grudzień 1970 r." N.d.

Bobkowska, Cecylia. "Strach" (An account sent to Gdańsk Solidarity). N.d.

Budziński, Stanisław, Gdynia Paris Commune Shipyard. N.d.

Bżowy, Barbara, M.D. Gdynia-Śląska, November 19, 1980.

Cochola, Edward. Warski Shipyard, welder. N.d.

"Dane ewidencyjne dotyczące rannych załatwionych w Akademiii Medycznej w Gdańsku w czasie wydarzeń grudnia 1970." N.d.

Detlaff, Roman. Gdańsk Rail Repair Shop. N.d.

Drogosz, Ireneusz. Gdynia Youth Work Corps. A handwritten account. June 10, 1981.

Drożak, Mr. Gdynia Paris Commune Shipyard. N.d.

Duda, Bronisław. Gdańsk Lenin Shipyard. Letter to Gdańsk Solidarity. May 14, 1981.

Durski, Grzegorz. Warski Shipyard worker. N.d.

Galant, Andrzej. Gdynia. N.d.

Gdynia, "Lekarz-ortopeda, R.O." (An anonymous account of a Gdynia orthopedist.) N.d.

Gdynia City Hospital. Hospital log, "Ranni z dnia 17 Grudnia." December 17, 1970.

Gintrowski, Marian. Gdynia. Letter to Gdańsk Solidarity. N.d.

Górnicki, Henryk. 2nd Regiment Fighter Squadron "Krakow," Goleniów, Szczecin. N.d.

Gotner, Adam. Gdynia Paris Commune Shipyard. N.d.

Grela, Henryk. Szczecin bus driver. N.d.

"Grudniowe Dni 1970 roku." An anonymous account of an administrative worker in the Gdańsk Lenin Shipyard. N.d.

"Grudzień 1970." Anonymous anesthesiologist, Gdynia. December 1980.

Hallmann, Henryka. Nurse, Gdynia. N.d.

Hulsz, Edmund. Gdynia Dalmor. N.d.

Jagielski, Henryk. Gdańsk Lenin Shipyard. N.d.

Jagielski, Krzysztof. Szczecin seaman (PLO). N.d.

Jakubowski, Zdzisław. Gdańsk Provincial Center for Mothers and Children. Letter to Gdańsk Solidarity. March 30, 1981.

Janczyszyn, Ludwik, Admiral. Commander in Chief of the Polish Navy in 1970. Interview by Wiesława Kwiatkowska. 1981.

Jaroszyński, Tadeusz. Gdynia Paris Commune Shipyard, Shop E. "Mój grudzień 1970." N.d.

Jurkowska, Mrs. Gdynia. N.d.

Kaczkan, Hubert. Gdynia Port. N.d.

Kalanowski, Zdzisław. Gdynia. N.d.

Karczewska, Eleonora. Gdynia. Interview by Wiesława Kwiatkowska. N.d.

Kasprzyk, Mr. Gdynia longshoreman. N.d.

Kaszubowski, Franciszek. Priest, Gdynia. N.d.

Kaszubowski, Leon. Gdynia. N.d.

Kij, Antoni. Warski Shipyard worker. N.d.

Klamecki, Stanisław. Szczecin Repair Shipyard, Gryfia. N.d.

Kłyś, Ryszard. Ortal Factory, Łódź; in 1971, Defenders of Peace Textile Plant, Łódź. N.d.

Kodzik, W. Apprentice, Gdynia Paris Commune Shipyard. N.d. [In the transcript in the 1970 Archive, he appears as W. Kodzik; in *Grudzień 1970* (1986), pp. 348–49, he appears as Stanisław Kodzik.]

Kopeć, Mr. Locomotive Works worker, Szczecin Main Rail Station. N.d.

Kraczkiewicz-Dulas. Irena, Gdynia Repair Shipyard. March 2, 1981.

Krajewski, Wiesław, Szczecin Warski Shipyard. N.d.

Kropielnicka, Renata. Letter to Gdańsk Solidarity concerning the death of her father in Gdynia. October 10, 1980.

Kubaly, Stefan. Gdynia Paris Commune Shipyard. N.d.

Kucner, Mr. Gdańsk Lenin Shipyard. May 30, 1981.

Kunert, Kazimierz, M.D. Lieutenant "Notatka z przebiegu pracy w punkcie pomocy lekarskiej w Prezydium Miejskiej Rady Narodowej w Gdyni w dniach 15–20, 12, 1970r." N.d.

Kwasigroch, Edmund. Welder, Gdańsk Heating Enterprise. Letter concerning his participation in the December 1970 events. June 26, 1981.

"Lekarz chirurg zatr. w Szpit. Wojew. w Gdańsku." N.d.

"Lekarz-pracownik Chirurgii Akad. Med. w Gdańsku, 'Wspominenia z grudnia 1970r.' " N.d.

Lidzbarski, Roman. Warski Shipyard. N.d.

Lityński, Wojciech. Marchlewski Textile Plant, Łódź. N.d.

Lubarczewski, Mr. Gdynia Paris Commune Shipyard. N.d.

Malinowski, Hugon. First Secretary of the Gdynia Party Committee in 1970. Interview by Wiesława Kwiatkowska. 1981.

Marciniak, Mirosław. S-5, Gdańsk Lenin Shipyard, June 1, 1981.

Mariański, Jan. Chairman of the Gdynia National Council in 1970. Interview by Wiesława Kwiatkowska, 1981.

Matuszewski, H. Gdynia. A handwritten account. December 15, 1980.

Matuszyński, Mr. Defenders of Peace Textile Plant, Łódź. N.d.

Michel, Stanisław, "Wspomnienia z dni grudniowych." Gdańsk Miastoprojekt. N.d.

Micoch, Romuald. Gdańsk longshoreman. Interview conducted June 16, 1981.

Mierzejewski, Mieczysław. Gdynia Paris Commune Shipyard. Interview by Wiesława Kwiatkowska. N.d.

Militia Sergeant. [Militia Sergeant Interview.] Szczecin, Central District. N.d.

Muszyński, Eugeniusz. Party First Secretary, Warski Shipyard. N.d.

Nastały, Zbigniew. Wejherowo, father of a victim. N.d.

Niemiec, Roman. Letter concerning his firing from the Gdańsk Repair Shipyard on December 22, 1970, addressed to Gdańsk Solidarity. N.d.

Nowak, Gerard. Gdańsk Repair Shipyard. August 19, 1981.

Nowak, Tadeusz. Gdynia Paris Commune Shipyard. N.d.

Nowakowski, Wincenty. Gdynia bus driver. Interview by Ewa Dering and Aleksander Klemp. N.d.

Nowicki, Edward, Gdańsk Lenin Shipyard. May 18, 1981.

Olszewski, Mieczyslaw. Gdańsk Lenin Shipyard. June, 1981.

Ostrowski, Ryszard. Gdańsk Lenin Shipyard. "Ankieta Grudzień 1970." November 13, 1980.

Ostrowski, Włodzimierz. Gdańsk Lenin Shipyard. June 6, 1981.

Pepliński, Edmund. Photographer, Gdynia. N.d.

Pietrzak, Henryk. Student, Gdańsk Polytechnic. N.d.

Piłasiewicz, Józef. "Relacja uczestnika zdarzeń." Szczecin Port, December 17, 1970–January 24, 1971. [A diary.]

Portych, Leszek. Director of traumatic surgery in the Gdańsk Medical Academy. Interview by Henryk Majewski. July 20, 1981.

Porzycki, W. First Secretary of the Paris Commune Party Committee in December 1970; subsequently First Secretary of the Gdynia Party Committee. Interview by Wiesława Kwiatkowska. 1981.

Poświatowski, Henryk. Szczecin Repair Shipyard, Gryfia. N.d.

Pranga, Paweł. Gdynia longshoreman. "Diariusz grudniowyj" (including notes of the meeting in Gdańsk with Gierek, Szlachcic, and Jaroszewicz on January 25, 1971). N.d.

————. "Wspomnienia o wypadkach grudniowych 1970 r." N.d. An autobiographical account from World War II to 1970 of a Gdynia longshoreman and union activist). N.d.

Referiowska, Maria, M.D. "To co pamiętam z grudnia 1970 r., lekarz anestezjolog pracujący w Szpitalu Wojew. w. Gdańsku w Klinice Ortopedycznej." N.d.

"Relacja lekarza sądowego." N.d.

"Relacja matki poległego w. grudniu 1970 r. studenta." N.d.

"Relacja pielęgniarki—matki poszkodowanego w wypadkach grudniowych 1970 r." N.d.

"Relacja pielęgniarki na temat pracy w szpitalu w okresie wypadków grudniowych 1970 r. Gdynia—Grabówka Hospital." N.d.

"Relacja z Grudnia." 1970 Roku. Interviews with Józef Kasprzycki, Kazimierz Szmurło, Józef Fischbein, and Mieczysław Dopierała. Szczecin Warski Shipyard and Planning Bureau (COKB). N.d.

Remiszewska, Teresa. Gdynia Paris Commune Shipyard. N.d.

Rosiak, Tadeusz. Gdynia Port Director in 1970; in 1981, First Secretary of the Gdynia Party Committee. Interview by Wiesława Kwiatkowska. 1981.

Ruczynska, Marianna. Gdynia. N.d.

Sarad, Adam. Gdańsk Lenin Shipyard. Letter to Gdańsk Solidarity. N.d.

Sieradz, Stanisław. Gdynia Vocational Refrigeration School. N.d.

Ślesarow, Zdzisław. Gdynia Paris Commune Shipyard. N.d.

Steńka, Stanisław, Gdynia Paris Commune Shipyard. May 19, 1981.

Stobiński, Edward. Gdynia Hotel apprentice worker. N.d.

Szorc, Henryk. Szczecin Repair Shipyard, Gryfia. N.d.

Szpital Morski im. P.C.K., Gdynia-Redłowo. Hospital log for December 17, 1970.

Szylar, Jan. Szczecin Odra Shipyard. N.d.

Szymański, Mr. Construction worker of the Gdańsk Power Works. N.d.

Tomaszewski, Antoni. Gdańsk Lenin Shipyard. Letter to Gdańsk Solidarity. January 2, 1981.

Tymiński, Michał, Director of the Paris Commune Shipyard in 1970. Interview by Wiesława Kwiatkowska. 1981.

Walentynowicz, Anna. Gdańsk Lenin Shipyard. June 20, 1981.

Wąsik, Ryszard. Mechanic, Defenders of Peace Textile Plant, Łódź. N.d.

Watkowski, Edmund. Chief Mechanic, Przedsiębiorstwo Transportu Handlu Wewnętrznego. Letter to Gdańsk Solidarity. May 8, 1981.

Weber, Stanisław. Gdynia. N.d.

Węglarz, Jacek. Gdynia Paris Commune Shipyard. N.d.

Winnicki, Paweł. Szczecin Port. N.d.

"Wspomnienia zespołu anestezjologów szpitala morskiego w Gdyni." Kierownik dr. med. Marian Wroczyński, lek. med. Hanna Topolewicz-Broda, lek. med. Jolanta Misterek, lek. med. Andrzej Kozielecki. N.d.

"Wspomnienia z grudnia 1970, lekarz ortopeda pracujący w klin. ortop. w szpitalu wojew. w Gdańsku." N.d.

Wyciechowski, Zbigniew. Gdynia. N.d.

Wysoczański, Emil. Chemical Factory "Police," Szczecin. N.d.

Wyszyński, Stefan Cardinal. Letter to Father Hilary Jastak, February 15, 1971. From the Archive of the Parish of the Sacred Heart of Jesus, Gdynia.

"Wywiad z lekarzem na temat wypadków grudniowych, 1970 r." N.d.

"Wywiad z pielęgniarką na temat wypadków grudniowych 1970 r." Gdynia. N.d.

Zając, Rudolf. Gdańsk longshoreman. Interview conducted June 16, 1981.

Zajeczonko, Krystyna. Gdynia. N.d.

Zieliński, M.D. Szczecin Pomorzany Hospital. N.d.

Zimowski, Jerzy. Szczecin District Court prosecutor. N.d.

*Other Documents and Historical Materials*

Central Committee Report. See "Informacja o Wydarzeniach Grudniowych 1970 r. na Wybrzeżu."

"Informacja o strajkach i zjawiskach towarzyszących 'wydarzeniom grudniowym' w Zarządzie Portu Szczecin." Szczecin. April 1971. An internal report on the strikes in the Szczecin Port prepared for the management.

"Informacja o Wydarzeniach Grudniowych 1970 r. na Wybrzeżu," with the notice on the top margin, "To be transmitted only by word of mouth." [Central Committee Report.] According to the party-connected scholar A. Głowacki in his article in *Zapiski Historyczne* (Toruń) (1981): 128, this document dates from February-March 1981 and was issued by the Central Committee.

Jundziłł Report. See "Notatki ze spotkania z sekretarzami KW."

Kołodziejczyk, Tadeusz. Journalist. Letter to Jan Mariański, president of the Gdynia National Council. March 18, 1971.

Matusiak, Małgorzata. "Kalendarium" (A chronology of events in Szczecin), December 17, 1970–January 25, 1971. N.d.

"Nagranie milicyjne." Approximately six hours of taped conversations between militia patrol cars and their command post, Gdynia, December 17, 1970.

"Notatki ze spotkania z sekretarzami KW." [Jundziłł Report.] Notes from a meeting of Secretaries Karkoszka and Jundziłł with the Secretaries of the Provincial Committee. Gdańsk. December 22, 1970.

Paris Commune Shipyard, Gdynia. [Paris Commune Log.] "Opis Przebiegu Wydarzeń w Stoczni im. Komuny Paryskiej w Gdyni w dniach od 14 do 21 grudnia 1970 r." [15 typed single-spaced pages with the handwritten notation that they were made during the events by the order of the shipyard director.]

———. "Treść komunikatów nadawanych przez rozgłośnie . . . [illegible] w rejonie wiaduktu i stacji kolei elektrycznej Gdynia-Stocznia w dniu 17 grudnia 1970 r. w godzinach od. 5:50 do godz. 16:00." (Announcements made over the loudspeakers in the vicinity of the viaduct and the Gdynia Shipyard station of the electric railway line on December 17, 1970, from 5:50 A.M. to 4:00 P.M.

Paris Commune Shipyard, Gdynia, Dział Organizacji. "Przebieg pracy w Dziale

Organizacji w okresie od 14 do 21 grudnia 1970." (Events in the personnel office of the Paris Commune Shipyard, December 14–21, 1970.)

"Postanowienie o umorzeniu dochodzenia w sprawie przeciwko Stanisławowi Słodkowskiemu i innym podejrzanym o udział w okresie 11–13 stycznia 1971 r. w związku, którego istnienie, ustrój i cel miały pozostać tajemnicą wobec organów państwowych." April 3, 1971. (Prosecutor's account of the anti-Communist party formed by Gdynia workers.)

"Protokól ustaleń między delegatami robotniczymi i Janem Mariańskim podpisany w Gdyni 15 grudnia 1970."

Protokól z ogólnego zebrania załogi Fabryki Urządzeń "Techmet." Pruszcz Gdański. 21 stycznia 1971.

"Protokól z posiedzenia Egzekutywy Komitetu Miejskiego w Gdyni w dniu 23 stycznia 1971 r."

Requiem Mass for the dead, performed in Gdynia, December 21, 1971, with notes on the sermon preached by Fr. R. Tadrowski. Archive of the Parish of the Sacred Heart of Jesus, Gdynia.

"Solidarny bunt." A chronology of events in Szczecin, December 17–22, 1970. N.d.

"Spotkanie z sekretarzem KC PZPR, tow. E. Gierkiem i Premierem Tow. P Jaroszewiczem." Typewritten notes of the encounter between party leaders and Gdańsk workers, January 25, 1971.

1980 ARCHIVE, SOLIDARITY COLLECTION. HOUGHTON LIBRARY, HARVARD UNIVERSITY, CAMBRIDGE, MASSACHUSETTS

At the conclusion of the August 1980 strike, the interfactory strike committee based in the Lenin Shipyard deposited its records in the Gdańsk Solidarity Archive. This August 1980 archive essentially consists of demands written by 305 factories supporting the strike, along with supporting letters and telegrams. All filmed demands in this archive along with many supporting documents are deposited in the Houghton Library, Harvard University, Cambridge, Massachusetts.

OTHER UNPUBLISHED MATERIALS (IN AUTHOR'S POSSESSION)

Kurczewski, Jacek. "Solidarność od wewnątrz," August 1981. [Unpublished report on Solidarity's internal structure.]

Lenin Shipyard Internal Report. "Płynność kadr w Stoczni." November 29, 1974.

———. "Praca i życie załogi Stoczni Gdańskiej w świetle jej oceny i opinii." Pracownia Socjologii Pracy Stoczni Gdańskiej im. Lenina. June-July 1972.

———. "Przyszli stoczniowcy o sobie." N.d.

———. "Wyniki sondażu przeprowadzonego wśród załogi robotniczej K-2." N.d.

"Robotnicy 80." Transcript of the session sponsored by the Forum of the Association of Polish Journalists, Warsaw, December 12, 1980.

Strzelecka, Jolanta. Interview by the author. Warsaw. February 1982.

Wałęsa, Lech. Interview by the author. Gdańsk. April 1981.

Wyszkowski, Krszsztof. Interview by the author. Warsaw. March 1982.

Żórowski, Krzysztof. Interview by the author. Szczecin. November 1982.


PUBLISHED ACCOUNTS AND SECONDARY SOURCES

Adamczuk, Lucjan. "La révolte des années 70 à Szczecin: les enseignements de l'histoire." *Économie et Humanisme* 278 (July-August 1984): 8–20.

*Affiches et Imageries Russes 1914–21* (catalogue). With an introduction by Marc Ferro and an article by Wladimir Berelovitch, "Huit années de tourmente en images." Paris: Musée des deux guerres mondiales et B.D.I.C., 1982.

Andrews, Nicholas G. *Poland 1980–81*. Fort Lesley J. McNair, Washington, D.C.: National Defense University Press, 1985.

Andrzejewski, Jakub, ed. *Gomułka i inni: Dokumenty z Archiwum KC 1948–1982*. Warsaw: Krąg, 1986.

Ansart, Pierre. *Idéologies, Conflits et Pouvoir*. Paris: Presses Universitaires de France, 1977.

Arendt, Hannah. *On Revolution*. New York: Viking Press, 1963.

Ascherson, Neal. *The Polish August*. London: Allen Lane, 1981.

Aulard, A. "Le tutoiement pendant la révolution." *Études et leçons sur la révolution française*, 3rd ser., vol. 28, no. 1 (1914).

B., Bogdan. [Bogdan Borusewicz.] Interview. "Grudzień 70," special issue, reprint from no. 5. Biuletyn NZS UJ (n.p.. n.d.):39–42.

Bałuka, Edmund. "Drugi strajk szczeciński." *Na Antenie* (September 1973):22–25; (October 1973):15–17.

Bauman, Zygmunt. "Intellectuals in East-Central Europe: Continuity and Change." *Eastern European Politics and Societies* 1, 2 (Spring 1987):162–86.

Bernhard, Michael. "The Strikes of June 1976 in Poland." *Eastern European Politics and Societies* 1, 3 (Fall 1987):363–92.

Bernstein, Irving. *Turbulent Years: A History of the American Workers, 1933–1941*. Boston: Houghton Mifflin, 1971.

Bethell, Nicholas. *Gomułka*. New York: Holt, Rinehart and Winston, 1969.

Bianchi, Serge. *La révolution culturelle de l'an II: Élites et peuple (1789–1799)*. Paris: Aubier Montaigne, 1982.

Billington, James H. *Fire in the Minds of Men*. New York: Basic Books, 1980.

———. "Introduction." In *Solidarity and Poland*, edited by Steve W. Reiquam, pp. 1–4. Washington, D.C.: Wilson Center Press, 1988.

*Biuletyn Informacyjny Solidarność* (Gdańsk) 27 (December 21, 1980). (Special issue for the anniversary of 1970.)

Bonnell, Victoria E. *Roots of Rebellion: Workers' Politics and Organizations in St. Petersburg and Moscow, 1900–1914*. Berkeley: University of California Press, 1983.

*The Book of Lech Wałęsa*. Introduction by Neal Ascherson. New York: Simon and Schuster, 1982.

Borowczak, Jerzy, Bogdan Felski, and Lucjan Prądzyński. "Człowiek rodzi się i żyje wolny." *Tygodnik Solidarność* 20 (August 14, 1981).

Brody, David. "The Expansion of the American Labor Movement: Institutional Sources of Stimulus and Restraint." *In Institutions in Modern America,* edited by Stephen E. Ambrose, pp. 11–36. Baltimore: Johns Hopkins University Press, 1967.

Brogowski, Leszek. *Wydarzenia: Dokumenty z historii Solidarności.* Gdańsk: Galeria GN, 1981.

Bromke, Adam. *Poland: The Protracted Crisis.* Oakville, Ontario: Mosaic Press, 1983.

Brumberg, Abraham, ed. *Poland: The Genesis of a Revolution.* New York: Random House, 1983.

Brzosko, Eugenia. *Problemy zatrudnienia w przemyśle Województwa Szczecińskiego.* Poznań: UAM, 1971.

Butnyk-Siversk'yi, Borys Stepanovich. *Sovetskii plakat epokhi grazhdanskoi voiny.* Moscow: Izdatelstuo vsesoiuznoi knizhnoi palaty, 1960.

Cassirer, Ernst. *The Philosophy of Symbolic Forms.* Translated by Ralph Manheim. 3 vols. New Haven: Yale University Press, 1953, 1955, 1957.

Checinski, Michael. *Communism, Nationalism, Anti-Semitism.* New York: Karz, Kohl, 1982.

———. "Poland's Military Burden." *Problems of Communism* 36 (May-June 1983):31–44.

Ciechocińska, Maria. *Położenie klasy robotniczej w Polsce 1929–1939.* Warsaw: Książka i Wiedza, 1965.

Cobb, Richard. *French and Germans, Germans and French.* Hanover and London: New England Universities Press, 1983.

———. *The Police and the People.* London: Oxford University Press, 1970.

Connor, Walker. *The National Question in Marxist Leninist Theory and Strategy.* Princeton, N.J.: Princeton University Press, 1984.

Connor, Walter D. *Socialism, Politics and Equality.* New York: Columbia University Press, 1979.

Damus, Martin. *Sozialistischer Realismus und Kunst im Nationalsozialismus.* Frankfurt am Main: Fischer Taschenbuch Verlag, 1981.

Davies, Norman. *God's Playground,* Vols. 1, 2. New York: Columbia University Press, 1982.

De Weydenthal, Jan B. *The Communists of Poland.* Stanford, Calif.: Hoover Institution Press, 1978.

———. "Martial Law and the Reliability of the Polish Military." In *The Warsaw Pact and the Issue of Reliability,* edited by Daniel W. Nelson, pp. 225–49. Boulder, Colo. and London: Westview Press, 1984.

———. "The Worker's Dilemma of Polish Politics: A Case Study." *East European Quarterly* 13, 1 (1977):95–119.

Dommanget, Maurice. *Histoire du Premier Mai.* Paris: Éditions de la tête des feuilles, 1972.

Drescher, Seymour, David Sabean, and Allan Sharlin. "George Mosse and Political Symbolism." In *Political Symbolism in Modern Europe: Essays in Honor of George Mosse,* edited by Seymour Drescher, David Sabean, and Allan Sharlin, pp. 1–10. New Brunswick, N.J. and London: Transaction Books, 1982.

*Dyskusja nad programem i taktyką związku.* Gdańsk: BIPS, August 1981.

Dzięciołowski, Jerzy. "Druga zmiana w Trójmieście." *Życie Gospodarcze* 38 (September 20, 1970).

Edelman, Murray. *Constructing the Political Spectacle.* Chicago and London: University of Chicago Press, 1988.

————. *The Symbolic Uses of Politics.* Urbana: University of Illinois Press, 1967.

Fikus, Dariusz. *Foksal 81.* London: Aneks, 1984.

Fikus, Dariusz, and Jerzy Urban. "Szczecin." *Polityka* (February 6, 1971).

Fine, Sidney. *Sit-Down: The General Motors Strike of 1936–37.* Ann Arbor: University of Michigan Press, 1969.

Forment, Carlos A., "Socio-Historical Models of Spanish-American Democratization: A Review and a Reformulation," Harvard University, Sociology Department, Center for Research on Politics and Social Orgaization, Working Papers Series, October 1988.

Franqui, Carlos. *Family Portrait with Fidel.* New York: Random House, 1984.

Friedman, Edward. "Modernization and Democratization in Leninist States: The Case of China." *Studies in Comparative Communism* 22, 2–3 (Summer/Autumn 1989):251–64.

Furchel, Antoni. "Mimo tragedii wierzę w partię." *Polityka* (February 13, 1971).

Gajda, J. "August 1980 as I Saw It." *Sisyphus.* Polish Academy of Sciences, Institute of Philosophy and Sociology, vol. 3 (1982): 236–52.

Garton Ash, T. *The Polish Revolution: Solidarity.* New York: Vintage, 1985.

Geary, Dick. *European Labor Protest, 1848–1939.* London: Croom Helm, 1981.

Gella, Aleksander. "The Life and Death of the Old Polish Intelligentsia." *Slavic Review* 30, 1 (March 1971):1–27.

Gendron, François. *La Jeunesse Doreé.* Sillery, Québec: Presses de l'université de Québec, 1979.

Genovese, Eugene D. *Roll Jordan, Roll: The World the Slaves Made.* New York: Vintage, 1974.

Gerlach, L. P., and V. H. Hine. *People, Power, Change: Movements of Social Transformation.* Indianapolis: Bobbs-Merrill, 1970.

Giedroyć, Jerzy. "Rozmowa z Jerzym Giedroyciem sprzed dwunastu lat." *Aneks* (London) 44 (1986).

Glemp, Józef Cardinal. Interview, in *O Estado de São Paolo* (March 2, 1983).

*Głos Wolny* (Warsaw) 6 (January 17, 1981). Special issue, "December 1970."

Głowacki, Andrzej. *Kryzys polityczny 1970 roku w świetle wydarzeń na Wybrzeżu Szczecińskim.* Szczecin: Szczecińskie Towarzystwo Naukowe, 1985.

————. "Wydarzenia grudnia 1970 r.-stycznia 1971 r. w Szczecinie." *Zapiski Historyczne* (Toruń) 46, 4 (1981):127–54. Also published in *Vacat* 11–12 (November-December 1983):58–73.

Goldstone, Jack A., ed. *Revolutions.* New York: Harcourt Brace Jovanovich, 1986.

Gömöri, George. "The Cultural Intelligentsia: The Writers." In *Social Groups in Polish Society,* edited by David Lane and George Kolankiewicz, pp. 152–79. New York: Columbia University Press, 1973.

Green, Peter. "The Third Round in Poland." *New Left Review* 101–2 (1977): 69–109.

Gross, David. "Myth and Symbolism in Georges Sorel." In *Political Symbolism in Modern Europe*, edited by Seymour Drescher, George Sabean, and Allan Sharlin, pp. 101–17. New Brunswick, N.J. and London: Transaction Books, 1982.

*Grudzień 70.* Warsaw: Biblioteka Głos, 1981. [Documents and interviews concerning 1970.]

*Grudzień 1970.* Paris: Éditions Spotkania, 1986. [Containing the interviews and documents gathered by the 1970 research team in Gdańsk.]

*Grudzień 1970, Wybór Dokumentów.* Warsaw: Gdański Sierpień, 1981. [A collection of documents from 1970.]

Grudzinska-Gross, Irena. "The Art of Solidarity." *International Popular Culture* 3 (1985). [A special issue on the art of Solidarity.]

Gusfeld, Joseph. *Symbolic Crusade: Status Politics and the American Temperance Movement.* Urbana: University of Illinois Press, 1963.

Hahn, Werner G. *Democracy in a Communist Party.* New York: Columbia University Press, 1987.

Hann, C. M. *A Village without Solidarity.* New Haven: Yale University Press, 1985.

Herspring, Dale, R.. "The Polish Military and the Policy Process." In *Background to Crisis: Policy and Politics in Gierek's Poland*, edited by Maurice D. Simon and Roger E. Kanet, pp. 221–38. Boulder, Colo.: Westview Press, 1981.

Hinz, Berthold. *Art in the Third Reich.* New York: Pantheon, 1979.

Hobsbawm, Eric J. *Primitive Rebels.* Manchester: Manchester University Press, 1959.

Holzer, Jerzy. *Solidarność, 1980–1981.* Paris: Instytut Literacki, 1984.

Holzman, Franklyn. *The Soviet Economy.* New York: Foreign Policy Association, 1982.

Jagiełło, Krystyna. "Koniec wielkiego strachu." *Tygodnik Solidarność* 19 (August 7, 1981). [Interviews with Jozef Tabin and Jan Pydyn, workers of the Lenin Shipyard.]

Janion, Maria. "On the Difference between a Worker and a 'Representative of the Working Class.'" In *The Book of Lech Wałęsa.* pp. 126–37. New York: Simon and Schuster, 1982.

Janion, Maria, and Maria Żmigrodzka. *Romantyzm i historia.* Warsaw: Państwowy Instytut Wydawniczy, 1978.

Janiszewski, Jerzy. Interview. *Tygodnik Solidarność* 1 (April 5, 1981).

Jankowsky, Rudolf. "History and Tradition in Contemporary Poland," *East European Quarterly* 19, 3 (September 1985):349–62.

Jarecki, Edward. *Stocznia Gdańska im. Lenina.* Warsaw: Książka i Wiedza, 1985.

*Jedność (Szczecin)* 17 (December 17, 1980). [An issue devoted to December 1970.]

Jędrychowski, Stefan. "Mój pogląd na źródła kryzysów w Polsce Ludowej." *Zdanie* 1 (April 1982).

Johnson, A. Ross, Robert W. Dean, and Alexander Alexiev. *East European Military Establishments: The Warsaw Pact Northern Tier.* Santa Monica, Calif.: Rand, 1980.

Kaczyńska, Elizabeth. "Les symboles traditionnels dans le mouvement ouvrier d'aujourd'hui en Pologne." Presented at "La cultura operaia nella industraia lizzaia," Convegno Internazionale, Torino, May 1982.

"Kalendarium kryzysów w PRL w latach 1953–1980." [The Kubiak Report.] *Zeszyty Historyczne* (Paris) 38, 66 (1983):144–95. [This detailed chronology of Polish crises was prepared by a Central Committee commission and escaped into public view during martial law.]

Kaufman, Michael T. *Mad Dreams, Saving Graces.* New York: Random House, 1989.

Kawalec, Stefan. *Demokratyczna opozycja w Polsce.* New York: Wydawnictwo Głos, 1982.

Kemp-Welch, A., ed. *The Birth of Solidarity.* London: Macmillan, 1983.

Kijowski, Andrzej. "Co się zmieni to. . . ." *Arka* 1–9, (Krakow, 1983–1984): 131–42.

Kirby, Andrew. "State, Local State, Context and Spatiality: A Reappraisal of State Theory." In *The Elusive State,* edited by James A. Caporaso, pp. 204–26. Newbury Park and London: Sage Publications, 1989.

Kirkpatrick, Ervin R. "Solidarity: A Documentary History." *World Affairs* 145, 1 (Summer 1982). [A special issue containing fundamental documents of Solidarity.]

Klandermans, Bert. "The Formation and Mobilization of Consensus." In *From Structure to Action: Comparing Social Movement Research across Cultures,* edited by Bert Klandermans, Hanspeter Kriesi, and Sidney Tarrow, pp. 173–96. Greenwich, Conn.: JAI, 1988.

Kociołek, Stanisław. Interview by Marzena and Tadeusz Woźniak. *Czas* (Gdańsk) (December 7, 1980).

Kołakowski, Leszek, "The Intelligentsia." In *Poland: The Genesis of a Revolution,* edited by Abraham Brumberg, pp. 54–67. New York: Random House, 1983.

Kolankiewicz, George. "Poland, 1980: The Working Class under 'Anomic Socialism.' " In *Blue-Collar Workers in Eastern Europe,* edited by J. F. Triska and Charles Gati, pp. 136–56. London: Allen and Unwin, 1981.

———. "The Polish Industrial Manual Working Class." In *Social Groups in Polish Society,* edited by David Lane and George Kolankiewicz, pp. 88–151. New York: Columbia University Press, 1973.

Kołodziejczyk, Tadeusz. "Kontynuacja w nowych warunkach." *Rada Narodowa* 12 (March 20, 1971).

Korbonski, Andrzej. "The Dilemmas of Civil-Military Relations in Contemporary Poland, 1945–1981." *Armed Forces and Society* (Fall 1981):3–20.

———. "Poland: Changed Relationship between the Polish United Workers' Party and the Polish People's Army." In *Security Implication of Nationalism in Eastern Europe,* edited by Jeffrey Simon and Trond Gilberg, pp. 257–75. Boulder, Colo. and London: Westview Press, 1986.

Korboński, Andrzej, and Sarah M. Terry. "The Military as a Political Actor in Poland." In *Soldiers, Peasants, and Bureaucrats,* edited by Roman Kołkowicz and Andrzej Korboński, pp. 159–79. London: Allen and Unwin, 1982.

Korczyński, General Grzegorz. Obituary. *Wojskowy Przegląd Historyczny* 16, 4 (1971):354–55.

Korybutowicz, Zygmunt. *Grudzień 1970*. Paris: Instytut Literacki, 1983.

Kowalik, Tadeusz. "Experts and the Working Group." *The Birth of Solidarity*, edited by A. Kemp-Welch, pp. 143–167. London: Macmillan, 1983.

Kowalski, Sergiusz, and Jacek Kurczewski. *Sprawy Związkowe*. Biblioteka Biuletynu Informacyjnego Instytutu Badań Jądrowych, vol. 4, Warsaw, August 1981.

Kubiak Report. See "Kalendarium Kryzysów w PRL lata 1953–1980."

Kukliński, Ryszard J. "Wojna z narodem widziana od środka." *Kultura* (Paris) 4 (April 1987): 3–57.

Kuroń, Jacek. Interview. "Grudzień 70," special issue, reprint from no. 5. Biuletyn NZS UJ (n.p.. n.d.): 37–39.

———. Interview. *Les Temps Modernes* 372 (July 1977).

———. *Polityka i odpowiedzialność*. London: Aneks, 1984.

———. *Wiara: Wina*. London: Aneks, 1989.

Kuroń, Jacek, and Karol Modzelewski. "An Open Letter to Communist Party Members." In *Revolutionary Marxist Students in Poland Speak Out*. New York: Merit Publishers, 1969.

Kwiatkowska, Wiesława. *Grudzień 1970 w Gdyni*. Archiwum Solidarności, vol. 11, Relacje i Opracowania. Warsaw: Wydawnictwo Pokolenie, 1986.

Laba, Roman. "La longue marche de la classe ouvrière polonaise." *Le Monde Diplomatique* (February 1983).

———. "Political Symbolism of Solidarity." *Vidnova* (Munich) (Winter 1985-Spring 1986): 204–33.

———. "Solidarité comme organisation." *L'Autre Europe* (Paris) 23 (1990).

———. "Solidarité et les luttes ouvrières en Pologne 1970–1980." *Actes de la Recherche en Sciences Sociales* (Paris) 61 (March 1986): 7–34.

———. "Worker Roots of Solidarity." *Problems of Communism* 35, 4 (July-August 1986): 47–67.

Lane, David. "The Role of Social Groups." In *Social Groups in Polish Society*, edited by David Lane and George Kolankiewicz, pp. 302–26. New York: Columbia University Press, 1973.

Lane, David, and George Kolankiewicz, eds. *Social Groups in Polish Society*. New York: Columbia University Press, 1973.

Łapiński, Ireneusz, ed. *Gdańsk, Sierpień 1980*. Warsaw: Instytut Wydawniczy Związków Zawodowych, 1981.

Latawski, Paul C. "The Polish Military and Politics." In *Polish Politics: Edge of the Abyss*, edited by Jack Bielasiak and Maurice D. Simon, pp. 268–92. New York: Praeger, 1984.

Leinhardt, Peter. "The Interpretation of Rumour." In *Studies in Social Anthropology: Essays in Memory of E. E. Evans-Pritchard*, edited by J.H.M. Beattie and R. G. Leinhardt, pp. 105–31. Oxford: Clarendon Press, 1975.

Lepak, Keith John. *Prelude to Solidarity*. New York: Columbia University Press, 1988.

Lévi-Strauss, Claude. *Structural Anthropology*. Translated by Claire Jacobson and Brooke G. Schoepf. New York: Basic Books, 1963.

Lipset, Seymour Martin. "Industrial Proletariat in Comparative Perspective." In

*Blue-Collar Workers in Eastern Europe*, edited by Jan F. Triska and Charles Gati, pp. 1–28. London: Allen and Unwin, 1981.

Lipski, Jan Józef. *KOR*. Berkeley: University of California Press, 1985.

Łopiński, Maciej, Marcin Moskit, and Mariusz Wilk. *Konspira*. Paris: Éditions Spotkania, 1984.

Lukes, Steven. *Essays in Social Theory*. New York: Columbia University Press, 1977.

Machejek, Władysław. "Renesans Gomułki: Był 'satrapą'?" *Życie Literackie* (Kraków) (June 20, 1982).

Maciejewski, Jarosław, and Zofia Trojanowicz, eds. *Poznański Czerwiec 1956*. Poznań: Wydawnictwo Poznańskie, 1981. [Documents of the Poznań uprising of 1956.]

Majkowski, Władysław. *People's Poland*. Westport, Conn. and London: Greenwood Press, 1985.

Makowska, Teresa J., and Lucjan Adamczuk. "Robotnicy w dwu sytuacjach konfliktowych." *Studia Socjologiczne* 4 (1983):53–72.

Malanowski, Jan. *Polscy robotnicy*. Warsaw: Książka i Wiedza, 1981.

Malara, Jean, and Lucienne Rey. *La Pologne d'une Occupation à l'autre*. Paris: Éditions du Fuseau, 1952.

Mann, Michael. "The Social Cohesion of Liberal Democracy." *American Sociological Review* 35, 3 (June 1970):423–39.

Marshall, T. H. *Citizenship and Social Class*. Cambridge: Cambridge University Press, 1950.

Marx, Karl. "Contribution to the Critique of Hegel's Philosophy of Right." In *The Marx-Engels Reader*, edited by Robert C. Tucker, pp. 53–65. New York: Norton, 1972.

———. "The Poverty of Philosophy." In *Karl Marx, Selected Writings*, edited by David McLellen, pp. 195–215. Oxford: Oxford University Press, 1977.

Michel, Patrick. *La societé retrouvée*. Paris: Fayard, 1988.

Michels, Robert. *Political Parties: A Sociological Study of the Oligarchical Tendencies of Modern Democracies*. New York: The Free Press, 1962.

Michnik, Adam. "KOR i Solidarność." *Zeszyty Historyczne* (Paris) 64 (1985): 67–106.

———. *Letters from Prison*. Berkeley: University of California Press, 1985.

Michta, Andrew A. *Red Eagle: The Army in Polish Politics, 1944–1988*. Stanford, Calif.: Hoover Institution Press, 1990.

Mickiewicz, Adam. *Forefathers*. Translated by Count Potocki of Montalk. London: Polish Cultural Foundation, 1968.

*Miesiące* 1 (1981), Region Środkowo-Wschodni NSZZ Solidarność. [A special issue devoted to the July 1980 strikes in Lublin.]

Mills, C. Wright. *Power, Politics and People: Collected Essays of C. Wright Mills*. Edited by I. L. Horowitz. New York: Oxford University Press, 1960.

Miłosz, Czesław. "To the Tyrant." Translated by Michael J. Mikos. *The Polish Review* 16, 2 (1981).

Mink, Georges. "La classe ouvrière en Pologne." In *Structures sociales en Europe de l'ést*, no. 2, *Transformation de la classe ouvrière*, coordinated by Georges

Mink. *Notes et études documentaires*, no. 4511–4512. La Documentation Française, 10 Mai 1979, pp. 81–112.

Montias, J. M. "Observations on Strikes, Riots, and Other Disturbances." In *Blue-Collar Workers in Eastern Europe*, edited by Jan Triska and Charles Gati, pp. 173–86. London: Allen and Unwin, 1981.

Moore, Barrington, Jr. *Authority and Inequality under Capitalism and Socialism.* Oxford: Oxford University Press, 1987.

————. *Injustice: The Social Bases of Obedience and Revolt.* White Plains, N.Y.: M. E. Sharpe, 1978.

————. *Social Origins of Dictatorship and Democracy.* Boston: Beacon Press, 1966.

Morawska, Ewa. "Civil Religion vs. State Power in Poland." *Society* (May-June 1984): 29–34.

*Morze i Ziemia* (Szczecin) 2 (1981). [A special issue devoted to December 1970 and January 1971 in Szczecin.]

Mosse, George L. *The Culture of Modern Europe: The Nineteenth and Twentieth Centuries.* Chicago: Rand McNally, 1961.

————. *The Nationalization of the Masses.* New York: Howard Fertig, 1975.

Muskat, Mariusz. "Grudzień przed Sierpniem." Interview with Bogdan Borusewicz and Błażej Wyszkowski. *Tygodnik Solidarność* 37 (December 11, 1981).

Nelson, Daniel. "Origins of the Sit-Down Era: Worker Militancy and Innovation in the Rubber Industry, 1934–1938." *Labor History* 23 (Spring 1982): 198–225.

Niezabitowska, Małgorzata. "Sztandar i drzwi." *Tygodnik Solidarność* 37 (December 11, 1981).

*Niezależność* (Warsaw) 10 [December 22, 1980]. (A special issue for the anniversary of December 1970.]

Nipperday, Thomas. "Nationalidee und Nationaldenkmal in Deutschland im 19. Jahrhundert." *Historische Zeitschrift* 206, 3 (1968):529–85; reprinted in Thomas Nipperday, *Gesellschaft, Kultur, Theorie.* Göttingen, 1976.

Nove, Alec. *The Economics of Feasible Socialism.* London: Allen and Unwin, 1983.

Nowak, Jan. *Wojna w eterze.* Vol. 1, *1948–1956.* London: Odnowa, 1985.

*Nowe Drogi* (special issue) (February 1971).

O'Donnell, Guillermo, Philippe C. Schmitter, and Laurence Whitehead. *Transitions from Authoritarian Regimes.* Baltimore: The Johns Hopkins University Press, 1986.

Olbrycht, Jerzy. "Raport ze Stoczni Gdańskiej." *Życie Partii* (August 1971): 2–5.

*Opis.* Seria Historyczna "Grudzień 1970–Relacje" Część 1 (Gdańsk: Ośrodek Prac Społeczno-Zawodowych, MKZ NSZZ Solidarność, 1981). [A pamphlet containing several eyewitness accounts of December 1970.]

Orwell, George. *Homage to Catalonia.* In *The Orwell Reader.* New York: Harcourt Brace, 1956.

Owszany, Ewa, Tadeusz Stec, and Marian Szulc. "Dziesięć lat później." *Gazeta Południowa* (Kraków) (December 24–28, 1980).

Ozouf, Mona. "La Révolution Française et la perception de l'espace national:

fédérations, fédéralisme, et stéréotypes régionaux." In *L'École de la France*, pp. 27–54. Paris: Gallimard, 1984.

Panné, J.-L., and E. Wallon. *L'enterprise sociale: le pari autogestionnaire de Solidarność*. Paris: L'Harmattan, 1986.

Paret, Peter, and Beth Irwin Lewis. "Art, Society and Politics in Wilhelmine Germany." *Journal of Modern History* 57, 4 (December 1985):696–710.

Parkin, Frank. *Class Inequality and Political Order*. New York: Praeger, 1971.

Pelczynski, Z. A. "The Downfall of Gomułka." *Canadian Slavonic Papers* 15, 1–2 (1973): 1–23. Reprinted in *Gierek's Poland*, edited by Adam Bromke and John W. Strong, pp. 1–23. New York, Washington, D.C., and London: Praeger, 1973.

———. *The History of Poland since 1863*, edited by R. F. Leslie, chs. 12–17. Cambridge: Cambridge University Press, 1983.

———. "Solidarity and the 'Rebirth of Civil Society' in Poland, 1976–81." In *Civil Society and the State*, edited by John H. Keane, pp. 361–80. London: Verso, 1988.

Persky, Stan. *At the Lenin Shipyard*. Vancouver: New Star Books, 1981.

Pietruszak, Bohdan. Interview. "Grudzień 70," special issue, reprint from no. 5, Biuletyn NZS, UJ (n.p., n.d.):43–47.

Pirie, Donald. "The Agony in the Garden: Polish Romanticism." In *Romanticism in National Context*, edited by Roy Porter and Mikuláš Teich, pp. 317–44. Cambridge and New York: Cambridge University Press, 1988.

Piven, Frances Fox, and Richard A. Cloward. *Poor People's Movements: Why They Succeed, How They Fail*. New York: Vintage, 1979.

Ploss, Sidney. *Moscow and the Polish Crisis*. Boulder, Colo. and London: Westview, 1986.

Polish Helsinki Watch Committee. *Prologue to Gdańsk*. New York: U.S. Helsinki Watch Committee, 1980.

"Polish Workers and Party Leaders—A Confrontation." *New Left Review* 72 (March-April 1972): 35–53. [English-language excerpts of the meeting of Gierek and other party officials with Szczecin workers in January 1971.]

Pomian, Krzysztof. *Pologne: Défi à l'impossible*. Paris: Les éditions ouvrières, 1982.

———. *Wymiary polskiego konfliktu 1956–1981*. London: Aneks, 1985.

Potel, Jean-Yves, ed. *La Mémoire Ouvrière 1970–1980*. Paris: F. Maspero, 1982. [An edited collection of interviews, documents, and analysis of 1970.]

———. *The Promise of Solidarity*. New York: Praeger, 1982.

"Powstanie KKP (Posiedzenie delegacji MKZ-17 IX 1980 w Gdańsku)." (The creation of the National Coordinating Commission of Solidarity, September 17, 1980.) *Krytyka* 18 (1984):87–127.

Pravda, Alex. "The Workers." In *Poland: The Genesis of a Revolution*, edited by Abraham Brumberg, pp. 68–91. New York: Random House, 1983.

*Protokoły porozumień, Gdańsk, Szczecin, Jastrzębie, Statut NSZZ Solidarność, Założenia ustawy o związkach zawodowych*. Warsaw: Krajowa Agencja Wydawnicza, 1981.

Przeworski, Adam. "The Man of Iron and Men of Power in Poland." *Political Science* 15, 1 (Winter 1982):8–21.

Przybylski, Józef. "Wspomnienia." *Kontakt* (Paris) 1, 21 (January 1984): 29–38.

*Punkt* 12. Gdańsk: Gdańskich Środowisk Twórczych, October-December, 1980. [A special issue with documents and commentary on the August 1980 strike.]

Rakowska-Harmstone, Teresa. "Poland." In *Warsaw Pact: The Question of Cohesion*, phase 2, vol. 2, *Poland, German Democratic Republic, and Romania*, edited by Teresa Rakowska-Harmstone, Christopher D. Jones, and Ivan Sylvain. Ottawa: DND, 1984.

Rakowski, Mieczysław F. *Przesilenie grudniowe.* Warsaw: Państwowy Instytut Wydawniczy, 1981.

*Raport o stanie rzeczpospolitej i o drogach do jej naprawy—wersja wstępna i Jak z tego wyjść? (Opracowanie wyników ankiety.)* Paris: Instytut Literacki, 1980.

Reiquam, Steve W., ed. *Solidarity and Poland.* Washington, D.C.: Wilson Center Press, 1988.

Remington, Robin Alison. "Foreword." In Jerzy J. Wiatr, *The Soldier and the Nation: The Role of the Military in Polish Politics.* Boulder, Colo. and London: Westview, 1988.

Reynolds, Jaime. "Communists, Socialists and Workers: Poland 1944–48." *Soviet Studies* 30, 4 (October 1978):516–39.

*Robotnik* (Warsaw) 70–71 (December 12, 1981). [A special issue for the anniversary of December 1970.]

Rogowski, Wiesław. *Biały punkt.* Szczecin: Krajowa Agencja Wydawnicza, 1986. [A novel.]

Rothschild, Joseph. *East Central Europe between the Two World Wars.* Seattle: University of Washington Press, 1974.

Schell, Jonathan. "Introduction." In Adam Michnik, *Letters from Prison*, pp. xvii–xlii. Berkeley: University of California Press, 1985.

Schenk, H. G. *The Mind of the European Romantics.* New York: Doubleday, 1969.

Scott, James C. *Moral Economy of the Peasant.* New Haven: Yale University Press, 1976.

———. *Weapons of the Weak.* New Haven: Yale University Press, 1985.

Seidler, Barbara. "Gdańsk-Gdynia, Grudzień-Luty." *Życie Literackie* (February 21, 1971).

*Sierpień 1980 roku w Szczecinie.* Szczecin: Socjalistyczny Związek Studentów Polskich, n.d. [A collection of documents of the 1980 strikes in Szczecin.]

Simon, Henri. *Lutte des classes et crise de capital, Pologne 1980–82.* Paris: Spartacus, René Lefeuvre, 1982.

Smolar, Aleksander. "Contestation Intellectuelle et Mouvement Populaire." In *Solidarité Résiste et Signe*, pp. 135–51. Paris: Nouvelle Cité, 1984.

———. "The Rich and the Powerful." In *Poland: The Genesis of a Revolution*, edited by Abraham Brumberg, pp. 42–53. New York: Random House, 1983.

*Solidarność Dolnośląska* (Wrocław) 13 (December 16, 1980). [Special issue for the anniversary of December 1970.]

*Solidarność Gdańsk* 13 (April 23, 1981). [Special issue for the founding of the Free Trade Unions of the Baltic.]

Staniszkis, Jadwiga. *Poland's Self-Limiting Revolution.* Edited by Jan T. Gross. Princeton, N.J.: Princeton University Press, 1984.

Starski, Stanisław. *Class Struggle in Classless Poland.* Boston: South End Press, 1982.

Steven, Stewart. *The Poles.* New York: Macmillan, 1982.

Sulik, Bolesław. "Robotnicy." *Kultura* (Paris) 10 (October 1976):65–77. Reprinted as "Les Ouvriers," in *La Pologne: Une société en dissidence,* edited by Z. Erard and G. M. Zygier, pp. 51–66. Paris: François Maspero, 1978.

———. *Three Days in Szczecin.* Boston: WGBH Educational Foundation, 1978. [The transcript of a documentary film on the January 1971 strike in Szczecin.]

Surdykowski, Jerzy. *Notatki gdańskie.* London: Aneks, 1982.

———. "Przemysl okrętowy." *Perspektywy* (September 10, 1970).

Szafar, Tadeusz. "Anti-Semitism: A Trusty Weapon." In *Poland: The Genesis of a Revolution,* edited by Abraham Brumberg, pp. 109–22. New York: Random House, 1983.

Szajkowski, Bogdan. *Next to God ... Poland.* New York: St. Martin's Press, 1983.

Szczęśniak, Edmund. "Dusza rogata." *Czas* (Gdańsk) 42, 299 (October 19, 1980); 43, 300 (October 26, 1980). [A profile of Henryk Lenarciak, a worker of the Gdańsk Lenin Shipyard.]

Szczypiński, Zbigniew. (Industrial sociologist, Gdańsk Lenin Shipyard.) Interview, "Grudzień 70," special issue, reprint from no. 5. Biuletyn NZS UJ (n.p., n.d.): 17–22.

Szejnert, Małgorzata and Tomasz Zalewski. *Szczecin: Grudzień-Sierpień-Grudzień.* London: Aneks, 1986.

Tarrow, Sidney. *Struggle, Politics and Reform: Collective Action, Social Movements and Cycles of Protest.* Western Societies Program, Occasional Paper no. 21. Ithaca, N.Y.: Center for International Studies, Cornell University, 1989.

Tilly, Charles. "Collective Violence in European Perspective." In *A History of Violence in America,* vol. 2, edited by Ted Robert Gurr, pp. 62–100. Newbury Park, Calif.: Sage Publications, 1989.

"To mi utkwiło w pamięci." ("Press Conference with the participation of the Citizens' Committee for the building of the monument and the families of the victims of the December 1970 events.") *Kontakt* (Paris) 12 (December 1983): 40–44.

Touraine, Alain, François Dubet, Michel Wieviorka, and Jan Strzelecki. *Solidarity: The Analysis of a Social Movement, Poland 1980–1981.* Cambridge: Cambridge University Press, 1983.

Triska, Jan F., and Charles Gati, eds. *Blue-Collar Workers in Eastern Europe.* London: Allen and Unwin, 1981.

Trotsky, Leon. *The History of the Russian Revolution.* Ann Arbor: University of Michigan Press, 1960.

———. *1905.* New York: Pathfinder Press, 1972.

Turner, Victor. *Dramas, Fields and Metaphors.* Ithaca, N.Y.: Cornell University Press, 1974.

———. "Religious Celebrations." In Victor and Edith Turner, *Celebration,* pp. 201–19. Washington, D.C.: Smithsonian Institution Press, 1982.

————. *The Ritual Process*. Ithaca, N.Y.: Cornell University Press, 1977.

Van Gennep, Arnold. *The Rites of Passage*. Chicago: University of Chicago Press, 1960.

Volgyes, Ivan. "Military Politics of the Warsaw Pact Armies." In *Civil-Military Relations*, edited by Morris Janowitz, pp. 183–230. Beverly Hills, Calif. and London: Sage Publications, 1981.

Wacowska, Ewa, ed. *Poznań 1956—Grudzień 1970*. Paris: Instytut Literacki, 1971.

————, ed. *Rewolta Szczecińska i jej znaczenie*. Paris: Instytut Literacki, 1971.

Wądołowski, Stanisław. "Nigdy nie będę szedł bezbronny z rękami do góry." *Tygodnik Solidarność* 21 (August 21, 1981).

Walentynowicz, Anna. "Autobiography." Edited by Tomasz Jastrun. *Tygodnik Solidarność* 9 (May 20, 1981).

————. "Odpowiada Anna Walentynowicz." In *Gdańsk-Sierpień 1980*, edited by Ireneusz Łapiński. Warsaw: Instytut Wydawniczy Związków Zawodowych, 1981.

Wałęsa, Lech. Interview. *Kontakt* (Paris) 11 (November 1983).

————. *Un Chemin d'Espoir*. Paris: Fayard, 1987. [Published in English as *A Way of Hope*. New York: Henry Holt, 1987.]

Walicki, Andrzej. *Philosophy and Romantic Nationalism*. New York: Oxford University Press, 1982.

Wąsowski, Br. (Retired colonel of border guards). Letter to *Życie Warszawy* (December 27–28, 1980).

Watts, Larry. "Civil-Military Relations in Eastern Europe: Some Reflections on the Polish Case." *Nordic Journal of Soviet and East European Affairs* 2, 4 (1985):1–92.

Weber, Max. *From Max Weber*. Edited by Hans H. Gerth and C. Wright Mills. New York: Harcourt Brace Jovanovich, 1986.

Weit, Erwin. *Eyewitness*. London: Andre Deutsch, 1973.

Weschler, Lawrence. *Solidarity: Poland in the Season of Its Passion*. New York: Simon and Schuster, 1982.

*Who's Who Solidarność, leksykon związkowy*. Gdańsk: BIPS, 1981.

Wiatr, Jerzy T. *The Soldier and the Nation: The Role of the Military in Polish Politics*. Boulder, Colo. and London: Westview, 1988.

Wolf, Eric R. "The Virgin of Guadalupe: A Mexican National Symbol." *Journal of American Folklore* 71, 279 (January-March 1958):34–39.

Wolin, Sheldon S. *Politics and Vision*. Boston: Little, Brown and Company, 1960.

Woźniak, Marzena, and Tadeusz Woźniak. "Wałęsa—An Action Portrait." In *The Book of Lech Wałęsa*, pp. 188–203. New York: Simon and Schuster, 1982.

Wyszkowski, Krzysztof. "Od WZZ do Sierpnia." *Tygodnik Solidarność* 5 (May 1, 1981).

*WZZ a Solidarność*. Fakt: n.p., 1981. [A transcript of a meeting of former activists of the Free Trade Unions of the Baltic in 1981.]

Zalecki, Marian. *Theology of a Marian Shrine Our Lady of Czestochowa*. Dayton, Ohio: University of Dayton Press, 1976.

Zambrowski, Roman. "Dziennik." *Krytyka* (Warsaw and London) 6 (1980): 20–107.

Zamorski, Kazimierz. "Kronika wydarzeń." In *Poznań 1956—Grudzień 1970*, edited by Ewa Wacowska, pp. 19–66. Translated and published as "A Chronicle of Events" (December 1970-February 1971). Radio Free Europe Research, Poland 16 (June 15, 1971).